Of Innocence
The Murder of Shoeshine Boy, Emanuel Jaques

By
Robert J. Hoshowsky

OUTRAGED

The Murder of Shoeshine Boy, Emanuel Jaques
By
Robert J. Hoshowsky

Copyright ©2017 by Robert Hoshowsky
Cover Photo by Citatus

Book Cover by *Aeternum Designs*

VP Publication an imprint of
RJ Parker Publishing

ISBN 13: 978-1978415959
ISBN 10: 1978415958

www.RJParkerPublishing.com

Published in Canada

The Murder That Changed a City

The tragic story of Shoeshine Boy Emanuel Jaques has been the basis of novels, short stories, a documentary, a play, songs, a children's book on the dangers of abduction, and dozens of essays, but never a True Crime book...until now.

The torture and killing of Emanuel over a 12-hour period above a seedy Toronto body rub parlour outraged citizens who demanded change to Toronto's Yonge Street strip, which by 1977 resembled New York's grimy 42nd Street with its many X-rated movie theatres, massage parlours, pornographic bookstores, and prostitutes.

Through a series of original interviews, archival research, and previously unpublished documents, author Robert J. Hoshowsky recreates in detail Emanuel's brutal death, the hunt for the boy's killers, the shocking trial and press coverage, the controversial Yonge Street clean-up, and what remains one of the most sensational True Crime cases in Canadian history.

Dedication

I dedicate this book to my wife and best friend, Liz, for her love, patience, and understanding.

Table of Contents

Dedication...4
Introduction...6
   A Note on the Trial..21
Chapter One: "How'd You Like to Make Thirty-Five Dollars an Hour?"..22
Chapter Two: Murder on the Sin Strip..........................43
Chapter Three: Burial of an Innocent...........................56
Chapter Four: Backlash...77
Chapter Five: "Hanging is for murderers!"...................99
Chapter Six: Where the Public and Punk Collide: The Curse and Shoeshine Boy..119
Chapter Seven: The Trial..128
Chapter Eight: Parallels to the Murder of Kirkland Deasley...135
Chapter Nine: Troubling Testimony............................145
Chapter Ten: Saul David Betesh: From Heaven to Hell 183
Chapter Eleven: The Campaign to Clean-Up Yonge Street...235
Chapter Twelve: Enter Morris Manning......................263
Chapter Thirteen: The Legacy of the Shoeshine Boy. 296
Chapter Fourteen: The Disappearing Werner Gruener 335
Acknowledgements..340
About the Author..342
Bibliography...343
   Books..343
   Thesis...344
   Magazines..344
   Endnotes..345

Introduction

For some, the words 'shoeshine boy' brings back nostalgic images of a bygone era, a simpler time when eager kids were out on the streets looking to make a few dollars. For others, 'shoeshine boy' means something far more nefarious, and remains forever tied to the brutal murder of an innocent boy.

What began as a sunny, hot, and otherwise uneventful Thursday in late July of 1977 soon turned into a city-wide police hunt for an abducted child. Just days after disappearing, news broke on the front page of Toronto newspapers about the naked body of Emanuel Jaques found on the roof of a body rub parlour on the city's infamous Yonge Street strip. Many believed at the time that not only were the killers to blame, but Toronto itself was culpable for allowing the downtown core of one of the nation's largest cities to turn into a dismal array of porno theatres, X-rated bookstores, and prostitution thinly disguised as health spas and massage parlours.

Just 12 years old when he was murdered, the shocking death of Emanuel did not just signal the end of Toronto's so-called 'innocence' with a bang, but an earth-splitting explosion heard across Canada, the United States, and even Europe. Stories spread overnight about a Portuguese immigrant child shining shoes on the Yonge Street strip being lured to a filthy apartment, repeatedly raped, and ultimately murdered. As revolting as the crime was for 'Toronto the Good' — a slogan coined the previous century by then-mayor and champion of religion and morality William Holmes — Yonge Street had decomposed into a place where anything *but* ethics and decency were to be found.

In the downtown core, the sex industry was growing at an uncontrollable rate. Prostitution, common in major cities like Montreal and Vancouver, started taking the form in Toronto of body rubs, which saw their numbers swell in the early to mid-1970s. Young women working in these establishments — many located on second-floors of buildings along the street's east side — were advertised through handouts and street-level posters where anyone, adult or child, could see them. Places like Le Strip and Samantha's Nude Body rub promised private shows with 'beautiful nude attendants,' and the guarantee of a good time. Women featured on ads were often photographed in silhouette, or skimpy bikinis. Immoral? Perhaps. Illegal? No.

Two of Yonge Street's well-known sex shops, Lady Love and Lady Jane, in the mid-Seventies (Courtesy George Rust-D'Eye)

To sidestep existing by-laws, and ensure premises weren't raided by police, operators of these body rub and massage parlours devised cunning schemes that would make Machiavelli blush, with signage and advertising stopping tantalizingly short of mentioning sexual acts for money. As soon as new laws governing these establishments were announced, as happened in August of 1975, services were promoted differently. Euphemisms abounded, with some owners calling them 'nude encounters.' Anyone walking along Yonge Street back then knew what they really were — they just refrained from saying it with any specificity.

In mid-September of that year, the *Toronto Star* newspaper published a front cover story on the price war going on in Toronto's dozens of body rub parlours before a 60-day licensing deadline came into effect on October 25 to reduce the number of these establishments. To generate business, some were offering special deals for as little as ten dollars. Among those interviewed for the article were Arnold Linetsky, owner of Mr. Arnold's Men's Club and founder of the Yonge Street Adult Entertainment Association, along with the managers of the Play Dance Club, and Delilah's Den. Less than two years later, after the sex slaying of Emanuel Jaques, these and other body rubs would be targeted by police, the city, and the province of Ontario, and closed forever.

One of those quoted in the feature was Werner Gruener, who would be charged with second-degree murder in the death of the shoeshine boy, along with Robert Wayne Kribs, Saul David Betesh, and Josef (sometimes spelled Joseph) Woods. All four men had been involved in

Toronto's sex industry as bouncers, managers, or — in the case of Betesh — as a dancer in gay nightclubs, and as a male prostitute specializing in sadomasochistic fetishes.

As then-manager of the Pleasure Palace body rub parlour, Gruener stated the business was actually a "nude meditation" centre, where men paid to take off their clothes, sit down, and read books with naked women. While this sounded absurd, it remained legal. "That's what we are doing so we won't have to get a licence," he said. Other sex clubs were equally inventive in their methods to elude upcoming changes to legislation. Some, like Delilah's Den on the Yonge Street strip, already had other schemes in place to keep themselves in existence, ranging from talking to a nude girl for twenty minutes for twenty dollars, or dancing with a naked female for fifteen minutes, also twenty dollars. One of the most ingenious ploys saw customers paying thirty dollars and being handed a Polaroid instant camera and eight photo negatives for their own half-hour 'nude photo session.' Since none of these activities technically involved sex, they were not against the law.

For many of Toronto's residents, Yonge Street business owners, and city councillors, the growing number of body rub parlours was alarming; to others who lived or worked away from downtown, the strip's sex trade was largely met with indifference. Over the years, particularly in the early 1970s, a number of attempts were made by Metro and business associations to eliminate the sex industry from Yonge Street. One was Bill 107, which would give municipalities the power to regulate body rub parlours through licensing. On one side was Ontario Premier William Davis, Toronto Mayor David Crombie, a host of politicians, and the Downtown Council; on the other, the body rub owners, operators, employees, and the Yonge Street Adult Entertainment Association which, in a bizarre twist, promised to create its *own* task force to determine the "real cause" behind the pimps, prostitutes, drug-dealers, junkies, and panhandlers along Yonge Street.

It was against this backdrop of strip clubs, porno theatres, and thinly-veiled massage parlours that young Emanuel was lured to his death from a busy Yonge Street intersection.

Shoeshine Boy Emanuel Jaques

The story of Emanuel's abduction and murder before being found on the roof of a dumpy body rub parlour enraged the city like no other crime before or since. Coming to Canada from

Portugal with his family just a few years earlier, his gruesome death triggered residents into demanding something be done to clean-up — as Mayor David Crombie famously called it — the "yawning cesspool" that was Yonge Street, targeting the stretch from Gerrard Street in the North, to Queen Street in the South. A mish-mash of body rubs, porno shops, adult movie theatres, prostitutes both male and female, cross-dressers and smoke-filled bars stood alongside reputable establishments like Howard Johnson's restaurant, COLES The Book People!, and music stores A&A Books and Records, and Sam the Record Man. For owners of these businesses and many others, the horrific murder of the shoeshine boy was the impetus to change the city, but not without opposition, and permanent consequences.

*****

I was 13 back in 1977, a year older than Emanuel Jaques. Like many others living in Toronto at the time, I vividly remember the extensive coverage in the city's newspapers, on television, and the radio. Details of the atrocious crime were everywhere, and about as inescapable as a ferociously steamy summer in the city. If there was ever a time you could feel rage, pain, and frustration in the air, it was August of 1977.

To say Emanuel's permanently changed the city is not an overstatement. Often referred to as the moment when 'Toronto lost its innocence,' the reality remains: no major urban city is truly *innocent*, nor can it ever be. In the Seventies, the downward spiral of Yonge Street was obvious, yet tolerated by many. The murder of the shoeshine boy, an immigrant child from Portugal, changed that forever.

In the decades since Emanuel's death, much of Toronto's sex industry has gone underground. While some of today's massage parlours offer much more than temporary relief from back or neck pain, and street prostitutes can still be seen occasionally near the downtown core, escort ads in the back of free newspapers and the Internet have effectively changed how sin sells in big cities. The 'seedy side' of the city still exists, for those who want to find it.

And still, all those years ago, the Yonge Street strip had a quirky, intoxicating allure. Some of the hippies and folk music crowd of the late Sixties were still lingering, but were joined by punk rockers with studded leather jackets and spiked purple mohawks in the mid-Seventies, and the dance crowd getting into the then-new style of music, disco. Yonge Street's Sam the Record Man sold 45's and LP's in distinctive white plastic bags with red lettering, which were heat-sealed by cashiers to deter theft. Whenever I went downtown, it was with my parents or brother and his older friends, never alone, and always to the same haunts: grimy bookstores smelling like old man sweat and decades of stale cigarette smoke, selling used Superman and Spider-Man comics, and trading cards packed with a stick of gum for Star Wars, a new movie coming to theatres in 1977.

Passing stores on the street with their doors wide open and radios blaring, you would hear classic rock songs by groups like Creedence Clearwater Revival and the Beatles one minute, and *Anarchy in the U.K.* by the Sex Pistols the next, followed by Swedish pop group Abba's *Dancing Queen*.

And then, there was the other side of Yonge, where the so-called 'dirty stores' were. These were the strip joints, the body rubs, and the adult bookstores where you'd deliberately slow down while passing, or pretend to bend over and tie your shoelace so you could steal a quick peek inside from the sidewalk. If you were on the strip around noon, you would sometimes see young women standing outside these places, cigarette and coffee in hand, looking like they just slid out of bed, and threw on a bathrobe before getting ready for the day. Like most boys that age, I was mystified by Yonge Street, and what it had to offer.

And, like others kids, I wanted money to be able to pay for my own things, like records, candy, and the wonders that could be ordered from the back pages of comic books, ranging from top of the line toys like the Evel Knievel gryo-powered energizer stunt cycle and The Six Million Dollar Man action figure with a bionic arm, to less expensive items like X-Ray specs (which, to my great disappointment, did not allow me to see through clothing), Mexican jumping beans (seed pods with moth larvae inside struggling to get out), and a scary, life-size monster ghost 'promising to obey my commands' for just one American dollar (a white plastic sheet with black eyes on it, and an uninflated balloon for a head).

On Yonge Street, there were a lot of kids out shining shoes to make money. In fact, newspapers published photos of them in the mid-Seventies, industrious youngsters working downtown with their boxes, rags and polish. *Why couldn't I be one of them?* I wondered. Heading to the basement full of inspiration, I built a shoeshine kit out of some of my dad's old plywood scraps and nails, liberating some of his tins of Kiwi shoe polish, and a couple of brushes. The box was about a foot and a half long, and really rough-looking, like a hastily-constructed casket for a beloved family pet. Using leftover purple paint the shade of a bruised knee, I said nothing to my parents until early the next day, as I headed for the front door and what I believed to be my path to financial success at the time.

The conversation with my mother was both uncomfortable and brief, and went something as follows:

Mom: (slanting her eyes down, and looking at the box in my hand) What is *that*?
Me: (voice full of pride) A shoeshine kit I built.
Mom: And *where*, exactly, do you think you're going with it?

Knowing her tone extremely well, I tried to sound upbeat when I responded, "downtown, to shine shoes!" her response was a flat, "No, you're not," which effectively quashed my dreams of becoming rich by polishing the shoes of businessmen and women. Explaining to her the mutual benefits of part-time employment — and attempting to rationalize how it would help me to buy things like a new 10-speed bike with my own money, instead of theirs — she eventually said, "You're going to get a paper route." In this way, she would know where I was, street by street, how long I'd be out, and approximately what time I would return. Within a week, I started delivering the Sunday edition of the *Toronto Sun*, which cost a quarter an issue, and collecting from my customers once a month.

    This was late in the spring of 1977, before Emanuel Jaques was raped and murdered in an apartment above Charlie's Angels body rub parlour.

Street level outside 245 Yonge Street, with Charlie's Angels' body rub located on the second floor, with the apartment above where Emanuel Jaques was murdered (Courtesy Toronto Police)

For parents across the city, the death of the shoeshine boy justified them being viewed as 'over-protective' by their relatives and neighbours.

Not only downtown but over all of Toronto, mothers and fathers immediately re-evaluated their children's choice of friends, what they did at recess, where they were after school, and in some cases, even their teachers. Terrified their sons and daughters could meet the same fate as Emanuel, many parents kept their kids close to home. Block Parent and neighbourhood watch programs aimed at making communities safer increased in the weeks after the killing. And where there was once dozens of shoeshine boys at Yonge and Dundas — the same location where Emanuel was working before he was lured to his death — numbers plummeted, as parents forbade their youngsters from going there, with Toronto police officers chasing away the remaining few kids.

Like all major cities, Toronto experienced the horror of child murders long before Emanuel. In the mid-1950s, deeply disturbed teenager Peter Woodcock (who later changed his name to David Michael Krueger) wandered around Toronto, often on his prized red-and-white Schwinn bicycle, molesting children, eventually brutalizing and killing three: Wayne Mallette, seven, Gary Morris, nine, and Carole Voyce, just four years old. In and out of psychiatric treatment facilities Woodcock, who was adopted, was deemed to be a violent psychopath. In the early 1960s, Gary Alexander McCorkell, 19, raped and murdered two toddlers, Michael Atkinson and Ronald MacLeod. Sentenced to hang, a jury declared mercy, and his life was spared. Years later, McCorkell would be released, and immediately reoffended. In British Columbia in the 1980s, the infamous killer Clifford Olson confessed to murdering 11 children and young adults. This was followed by other child killers, such as husband and wife team Paul Bernardo and Karla Homolka in the early 1990s whose victims include Kristen French, 15, Leslie Mahaffy, 14, and Homolka's own sister, Tammy, 15.

Sadly, these children and many others were robbed of their lives, like Sharin' Morningstar Keenan, Christine Jessop, Alison Parrott, Kayla Klaudusz, Cecilia Zhang, Andrea Atkinson, Holly Jones, and Tori Stafford, preyed upon by twisted pedophiles who chose to kill their victims rather than let them survive. Still, the name Emanuel Jaques brings with it a certain sense of foreboding, and a reminder of the city that was, slowly fading into memory.

The murder of the shoeshine boy changed Toronto in every way imaginable: legally, politically, morally, socially, economically, criminally, sexually, and even aesthetically. Many of Yonge Street's buildings got a facelift in the years after Emanuel was killed, while others were demolished and rebuilt. The city's sex industry — at least the way the sex industry was at the time — is gone. Every few years, particularly around the anniversary of his death, Emanuel's name makes the news, a grim reminder of Toronto's past, but also an insight into what would become the future of the city.

*****

A Note on the Trial

The 1978 Ontario Supreme Court trial of the four men charged with the murder of Emanuel Jaques — Saul David Betesh, Robert Wayne Kribs, Josef Woods, and Werner Gruener — heard testimony from Toronto police officers and detectives, psychiatrists and psychologists, family members and friends of both the accused and the victim, among many others. A number of children also testified. While actual names are used throughout the book, the names of some individuals have been changed to protect their identities.

Chapter One: "How'd You Like to Make Thirty-Five Dollars an Hour?"

For the trio of young boys, Thursday July 28, 1977 started off like many other days that summer. The weather was ideal: bright, warm, with a clear blue sky. Although the summer solstice, the longest day of the year, had passed well over a month earlier, the kids knew the sun wouldn't be setting for hours yet, not until shortly before 9 o'clock that night. Plenty of time to shine shoes, and make money.

Although there were prohibitions under Ontario's Child Welfare Act at the time governing youngsters under specific ages — boys, 12, and girls less than 16 — from working any street trade between the hours of 9 p.m., and six a.m., a dozen or more kids were out hustling on Yonge Street. Their shoeshine boxes full, calls of "Mister, want a shine? Just 50 cents!" were heard. While police enforced the laws, there was some flexibility; after all, what harm was there in children making a few dollars shining shoes? Officers got to know many of the kids by name. The older ones usually got a pass, while the younger boys were told to go home to their parents when it got late, and the street lights went on.

Toronto, particularly the area around Yonge and Dundas in the city's core, was always active that time of year. A major artery, Dundas connected the city from east to west, while Yonge Street, another major route, stretched all the way from the shores of Lake Ontario in the South to Lake Simcoe in the North. For residents, tourists, and businesses alike, the area known as the Yonge Street strip was a mixed blessing. Extending from Gerrard Street down to Queen Street, it was home to music stores like Sam the Record Man, numerous discount jewellers, A&A Records, Howard Johnson's, and plenty of pinball arcades, with their doors open, music blasting, and the constant *ding-ding-ding* ringing out from machines like Bally's Captain Fantastic, named after Elton John's album *Captain Fantastic and the Brown Dirt Cowboy*, and Eight Ball, which featured unauthorized artwork resembling The Fonz, Laverne, and others from the TV sitcom Happy Days.

And then, there was the sleazier side of Yonge, namely the strip clubs, bars, body rub parlours, and adult movie theatres like Cinema 2000, which screened films and sold magazines and books during what some consider 'the Golden Age of Porn' of the Seventies. A few years earlier, in the late 1960s, adult movies grew bolder, showing more graphic sex acts and leaving less to the imagination, with movies like *Alice in Wonderland: An X-Rated Musical Comedy*, *Through the Looking Glass*, and *The Opening of Misty Beethoven*. If someone was feeling nostalgic, they could always catch older skin flicks on Yonge, like *The Devil in Miss Jones* or *Flesh Gordon*, an erotic parody of the Flash Gordon outer space serials of the 1930s.

The busy northeast corner of Yonge and Dundas, where shoeshine boys Emanuel Jaques, his older brother and their friend were approached by Saul Betesh (City of Toronto Archives)

Standing in complete contrast to the street's X-rated cinemas, bookstores, and massage parlours was the Eaton Centre. Announced over a decade earlier by the department store giant, the retail and restaurant development was like nothing ever seen before in the city, resembling a massive, modern suburban mall in the heart of downtown. First planned in the late 1960s, the Eaton Centre underwent a number of design changes in the early 1970s, which saw nearby historic structures — Toronto's Old City Hall and Trinity Church — preserved instead of demolished, as was initially planned.

Occupying the stretch of Yonge Street from Dundas to Queen on the west side, the Eaton

Centre was a sparkling, futuristic gem. With hundreds of glass panes in its vaulted galleria reaching to the sky, natural light flooded the Centre's lofty interior. Escalators seemed to seem to go on forever, while transparent elevators offered incredible views. Spread over nine levels, the complex boasted more than 250 stores, restaurants, and boutiques. The hype building up to the opening of the Centre in 1977 was enormous. Expensive full-page ads ran in all the major newspapers, comparing the new structure to legendary shopping districts such as New York's Fifth Avenue, Oxford Street in London, the Champs Elysées in Paris, and the legendary Galleria Vittorio Emanuele II in Milan. "The world's greatest shopping areas have one thing in common. All are in the heart of the city," stated one promotional piece. "Early in 1977, it comes to life. Consider yourself invited." At the time, the Eaton Centre was viewed not only as a destination, but as a saviour, a business to lead by example the revitalization of Toronto's downtown core.

A postcard of Yonge Street in the 1970s featuring the rarely-shown east side and its many undeveloped low-rise older buildings, standing in stark contrast to the new Eaton Centre on the west side. (Public domain)

Directly across from the Eaton Centre on the east side of Yonge, things were very different. Massage parlours and adult bookstores were plentiful. Many were located above regular, run-of-the-mill shops. At 245 Yonge was Orientique on street level, a retail gift store. On the second floor, accessible through a narrow stairway, was Charlie's Angels. A body rub parlour, it was listed in the County of York (Metro) tax assessment records for that year as, somewhat confusingly, under two entries: one stating "movie entertainment," the other "not used for business," which was absolutely not the case.

Passers-by were greeted by huge letters promoting Charlie's Angels, with the words "sexy" above "girls," which was repeated for emphasis.

The name of the body rub came from the ABC television series Charlie's Angels, which chronicled the adventures of three attractive female private investigators. Popular with viewers but labelled "jiggle TV" and "tits and ass television" by critics because of sexist plots, female leads often appeared in underwear, tiny bathing suits, or naked, barely concealed by a strategically-wrapped towel. Below the Charlie's Angels wording was the black key-shaped "Admittance Restricted" logo, followed by promises of movies, love aids, magazines, books, films, and more. Less prominent however, were smaller letters painted on a glass panel above the doorway, reading: "Come to world of love, your happiness may depend on it," which was the last thing anyone ascending the stairs to the body rub would see.

A close-up of the signage at Charlie's Angels, reading "Come to world of love, your happiness may depend on it," which was above the doorway leading to the apartment where Emanuel Jaques was raped and murdered. (Courtesy George Rust-D'Eye)

For Emanuel Jaques, the sleaze of the Yonge Street strip was about as far removed from his life back in Portugal as one could possibly imagine. Immigrating from the North Atlantic's Azores archipelago, Emanuel's father, Valdemiro, arrived in Toronto in 1972 and worked as a cleaner before arranging to bring over his wife and six other children in 1974. For the Jaques family — and thousands of others from Portugal — Canada and the United States were seen as lands of opportunity. In the Azores, much of the economy was founded on fishing, agriculture, and the meat and dairy industries; in Canada, South Africa, Venezuela or Brazil, the chances for advancement were much greater for their youngsters.

A number of cities at the time, Toronto in particular, had developed sizable Portuguese communities starting in the early 1950s, where new immigrants could feel more at home. In the growing "Little Portugal" area located west of the downtown core, shops soon appeared selling Portuguese products, along with restaurants and clubs, peaking in the early 1970s. It was during this period, 1971 to 1980, that Canada welcomed 76,602 immigrants from Portugal[1], the Jaques family among them.

Like many other immigrant families, they settled in an area of Toronto which was affordable, on Shuter Street in Regent Park, east of downtown. It was from here 12-year-old Emanuel, his brother Luciano, 14, and friend Shane McLean, 12, set out for the busy downtown intersection to make a few dollars. Although his parents were initially reluctant to let him go without adult supervision, Emanuel pressured them until they relented; after all, he was with his older brother. A number of other kids they knew had been shining shoes for weeks downtown, and the northeast corner of Yonge and Dundas — right near a streetcar stop and a subway entrance — wasn't some isolated part of the city, but a busy area populated with thousands of pedestrians and cars every day. The parents agreed the boys could head downtown to shine shoes, where they went every day, except Sundays.

Dutifully, Emanuel handed over his earnings to his mother, ranging from $10 to $20 a day, which went towards helping the family. His mother, in fact, had purchased the shoeshine kit for Emanuel, who was especially excited: a neighbor was going to give him a puppy, and he wanted to use some of the money to buy food for his future pet.[2]

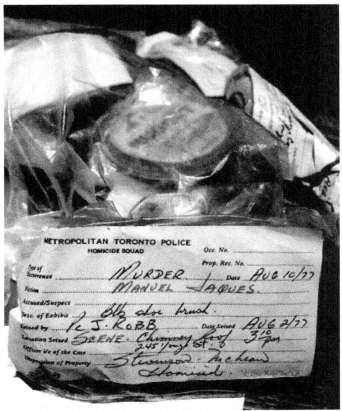

Part of Emanuel's shoeshine kit, including Nugget brand shoe polish, found on the roof of 245 Yonge Street, still sealed and tagged in its plastic evidence bag (Courtesy Toronto Police)

Business that hot July day was a bit slow. Around 5:30 p.m., the boys were approached by a man who looked like he was in his late twenties. About six feet tall, with long, light brown hair, he wore blue denim overalls, no shirt underneath, and looked like he had just come from a construction site. The interest from the boys wasn't in his clothes, however, but his shoes, and a pair of well-worn work boots he was carrying with him in a plastic bag from the Adam and Eve boutique.

Shane started shining the pair of brown shoes the man was wearing, while Emanuel and Luciano took one boot each from the bag. At one point, the man — who said he was an out-of-town visitor — started showing them some chops and kicks, claiming he knew Kung Fu, which was all the rage in the Seventies thanks to Bruce Lee movies like *Enter the Dragon*, and the TV series starring David Carradine. Showing off his moves, the stranger picked up Shane, and playfully threw him across his shoulders.

Initially a Missing Person, Metropolitan Toronto Police scoured Toronto's waterfront, alleyways, dumpsters, ravines, parks, hotels and other areas for a sign of missing 12-year-old

Emanuel Jaques. Interviewing dozens of potential witnesses including store owners, street vendors and other shoeshine boys, thoroughly detailed Supplementary Report pages were created. This one describes the suspect last seen with the boy, which turned out to be Saul Betesh (Courtesy Toronto Police)

Once the boys were done, the man handed them two dollars for shining his boots, and *another* two dollars for the shoes, much more than the 50 cents they usually charged. He then made an unbelievable offer, asking if they'd like to make $35 an hour to move some photographic equipment. The boys were told they could earn up to four hundred bucks, an amount that would take them many months to make just shining shoes. "Let me earn the money, let me earn the money!" cried Emanuel.

While the offer was enticing, Luciano and Shane were skeptical. Although the man looked normal, even friendly, there was something just not *right* about him, and the way they caught him quickly narrowing his eyes at them, particularly blond, mop-haired Shane, was creepy, and made them feel uneasy. Leaving his younger brother with the stranger at the crowded intersection, Luciano headed off with Shane up the street and around the corner to a pay phone outside a restaurant to call their mothers, and ask for permission, which was denied. Shane's mother, Bessie, told her son to come home immediately. Maria Jaques also instructed Luciano to get back to the house with his little brother, and not to go anywhere with the man. All three boys were to keep their promise of coming home no later than 9 o'clock that night. Shane, who had been working as a shoeshine boy for about a year, knew he would be grounded if he wasn't home on time, which meant he wouldn't be able to make money. The two promised to come home.

Returning to the intersection a few minutes later, the boys saw Emanuel and the stranger walking away in the distance. They yelled out to him, but the sidewalk was packed, with Emanuel and the man disappearing into the crowd, not seeing or hearing them shouting. Frantic, the boys began looking for a policeman. None could be found.

Rushing back to their homes, Shane and Luciano said Emanuel was missing. Fearing the worst, members of the Jaques family, including his father, went downtown to search for the child, knowing it would soon be dark. Neither parent spoke English well, making the search of Yonge and Dundas much more difficult. Soon, Toronto Police were alerted by one of the older Jaques children that their little brother disappeared, and was last seen with a strange man.

Emanuel, 12 lured away pals testify

Newspaper headline (author collection)

Immediately, Toronto officers from 54 Division along with volunteers began searching the city for any signs of the youngster. Copies of the missing boy's school photo were circulated to foot patrols and officers in the Yonge and Dundas Street area from the Ident Bureau, while 8" X 10" images were distributed to Toronto newspapers, which carried front-page stories about the missing 12-year-old, mistakenly referred to him as "Manuel" instead of Emanuel.

Hours turned into days, and with no sign of the missing shoeshine boy being uncovered, the number of police soon grew from about 50 to over 100. Some were dispatched to houses downtown, knocking on doors and showing Emanuel's picture to see if anyone knew him, or the man he was with.

Others went through Toronto's many alleys and laneways behind houses and industrial buildings, desperate to find some sign of the missing child. Still more officers, some on horseback and others on foot, scoured wooded areas of the city, including the Rosedale Ravine, the Don Valley Parkway, parks, the harbour, the Don River, trash cans, dumpsters, hotel parking lots and parked cars, and abandoned buildings. Persons interviewed included a girl who worked at Wendy's, who recalled seeing Emanuel in the restaurant with two or three young boys shortly before he disappeared, but she didn't remember seeing him with any older males.

Missing Person reports stated plainclothes officers were also dispatched to gay bars, "and any other 'Homo-hangouts'," including a gay drop-in centre on Granby Street. Also of interest were the city's youth hostels, hotels, and nightclubs, including the Hampton Court, Ramada Inn, Avonmore, Carriage House, Junction Hotel, Oxford Inn, Warwick, the St. Charles Tavern, Mo Mos Disco, Club Manatee, and many others. Expanding their search, Canadian National Railway police were notified to check train station lockers, and train tracks. No trace of the boy was uncovered.

Both Luciano and Shane were shown numerous "lookalike" photos by police to see if they could pick the man out of a list of suspects, including one known "to frequent juvenile boys and enter into sexual advances with such lads." The stranger wasn't in any of the images. One individual, a muscular young man with light brown/red hair and blue eyes, was described as a

CB Radio enthusiast who used the airwaves to pick up young boys, and had a habit of taking them for hamburgers once he met them, and teaching them Kung Fu. Arrested for vagrancy, the male also had been picked up for offences against young boys, but had been released. Another suspect, described as a young man with a lisp who lived at home, was interviewed by police due to a 1976 incident where he gave money to boys in exchange for taking nude photos of them.

During their search, police knocked on doors of persons suspected to have abducted Emanuel, particularly those resembling the man last seen with him. Interviewing downtown street vendors or "hawkers" who knew Emanuel, some stated he was a very friendly, bright kid. Others, including employees at the Pleasure Land Body Rub, referred to odd-looking characters seen the night of his disappearance, including one male known as "Blue," who hung out in pinball arcades, and had a previous arrest record for prostituting young boys. Stranger still, "Blue," a white male, was known for attempting to disguise himself as a Negro, blackening his face, and donning an afro wig.

Refusing to abandon their search, many of the officers had barely slept in days. Descriptions of the missing boy were widely circulated: four-feet-five inches tall, about 80 pounds, fair complexion, brown medium-length hair, and hazel eyes. At the time of his disappearance, Emanuel was wearing a short-sleeve yellow shirt with floral prints, dark blue pants, and blue and yellow running shoes. He also had a T-shirt given to him by a young woman working at a shop on Yonge Street, with her image silkscreened on the front.

According to Missing Person Reports from the Metropolitan Toronto Police, Emanuel's Cause of Absence was listed ominously as "lured away." Last seen by his brother Luciano, reports detailed how the three boys were approached by a man who "asked them if they would like to make $35 an hour helping him with photo equipment." Offering to buy them hamburgers, the man said at one point that he wanted more than one boy to accompany him. "Manuel *[sic]* has never been missing before and always phones and let his mother know where he is or if he will be late," stated one police report. "His family has only been in Canada for 3 ½ years and his father did not want the Police involved if he could help it and wanted to find the boy himself. He has been looking for Manuel *[sic]* since 2:00 am."

Speaking with Shane and Luciano, police were able to extract additional details about the stranger. Showing off a roll of $200 in cash, the man specifically said he was looking for boys between the ages of nine and 14 to help him carry photographic equipment; noticing a red stain on his left forearm, the man said it was the result of processing photo chemicals. At one point, he gave one of the boys some money and coins as a tip to run to a nearby store, Frank's Hamburger Shop, to get him a king-size package of Rothman's cigarettes.

Three anxious days passed for the family, with no sign of Emanuel. Then, on Sunday August 1, 1977 at 5:30 in the evening, a man named Saul David Betesh walked into 51 Division police station on Regent Street with a lawyer, Richard Parker. For Toronto Police Sergeant Paton Weir and other detectives, the hours to come would hear Betesh tell a story almost too bizarre to believe. During his 15 years on the force, Weir had listened to his share of tales, but few were as convoluted as the one he was about to hear. Opening his notepad, the Sergeant began writing down the words of an extremely animated Betesh. Among other things, he told the officer he was working on a news story about child prostitution in Toronto, which is why he approached Emanuel on the street for research. After walking with the boy to an apartment above the nearby Charlie's Angels body rub and realizing no one else was there, Betesh said he went back with Emanuel to the corner of Yonge and Dundas, where the two went into a Howard Johnson's restaurant for a burger before returning to the apartment.

Saul David Betesh, Toronto Police mugshot (Courtesy Toronto Police)

Betesh continued telling Weir his story, which grew more unbelievable, graphic, and grotesque with every word. If what he was saying was true — and not the words of a disturbed attention-seeker — it would be one of the most horrifying crimes in Toronto's history.

"Betesh had contacted a lawyer named Richard Parker when he went to the police," says Paul Tomlinson, the attorney who would later represent Betesh at trial. "That's when Betesh gave these interviews to the police. He sort of lead people to believe — including his lawyer at the time — that he was there to assist the police in the investigation, because he was the last person to see him [Emanuel]. After a number of hours of interviews, it became clear that Betesh had in fact been one of the perpetrators. Then after that, he contacted me."

Telling his tale, Betesh said the boy was photographed in an apartment above the body rub, fully-clothed at first, then persuaded to strip off his shirt, pants, and underwear until he was naked. Tied to a stained bed, he was tortured, repeatedly raped, drugged, choked with a stretch cord and then, when this attempt to kill him was not successful, held upside-down and *drowned* in a kitchen sink. Adding to the horror, he had been attacked by not just Betesh, but other men. The officer was practically speechless. As he jotted down the statement, Sergeant Weir asked Betesh why the boy had to die. In a calm, monotone voice, he responded: "We knew he couldn't let him go. We knew that all along...no, that's not right. We never intended to kill him, we had to."

Was the man sitting across the desk telling the Sergeant the truth, or spinning a sick string of lies? Hours passed, and by 5:30 the next morning, both Betesh and Weir were exhausted. With daybreak less than an hour away, Betesh suddenly said he wanted to "be more explicit." The boy's body, he announced, was "on the roof at the back" of the Yonge Street body rub, less than 100 yards from where Emanuel was last seen at his corner shoeshine stand. Betesh then proceeded to tell police he did not act alone. Three others were involved: Robert Wayne Kribs, Josef Woods, and Werner Gruener, who were at that moment on a Canadian National Railway train out of Toronto, heading to Vancouver.

Was it possible to stop the train before it left the province? The Ontario Provincial Police, one of the largest services in Canada, was contacted immediately. At the same time, Metro officers were sent to Charlie's Angel's body rub. Smashing the glass door to gain access, the search for Emanuel Jaques ended when they found his naked body on the third-floor rooftop, wrapped in garbage bags, crammed into an unused metal air vent, and buried beneath trash. No longer a missing child case, it was now murder, and the weeks, and months to come would see Torontonians united, and divided, as never before.

Chapter Two: Murder on the Sin Strip

Four Men charged with murder; missing boy, 12, was drowned
-The *Globe and Mail*, Tuesday August 2, 1977, Cover

The same day newspapers published articles about the latest victims of deranged serial killer Son of Sam taking the lives of a young couple — his thirteenth and fourteenth victims — in Brooklyn, New York, stories broke in Toronto about a missing shoeshine boy being found murdered on the roof of a Yonge Street body rub parlour. The city would never be the same again.

While plenty of residents still referred to it as 'Toronto the Good' back then, Yonge and Dundas was anything but good, more closely resembling New York City's 42nd Street of the Seventies, with its many topless bars, 25-cent peep shows with live nude girls, X-rated adult book stores and movie theatres, gay clubs like 'Follies Burlesk,' and sketchy-looking joints like the Avon 42st promising live acts on stage. And like Toronto, there were downtown massage parlours providing 'sensitive meeting places,' and lovely girls.

One of Yonge Street's many body rub parlours (Courtesy George Rust-D'Eye)

As is the case with every homicide, Emanuel Jaques could have been killed virtually anywhere in the city, from the palatial 'Millionaires' Row' mansions of the Bridle Path in North Toronto to

The Beaches in the East, The Junction neighbourhood in the West, or the Southern part of the city near Lake Ontario. Instead, Emanuel was slain in the very *heart* of Toronto, on the Yonge Street strip, a section of town which was allowed to decay like a neglected, misshapen mole that eventually turns into cancer. Over the years, the strip was viewed in a number of ways. For local teenagers out to have fun in arcades or hang out in movie theatres, it was a guaranteed good time.

Some would come in from smaller cities like Oshawa, about 40 miles away, to drive up and down Yonge Street on Saturday nights for hours, blaring their horns and catcall girls walking the strip. Businesses in the sex trade loved the area, because of their steady and often repeat clientele, while other store owners were frustrated little was being done to stop the growth of body rubs, which they believed were hurting their establishments. Some adopted the 'out of sight, out of mind' method, avoiding the strip entirely. To many, Toronto's Yonge Street strip in the Seventies was the modern-day version of Sodom and Gomorrah, a place of depravity, overflowing with evil and moral corruption.

With practically every major Canadian newspaper reporting on what became known as 'the shoeshine boy murder' on August 2, avoiding the issue of the city's downtown sex trade was no longer possible. The fact the murder happened on the Yonge Street strip was bad enough; that it took place in a grimy apartment over a body rub parlour was even worse. Adding to this scandal were reports several of the men involved were gay, with Emanuel dying during a "homosexual orgy," a term used repeatedly in the months to come, much to the dismay of the city's gay and lesbian population, who were as horrified at the brutality of the crime as everyone else.

Reporters from TV, radio, and major daily newspapers The *Toronto Sun*, The *Toronto Star*, and The *Globe and Mail* soon provided details of the crime so gruesomely specific that they received tremendous criticism from readers. The death of a child was monstrous, and in itself was too much for many readers to tolerate; describing the exact way he was brutalized over the course of hours was excruciating, and provoked anger never before seen in the city. The young boy had been lured by an older male, Saul David Betesh. On Monday August 1, based on information provided by Betesh, police went to Charlie's Angels, where Emanuel's tiny body was discovered on the roof at 6:30 a.m., soon after sunrise. The missing person case was now a murder.

To preserve the crime scene, the corpse could not be removed by placing it on a stretcher and carrying it down the narrow flight of stairs. Instead, the Toronto Fire Department was brought in, and a crane was used to gently lift the remains to street level, and the body was transported to the nearby Centre of Forensic Sciences to be autopsied.

*Emanuel's body being removed from the crime scene
(Courtesy Toronto Police)*

Even before Emanuel could be examined by the coroner, Staff Sergeant Gerald Stevenson, one of the homicide officers investigating the scene, confirmed "the boy died of asphyxia due to drowning," which raised additional questions about the child's final hours. Interviewing Emanuel's brother Luciano and friend Shane, police were able to piece together the youngster's final hours before his disappearance until the discovery of his body days later. Initially reporting the remains showed no bruises or other signs of physical abuse, word quickly spread Emanuel had been repeatedly sexually assaulted. Luciano and Shane were able to describe the man last seen talking to them on Yonge Street, resulting in a composite drawing. Taken by police to 51 Division, the youngsters positively identified Saul Betesh as the man whose shoes and boots they shone, and the person who was last seen with Emanuel.

The murder of the 12-year-old shook Toronto to its core. A largely conservative city, it was still considered safe by many. Within hours of his death, there were enraged calls for the reinstatement of Capital Punishment in Canada, which had been abolished under the Liberal government of Prime Minister Pierre Elliot Trudeau just one year earlier, on July 14, 1976. [3]

For many, hanging the men arrested for the torture, rape and sadistic murder of Emanuel Jaques was exactly what they wanted. Headlines reading "4 held in sex slaying of boy over body rub joint" appeared in The *Toronto Sun*, which for years published articles and editorials highly critical of Yonge Street's decline, and what it perceived as a complete lack of action from politicians to rid the area of its thriving sex trade.

Once the forensic examination was complete, newspapers repeated Emanuel had been "sexually abused in a homosexual orgy," with the autopsy report of Dr. Francis MacDonald stating ligature marks and bruising on his neck were a sign of strangulation, with drowning being the cause of death. Worse still were rumours, which were later confirmed during the trial, of needle marks in his arms where the killers injected him with some substance, and tears in his rectum, further evidence of rape. His fate was at complete odds with Emanuel's school portrait photo, which was widely circulated. Smiling, eyes wide, hair falling over his forehead and his checked shirt buttoned to the top, he was a child embodying innocence, and a promising future.

In sharp contrast were newspaper images of the four accused men, handcuffed together by police, being led in and out of police stations and court over the coming months. Saul David Betesh, who lured Emanuel to his death, was the most ordinary-looking of the bunch. The others were downright menacing. Born in Germany, Werner Gruener, with his thick beard and long, greasy hair swept back from his face, bore a passing resemblance to Jim Morrison, lead singer from The Doors.

Werner Gruener, known for riding his bicycle outfitted with streamers and a radio up and down Yonge Street at all hours (Courtesy Toronto Police)

The other two men were another matter entirely. Josef Woods, dark-haired and with a goatee, wore thick black-rimmed glasses which magnified his penetrating eyes. His nickname was 'The Mad Scientist,' which suited him perfectly.

Josef Woods, the "mad scientist" of the group (Courtesy Toronto Police)

Woods looked, and acted, the part, inventing bizarre mind-control devices, and believing himself to be gifted with psychic abilities enabling him to look into the minds of others and read their thoughts, or make them do his bidding.

The most frightening remained Robert Kribs. Six and a half feet tall, Kribs was nicknamed

'Stretcher,' and had a longstanding reputation for his unpredictable, eruptive temper, which he used to his benefit while working as a bouncer at Charlie's Angels body rub. The idea that any of these grown men were sexually involved with a little boy was repulsive, with furious citizens taking to the streets in protest, calling for an end to the filth of the Yonge Street strip, and severe punishment for the men behind Emanuel's murder, including death.

Robert Kribs, six and a half feet tall, also known as "Stretcher"
(Courtesy Toronto Police)

Demonstrations started immediately after the discovery of Emanuel's body, culminating in a large gathering at City Hall. On Wednesday August 3, 1977, Reverend Harold Jackman helped organize a two-mile march from Emanuel's east end home in Regent Park, a public housing project, down

Yonge Street, with many of the 150 in attendance friends and neighbours of the Jaques family. On their way to City Hall and a meeting with Mayor David Crombie, the crowd paused for a minute of silence outside the body rub parlour where the boy's naked body was discovered on the roof. The large glass panel on the front door, smashed by police to gain access to the building, had jagged sections remaining in the steel frame, with police officers standing guard outside. Before the silence was over, someone yelled "Throw a goddamned match into the place!"

Citizens simply had enough of Yonge Street, and the murder proved to be a test of political will. The day before the march, Crombie's office received over 200 phone calls between 8:30 a.m., and 2:30 that afternoon. Many messages were from mothers of young children, who were angry, frustrated, and demanded what was being done to rid the strip of its many sex businesses.

While some of the protestors, including children who knew Emanuel, were sobbing at the loss of their friend, others were shaking in disbelief. *Why were these seedy places allowed to exist? Why wasn't the city doing anything, to close them permanently?* News emerged that shortly before the murder, Mayor Crombie wrote a letter to Ontario Premier William Davis, imploring the province to move quickly so the city could clean-up "the yawning cesspool of Yonge Street." Most terrifying of all was the belief held by many parents that if action wasn't taken quickly, there would soon be more children abducted and murdered by pedophiles.

Surrounded by a crowd carrying signs with a drawing of gallows and a hangman's noose reading "Up with capital punishment again! Down with body rub joints" and "Kill the dirty pigs," Reverend Jackman stood, arms outstretched like Christ on the cross, the sign from Charlie's Angels behind him promising dirty movies, love aids, and plenty of girls. For those gathered mourning the loss, it symbolized the exact moment good met evil. Good may have failed to prevent Emanuel's death, but the protest, and others to come in the following days and weeks, would do everything in their power to destroy the evil the Yonge Street strip had become.

Continuing down the strip, Mayor Crombie expressed his sympathy, and promised changes would be made to clean-up the area. Over the next few days the province, Metro, and the city were strategizing ways to close body rubs, including crackdowns, changes to existing legislation and licensing, and making Yonge Street owners and landlords responsible for any sexual activities going-on in their commercial properties, a move fiercely fought by sex shop owners who saw their livelihoods coming to an end.

Chapter Three: Burial of an Innocent

Shoeshine boy's funeral tugs at the hearts of strangers
-The Globe and Mail, Friday August 5, 1977

On Thursday, August 4, 1977, thousands came together to mourn the loss of Emanuel Jaques. It was a time for tears, anger, and unanswered questions. United by sadness, huge crowds attended the visitation for Emanuel at the Ryan & Odette Funeral Home on Dundas Street West. Inside the chapel, a gold-painted figure of Christ on a black cross was on the wall above the boy's casket, and over three dozen wreaths and bouquets filling the room. "We wanted to donate everything for free," said funeral home manager David Lasiuk to a reporter from the *Globe and Mail*, who also interviewed the gravedigger at Holy Cross Cemetery, a man from Portugal. "We felt it was the least we could do. It's such a terrible tragedy." Once the family members said their final goodbye, the funeral procession soon made its way to nearby St. Agnes, a Catholic church which had been transferred from the Italian to the Portuguese community a number of years earlier.

Packed to capacity, about 3,000 who were unable to get in the church waited patiently outside, standing on the entrance steps, and flooding the sidewalk. In attendance were not only family and friends of the Jaques, but schoolmates, neighbours from Regent Park, police officers and homicide detectives investigating the case, reporters, and politicians including Mayor Crombie, Metro Chairman Paul Godfrey, Alderman Art Eggleton, and hundreds of strangers who never met the young shoeshine boy in life, but wanted to express their sympathies at his death. Both Crombie and Godfrey had young children of their own, and recall the overwhelming grief at the time. "I remember how painful it was to sit there and view that tiny coffin, and thought how lucky I was to have my young sons who were four and less than a year old in 1977, and how those parents must've felt," says Godfrey. "It sort of tore the heart out of me."

Bishop Aloysius Ambrozic, along with five priests, conducted the funeral mass and Emanuel's final absolution. Inside, the church service went on for less than half an hour, as prayers were repeated by the congregation, asking for mercy upon their souls; outside, some questioned if the killers of Emanuel even had souls, and how they deserved to be tortured and executed.

Outside St. Agnes, a man stating he was from the Regent Park Community Improvement Association named Austin Raymond Miller was circulating a petition, STAMP OUT GAYS AND BODY RUBS. Claiming he had already amassed a thousand signatures, Miller promised he would get many more, and forward the petition to Mayor Crombie, who described Emanuel's murder as a "supreme tragedy." Earlier that week, a Grade 6 student named Luis Sequeira began collecting names for his own petition, which he was going to present to Premier William Davis. Obtaining over a thousand signatures, many of them from children, the 12-year-old said he began the petition to make Yonge Street safe for kids again, and remind the Premier that authorities needed to deal harshly with Emanuel's killers, since they "didn't want another boy or girl to suffer like this boy must have. We appeal to be very hard on the inhuman people and we appeal to take the Yonge Street sin strip out. Yours truly the Youth of Toronto." Many at the time were already referring to Emanuel as "a martyr to Torontonians."

    With many bursting into tears at the sight of the tiny white lambskin-covered casket emerging from the church, Emanuel's body was carried by relatives and friends about his age, including his older brother Luciano, and friend Shane McLean. Some reached out to touch the coffin as it passed, saying their final goodbyes. The huge, 250-car funeral procession was almost three miles long, with police officers on motorcycles speeding ahead, blocking-off intersections as the procession made its way to the burial site at Holy Cross Cemetery in Thornhill. Arriving 90 minutes later, the family was met by an open grave covered by a brown canvas tent. Suspended above the awaiting grave was a gold-painted concrete burial vault used to protect the casket, and keep the coffin from sinking into the earth.

For the family, particularly Emanuel's mother Maria and father Valdemiro, the funeral of their child was overwhelming beyond measure. To them, the hopes and dreams they had for 12-year-old Emanuel when they came to Canada were gone forever. Overcome by emotion, they were unable to walk to the gravesite without assistance. With the priest praying as Emanuel was lowered into the ground, sorrow turned to anger for some, who shouted that the boy's killers deserved to be murdered. A number of family members went limp and fainted. Valdemiro had to be held back as he tried to throw himself on his son's casket while Maria, dressed all in black, collapsed and was carried off to a waiting car by family friend Gordon Stuckless. With press present at the funeral, the tragic scene was captured by photographers, appearing in newspapers the next day.

Within days of Emanuel's murder, a number of fundraising efforts took place. Along with the Ryan & Odette Funeral Home covering the costs of the burial, there was the 'I Give a Damn' fund. Created by North York Mayor Mel Lastman, the charity ultimately raised $12,484.37 from 587 contributors. Another initiative, organized by a group of Citizen Band radio enthusiasts, raised $3,468, while the Emanuel Jaques Memorial Fund saw over $8,500 provided to the family. Many corporations also made generous donations, including CP Air, which provided tickets for the entire Jaques family so they could return back to Portugal for a vacation. It was reported that even sex shop operators and prostitutes — who considered the shoeshine boy as "one of us" — were in the process of creating a trust fund for the family.

During the visitation at the funeral home, many mourners also made donations, which were later taken to 51 Division Police Station on Regent Street, where Stuckless was photographed by The *Toronto Star* on August 3, 1977. Hair uncombed, wearing a white short-sleeved shirt with an open collar, the exhausted-looking Stuckless sat behind a table, surrounded by a pile of open envelopes, and bills of all denominations held together with elastic bands.

"Money flows in for family of murdered shoeshine boy. Gordon Stuckless, a friend of the Jaques family, counts over $2,695 left in envelopes at the funeral home where the body of murdered Manuel [sic] Jaques...by thousands of mourners. Stuckless was counting the money in #51 Metro Police Station on Regent Street," read the photo caption. [4]

The same week as Emanuel's funeral, security was extremely tight at Toronto's Old City Hall as three of the men charged with the slaying, Robert Wayne Kribs, Josef Woods, and Werner Gruener, made a brief court appearance at Toronto's Old City Hall. Outside, members of the public were denied entrance to Courtroom 21 as Justice of the Peace Larry Tatangelo remanded the three in custody to the following Tuesday, the same time as Saul David Betesh would appear in court. Although their courtroom appearance before Tatangelo was brief, it demonstrated the highly peculiar personalities of the men, which would become more apparent in the weeks and months to come.

Appearing gaunt, the trio rose as the judge entered the court. Woods, stone-faced, stared in front of him, while Kribs kept whispering to Gruener to put away the well-worn copy of The Bible he pulled out and started reading earlier.

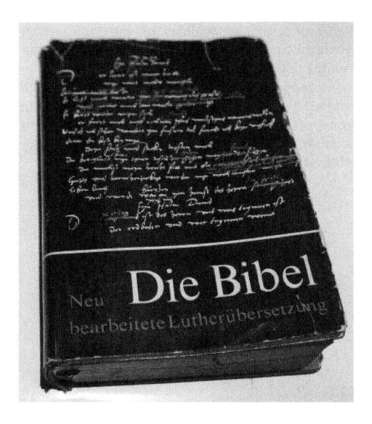

*Werner Gruener's German-language copy of The Bible
(Courtesy Toronto Police)*

Usually silent, Gruener, who often appeared dazed, was the only one to speak before the judge, stating he had already talked to a lawyer when asked if he had obtained legal representation. When asked the same question, Kribs and Woods nodded to indicate they had attorneys. Kribs, who had earlier run-ins with the law, was also due to stand trial that September on another matter. In May, before the murder of Emanuel, he had been arrested following a raid on Paradise Session House, was out on bail, and scheduled to appear in court on a charge of keeping a bawdy house.

Within days of Emanuel's funeral, news broke of politicians working on plans using whatever legal means necessary to close Yonge Street strip's sex industry. The goal at the time: police crackdowns, followed by changes to legislation. A team of politicians, lawyers, and licensing specialists was quickly assembled, including Metro Chairman and spokesman for a special Yonge Street committee Paul Godfrey, Mayor David Crombie, Director of the Metro Licensing Commission J.H. Neville, Ontario Assistant Deputy Attorney-General John Hilton, City Solicitor William Callow, Metro Solicitor Alex Joy, Toronto Aldermen Pat Sheppard, and Art Eggleton. A number of private meetings were held that week promising, according to Godfrey, that legal measures "some new and some not so new" would be swiftly implemented.

With the headline, "Politicians lay battle plans to clean up Yonge strip, the *Toronto Star* reported: "...draft legislation basically meets the requests that Metro has made to the province over the past several months," adding that Metro was in the process of seeking powers to license and control not only nude services and nude encounters, but the licensing of pinball machines in the city's many arcades, and the ability to apply for an injunction whenever licensing by-laws were violated. "The politicians were put under increased pressure to do something about the Yonge St. Strip after the sex slaying there of shoeshine boy Emanuel Jaques, 12, a week ago. Emanuel's body was found on the roof of a body rub parlour. Police said he had been made the victim of a sex orgy."[5]

Boy forced to commit sex acts at knifepoint, Jaques trial told

Newspaper headline (author collection)

Clean-up efforts included a number of police raids, which had been initiated just over two weeks prior to Emanuel's murder, resulting in 100 arrests, and over 150 charges laid. One of the body rub parlours raided was located close to where Emanuel was shining shoes at Yonge and Dundas, and a number of individuals were charged with keeping a common bawdy house.

Today Emanuel Dies, Tomorrow Others Might Die Too: Death to All Sex Criminals
-Protest sign carried outside Toronto City Hall

The murder of Emanuel Jaques saw the city, and its growing Portuguese community in particular, mobilize like no other time before or since. Founded by extremely industrious immigrants who did everything possible to build a better life for their families in Canada, the city's

Portuguese were outraged at the horrific murder of a child who could very well have been one of their own. Radio stations and newspapers like *Comunidade* covered the murder and trial of the four accused men.

Founded in June of 1975 by the Portuguese Development Committee/Movimento Comunitario Português, *Comunidade* was different from other Portuguese-Canadian newspapers, as its content was original, and not simply a collection of articles from newspapers in Portugal. Focusing on the lives of working-class immigrants in Canada rather than those back home, the newspaper "urged greater participation in Canadian society and sought to educate immigrants about their rights and responsibilities under the Canadian legal and political system."[6]

On Monday August 8, 1977, Toronto witnessed one of the largest marches in its history. Organized through the Portuguese Radio Club and its director Jose Rafael, an estimated 15,000 to 20,000 protestors — mainly of members of the Portuguese community — shouted slogans demanding a clean-up of downtown, and the return of capital punishment. On a scale unheard of at the time, some demonstrators drove in from cities and towns outside of Toronto for the rally. Marching along Dundas Street west behind a white car, sign-carrying protesters headed downtown, finally arriving at Nathan Phillips Square outside City Hall. Despite being the largest city square of its kind in the country, the demonstration was overflowing onto Queen and other surrounding streets.

For the crowd, prison wasn't enough for the sex killers of an innocent child. Strapped to a van was a black wooden gallows, a life-size dummy swaying back and forth from a noose tied around its neck, a nearby sign reading "Hang them."

A life-size effigy representing one of the four men charged with Emanuel's murder hangs from a noose during the August 8, 1977 protest at Toronto's City Hall (Courtesy York University Libraries, Clara Thomas Archives & Special Collections, Domingos Marques fonds, ASC17414)

Throughout the crowd, other placards had four drawings — one each for Woods, Gruener,

Betesh and Kribs — with the ages of each man, and the words "Justice as soon as possible." Many carried cardboard posters with Emanuel's public school portrait photo. Some shouted hanging the accused men was much too easy, and that they should be made to suffer, slowly and painfully, as had Emanuel.

The anger of the protestors was directed not only at the men responsible for the boy's death, but towards sex shop owners, along with the city and the province, for allowing the Yonge Street strip to decline in the first place. At one point, Toronto's acting mayor Art Eggleton spoke to the crowd: "I trust that Emanuel's death will not be in vain. The Strip is like a cancer spreading throughout our city." Many called for a greater police presence downtown. Others spoke angrily about Prime Minister Pierre Trudeau, under whose government Capital Punishment was abolished, and asked what he would do if it was one of *his* sons who was murdered?

After City Hall, the massive demonstration made its way to Queen's Park, where the crowd, demanding to see Premier William Davis, was growing angrier and more impatient while waiting for someone to come out and speak to them. Eventually a representative emerged and, despite promises that the province was looking into ways of preventing future murders on the infamous street, some hollered they would not vote for Crombie or Davis in future elections. Infuriated with being unable to walk down Yonge with their families without feeling harassed, intimidated or offended, Toronto didn't want more empty political promises, studies, committees, or reports: it wanted immediate action. Blame for the strip's steady decline was everywhere, from faulting police for not having enough officers patrolling Yonge to landlords renting their premises to body rub businesses, and politicians of all levels of government for failing to act on clean-up efforts.

Speaking on condition of anonymity, sources at Queen's Park told the press that powers had been in place to curtail the sex trade on Yonge Street, and Metro could have easily tapped-into existing measures available under the Ontario Municipal Act. While preparing legislation which would grant Metro powers over sex shops, including how many were allowed to exist, licensing, and display signage, one unnamed source stated, "It needn't have gone this far if they'd taken advantage of powers they've had for years." Citing Section 470 of the Municipal Act, and stating it could have been used to by the city and Metro to seek injunctions to close body rubs — as they were operating without a licence as required by bylaw — the individual told The *Toronto Star*, "They (Metro and Toronto) could have controlled them to a far greater degree than they have."[7] Likewise, the source stated other options had been readily available, including Metro having the ability to seek injunctions to shutter body rubs for contravening health or fire safety bylaws.

The discovery of Emanuel's naked corpse on the roof of a Yonge Street body rub parlour enraged Torontonians, particularly its Portuguese community. A number of demonstrations against the men charged with his murder were held across Canada, the largest in Toronto outside City Hall, where an estimated 15,000 men, women and children gathered to protest, and demand the reinstatement of Capital Punishment (Courtesy York University Libraries, Clara Thomas Archives & Special Collections, Domingos Marques fonds, ASC17414)]

For many years the press, The *Toronto Sun* in particular, had been after the city and the province to do something about cleaning-up the growing sex industry. To them, Emanuel's death was a vindication they were right all along, and cries to clean-up Yonge Street had gone unheard and unanswered for far too long. In January 1973, the *Sun* published an acerbic editorial critical of Mayor Crombie's efforts to rid the strip of its smut, calling it a "growing cancer." While average citizens overwhelmingly approved of a clean-up of body rubs and sex shops, others believed Crombie's efforts were reminiscent of censorship. Cautioning that the strip was fast becoming the Canadian version of New York's then-infamous 42nd Street, the *Sun* adopted a 'put up or shut up' attitude, remarkably, even of itself. Having published adult industry ads in the past — and profiting from some of the very same body rub parlours it chose to criticize — the paper conducted a survey of opinions about Yonge Street and, as of that March 1st, stated it would no longer be accepting display ads from many of those sex businesses.

"It was part of the job to get criticism coming your way usually on a daily basis, so there was nothing new about criticism of some event or some cause," says Crombie, who served as Mayor of Toronto from 1972 to 1978. "The *Toronto Sun* in those days was 'the little paper that grew,' and their views were quite clear."

For several years, the *Sun* fiercely expressed its opposition to not only the rising number of body rub parlours in the city, but the sex industry as a whole, particularly when it came to the availability of adult-only magazines to minors. In 1976, the year before Emanuel's murder, the newspaper ran a number of stories against the sex industry and pornographic publications, many making their way from being sold under the counter or behind wooden or plastic barriers with signs reading 'Adults Only' in bookstores and neighbourhood variety shops, in full view of children. This was no longer acceptable to moral Torontonians. Yonge Street stores, stocking magazines like *Penthouse*,

Oui, *Playboy*, and racy British import *Club International* was one thing, but many of these same titles out in the open in corner stores where kids bought pop, chocolate and *Archie* comic books would no longer be tolerated.

With the headline, 'Porn crackdown questioned,' a *Sun* article began, "One man's depraved filth is another man's way of life. At least that's what one manager of a Toronto adult bookstore says to Ontario Attorney-General Roy McMurtry's concern that hard-core pornography, once available only under the counter, is now being sold openly in neighbourhood variety stores in full view of children."[8] Much like the owners and operators of Toronto's many body rub parlours following Emanuel's murder, proprietors of adult bookstores were critical of any efforts on the part of the city, the province, or the federal government that would limit X-rated publications they were allowed to sell, with titles focusing on not only sex, but sadomasochism and domination, with titles like *Whimper: pain, torture, and incredible bondage photos teenage latex bitches*, and the *Photo-Guide to Spanking Schoolgirls*.

With politicians like Attorney-General McMurtry stating government regulations were required "to control this depraved filth," the province of Ontario was considering working with the federal government to strictly limit the types of publications that made their way into Canada, many of them skin mags with titles like *Barely Legal*, *Gallery*, and *Genesis* coming from the United

States. "Who's to say what's immoral? Is obscenity in the eye of the beholder? The people who yell the loudest don't buy these things," questioned Leo St. Louis, the manager of Times Square Bookstore in downtown Toronto, which had signage in place restricting access to certain sections of his store to adults 18 and older. Dismissive of McMurtry and inferring the Attorney-General had nothing better to do with his time, St. Louis added: "The hockey season's over and now he's got to find something else to stay in the public eye." Facing criticism from the media, The *Toronto Sun* ran an editorial about McMurtry's efforts to clean-up the province titled "McHeadlines."

Over several years, the Ontario government spearheaded a number of campaigns, ranging from seatbelt legislation to tougher drunk driving laws, and addressing the issue of hockey violence. The latest, aimed at curtailing pornography, was viewed by some with skepticism.

Now he [McMurtry] seems intent on being Mr. McClean by campaigning against sin and smut. At the moment he's particularly incensed at the 'depraved filth' one can purchase at bookstands. He's gone a step further than Mayor Crombie did when, soon after being elected Mayor, he won attention (and acclaim and abuse) for mentioning his intention to 'clean up Yonge Street.' Which he didn't do, but never mind, he made the purveyors of sex nervous. The trouble with such clean-up campaigns is that they seldom work. Those in charge become zealots fighting the devil (or attempt to stop the tide), or they give up and turn a blind eye to reality. In either case smut continues to exist.[9]

If 1977 was the year of outrage over Emanuel's death, 1976 was the lead-up to the war on pornography, and not just in Toronto. Police were stepping-up raids on shops in the city, and places like St. Catharines, seizing sex toys and other items, with criminal charges being laid. In May of 1976, Toronto Police Chief Harold Adamson, speaking at the Policeman of the Year awards dinner, said it was time to keep "depraved garbage" on newsstands and in variety and grocery stores out of sight from children, adding that Attorney-General McMurtry was right when it came to pornography coming to Canada being controlled by American organized crime. Solutions to keeping these glossy, hard-core magazines away from kids included licensing the distribution of these publications, and tighter screening at the border for adult books and magazines entering the country, with ones deemed unsuitable being rejected. In the first case, local government would be able to control which publications found their way to corner variety stores and newsstands; in the second, Canada Customs would make the decision over what was deemed to be pornographic, and unsuitable for young eyes.

Motivated by the potential of a ban, and fearful of a growing public controversy, the head office of The Becker Milk Company — a popular franchised chain of convenience stores —

voluntarily prohibited the sale of adult-oriented magazines in all of its stores, such as *Penthouse* and *Oui*; *Playboy*, less revealing than other magazines at the time, was relegated to behind-the-counter displays, which obscured the cover but left the title visible. Some Becker's store managers, afraid of losing revenue, were extremely unhappy with the decision. *Penthouse*, the Bob Guccione-founded magazine which was outselling *Playboy* two-to-one and printing photos far more explicit than its older counterpart, said it would challenge the ban.

Pornographic magazines seized from the apartment where Emanuel was slain. This issue of Oui from February 1975 had a feature article on the Children of God cult, of which Werner Gruener was a member (Courtesy Toronto Police)

Just over a year after the war on adult magazines was waged, Emanuel Jaques was murdered. Making news across Canada and the United States, few could anticipate just how swift reactions would be by the city against the sex industry, particularly body rub parlours, and the outrage in the months to come as the men charged with the vicious murder were put on trial.

Chapter Four: Backlash

> Police said the boy had been drowned in a sink after being subjected to a 12-hour orgy of abuse by homosexuals. The uproar was immediate and deafening. There were demands for the restoration of capital punishment. There were demands for reprisals against homosexuals. There were demands that body rub parlours be put to the torch, that their employees be tarred and feathered.
> -*Maclean's*, September 5, 1977

Within days of Emanuel's sex slaying, anger, fear, and blame was everywhere. The press was pointing fingers directly at municipal and provincial politicians, demanding to know why existing by-laws had not been used much more aggressively to close the doors on Yonge Street's many body rub parlours. Some faulted lawmakers and Toronto Police for not being tough enough when it came to dealing with prostitutes, pimps, and sex shop owners. And for the city's growing and increasingly prominent gay community, the timing of the murder could not possibly have been worse.

The year Emanuel Jaques was killed was 1977, 'the year of the child' — not according to the United Nations, however — but Anita Bryant. An icon to many at the time, Bryant was the embodiment of time-honoured American ideals of wholesomeness, and God-fearing values. Gifted with a beautiful voice, Bryant was a natural-born performer, winning prizes and securing a coveted spot on *Arthur Godfrey's Talent Scouts*, which featured legends like Tony Bennett, Eddie Fisher, Patsy Cline, and Pat Boone. Born and raised in an extremely religious household, Bryant's father was initially opposed to her talent show auditions. Winning first place, the teenager had a minor hit with the song *Sinful to Flirt* at age 16. Two years later, in 1958, Bryant won the Miss Oklahoma beauty pageant. From there, her career was set.

Emerging as second runner-up in 1959's Miss America beauty pageant, Bryant was viewed as a model of decorum. Marrying Miami disc jockey Bob Green in 1960, she soon raised a family, recorded a number of albums over the years with hits like *Paper Roses* selling over a million copies, and she was presented with a gold disc by the Recording Industry Association of America. In 1969, Bryant landed a lucrative endorsement deal, becoming the spokeswoman for the Florida Citrus Commission, and making the tagline famous: "Come to the Florida Sunshine Tree. A day without orange juice is like a day without sunshine." That same year, she was part of the Rally for Decency, which was held at the Orange Bowl in protest of rock band The Doors, and lead singer Jim Morrison's lewd behaviour on stage.

By early 1977, Bryant was far less known for her singing career than her stance on homosexuals. That year, she successfully campaigned against a human rights ordinance amendment in Florida's

Miami-Dade County, which made it illegal to discriminate based on "affectional or sexual preference" for housing, public accommodations, loans, and employment. Encouraged by her dedication, American evangelist Jerry Falwell — who told a crowd at a Miami rally before the referendum "so-called gay folks would just as soon kill you as look at you" — wholeheartedly supported Bryant's crusade. Years later, Falwell would find himself embroiled in numerous lawsuits, including one where he referred to the gay and lesbian-friendly Metropolitan Community Churches as "brute beasts," and products of a satanic system which would "one day be utterly annihilated and there will be a celebration in heaven." Once referring to homosexuality as a "character flaw" along with adultery and dishonesty, Falwell would later infamously say, "AIDS is not just God's punishment for homosexuals; it is God's punishment for the society that tolerates homosexuals."

Soon, the former singer and beauty pageant queen founded Save Our Children, an organization based on fears that youngsters would be targeted by gay pedophiles, stating, "As a mother, I know that homosexuals cannot biologically reproduce children; therefore, they must recruit our children." Due largely to Bryant's input, other local ordinances prohibiting discrimination on the basis of sexual orientation were repealed in St. Paul, Minnesota, Wichita, Kansas, and Eugene, Oregon. Fundraising cards were distributed with Bryant's image, stating "YES, ANITA! I want to help you bring America back to God and morality. Please send me all issues of your Protect America's Children *Newsletter*." At the bottom, a Miami Beach post office box address was included.

For gays and lesbians, Bryant's Save Our Children campaign was considered extremely dangerous to their civil rights, not just in the United States, but also in Canada. At times during her lectures, Bryant would cite contentious passages from the Bible, such as the Holiness Code from Leviticus, or Sodom and Gomorrah, to justify her homophobic beliefs. In response many gays, along with celebrities like Bette Midler, Barbra Streisand, and Jane Fonda, publicly protested Bryant and the Save Our Children organization. Boycotting — or as some called it at the time, "gaycotting" Florida orange juice — T-shirts, buttons, and bumper stickers soon appeared reading, "Squeeze a Fruit for Anita" and "Anita Bryant Sucks Oranges."

On June 25, just over a month prior to Emanuel's disappearance, rape and murder, a newly-created Toronto-based group called the Coalition to Stop Anita Bryant staged the first of two demonstrations, with the second march held in the city on July 22. The American anti-gay wave initiated by Bryant was creeping over the border, and threatening to further fuel discrimination in Canada, where homosexuals were faced with the likes of Reverend Ken Campbell. A Baptist minister, Campbell founded Renaissance Canada in 1974, a conservative lobby group promoting "parent power" in education, and Choose Life Canada a decade later, which picketed abortion clinics, and set-up an office adjacent to Dr. Henry Morgentaler's abortion clinic in Toronto.

High on the list of Campbell's causes was opposition to the inclusion of gays and lesbians in Canada's human rights code. Along with founding Renaissance Canada — which sponsored the Canadian leg of Anita Bryant's anti-gay tour to Ontario — Campbell was against books he considered unwholesome, including coming of age novel *The Catcher in the Rye* by J.D. Salinger, and Margaret Laurence's *The Diviners*, which deals with issues of race, sexuality, and abortion, and petitioned to having them removed from public schools.

Upon Bryant's arrival to the province, over 800 men and women marched on Yonge Street against her, marking the biggest gay and lesbian demonstration up to that time. While some in the media supported Bryant's anti-homosexual stance, many were opposed to her presence in Canada. In a tongue-in-cheek editorial, the *Montreal Gazette* referred to the spokeswoman as "the lady who has made it her business to tell us oranges are good for us and homosexuals bad." At the time, Bryant was receiving $100,000 a year for her work with the Florida Citrus Commission, which was growing concerned at the affect her fierce opinions would have on the massive industry in the sunshine state. "Evidently she likes $100,000 a year more than she dislikes homosexuals — or does she know something about the powers of OJ to set the world straight that the rest of us don't?" asked the editorial in the *Gazette* when Bryant began to back off from her hardline position on gays.

Underestimating how many people did not subscribe to her views, Bryant's career and personal life soon unravelled She lost her lucrative deal with the citrus industry, and was dropped by commercial advertisers she worked for such as Kraft Foods, sewing machine manufacturer Singer, and Coca-Cola. In 1980, her marriage to Bob Green ended in an explosive, highly publicized divorce. One of the biggest reasons for Bryant's downfall was her attempt to associate homosexuals to pedophilia, particularly through statements like "a particularly deviant-minded (gay) teacher could sexually molest children."

For homosexuals at the time, Bryant's comments were nothing less than incendiary. While gay rights were making advances over the years, there was now fear and anger that these gains would be stonewalled. Several of the men responsible for Emanuel's 12-hour ordeal were gay, which was repeated constantly in the media, stating the boy died during a "homosexual orgy." In many ways, the community was right to be afraid. In Toronto, well-established gay bars like the St. Charles Tavern — converted out of part of an old fire hall on Yonge Street — was frequently targeted by vandals. The bar's popular Halloween drag queen shows brought out crowds of thousands of fans, along with teenagers who drove up and down

Yonge Street screaming "faggots" and "queers" while hurling mushy tomatoes and rotten eggs at patrons standing outside. Worse still was the fear of gay bashing, with men being beaten simply because of their sexual orientation.

The controversy over Emanuel's death fueled action not only in Toronto against the city's growing sex industry, but other Canadian cities tiring of the many porno theatres, X-rated bookstores, and massage parlours in downtown areas of Montreal, Halifax, and Vancouver. Even normally staid *Maclean's* magazine published a feature entitled "Mean streets: The wages of sin is backlash." Uncharacteristically vitriolic, the piece stated that after a decade of "slow surrender to the siren song of the permissive society, Canada's biggest cities are fighting back against prostitution and pornography, mainstays of what has become a multi-million-dollar sex industry," which Canadian cities were accomplishing through the use of legitimate (non sex industry-related) businesses banding together, zoning restrictions, and licensing for body rub parlours with the goal of driving them out of existence permanently. Those opposed to sex shops in urban Canadian centres dogged them "...with the grim determination and frightening speed of lymphatic cancer and, civic officials fear, unless curtailed will ultimately kill off the areas they infest."[10]

Many gay and lesbian leaders across the country were nervous the backlash against the sex industry would see homosexual communities lumped-in with body rub parlours because of the murder, with them targeted by citizens, police, politicians, and law-makers. One of the most outspoken was George Hislop. Canada's best-known gay activist, Hislop was widely respected and fearless in his pursuit of equality for homosexuals. While many gays were closeted at the time, Hislop, an actor in his early days, was proud of his relationship with Ronald (Ronnie) Shearer, and would later fight for pension benefits. Becoming a public advocate in 1969 after Criminal Code amendments made sodomy illegal between consenting adults over the age of 21, Hislop formed the Community Homophile Association of Toronto, CHAT, in December of 1970, which acted as a social service and support agency for gay men and women, involved in public education and politics.

As CHAT President at the time of the murder, Hislop was the public face representing homosexuals in the city, and the person Saul David Betesh approached for advice days after Emanuel's death, with Hislop urging him to turn himself in to the authorities, and putting him in contact with his initial attorney Richard Parker, who accompanied him to the 51 Division police station where he made his lengthy statement. Parker would later terminate his arrangement with Betesh by mutual consent, following his advice that it would be in Betesh's best interests to be represented by another attorney.

By this point, Betesh's co-accused Kribs, Woods, and Gruener had left him in Toronto, and were fleeing by train to Vancouver, where they said they would later hook-up with him. Coming into the offices of CHAT a number of times over the previous two years, Betesh was known to Hislop, who would later testify at the Jaques murder trial of the four men. Instead of receiving any credit for imploring Betesh to confess — which led to the discovery of Emanuel's body on the roof of Charlie's Angels, and the arrest of the three other men — Hislop felt cast aside, stating "if I had been a counsellor or priest...I'd be a hero. Instead I get kooks phoning me up."

Considering the mounting public anger against gays following the murder, Hislop believed a tremendous gay backlash was possible, especially with the press stating a "homosexual orgy" took place the night of Emanuel's death. The concern was that *all* homosexuals would be guilty by association, perceived as pedophiles or worse, as child killers. "To a certain extent, the body rub shops absorbed the initial heat with this outrageous crime came to light," stated Hislop at the time. "But once they're gone, and once the trial begins and the sordid details become public, I fear that emotions will run strongly against gays. I can understand why, but it's a pity. The gay community was shocked by what happened as anyone else was."

In an attempt to steer attention away from homosexuals in the city, explain its position, and clear-up media misrepresentation following Emanuel's murder, a press conference was held in the Church Street office of CHAT. To quash growing anti-homosexual sentiments, a letter was sent to Mayor Crombie about the perils of associating all gays with the killers. In attendance at the press conference were CHAT President George Hislop, and Tom Warner, Co-ordinator for the Coalition for Gay Rights.

"Statements such as 'homosexual slaying' and 'homosexual orgy' result in indicting all homosexuals, thus making us co-accused," said Warner. "This assumes guilt by association and suggests that all gay people are at least indirectly responsible for the crime. Clearly, the gay community cannot be held responsible for the criminal action on the part of some of its members just as all heterosexuals cannot be held responsible for the actions of some." Frustration was also expressed over the "little acknowledgement given by the police, the media or community leaders to the contribution made by the gay community...in bringing to authorities information and assistance culminating in the apprehension of the four accused," a reference to Hislop advising Saul Betesh to contact the police, and arranging for a lawyer on his behalf, "because Betesh was afraid the police would beat him up" if he went into the station without an attorney by his side.

Objecting to the notion the press was somehow complicit in spreading homophobia, *Globe and Mail* columnist Dick Beddoes addressed Warner's comments about "media misrepresentation of gay people in the sensationalistic coverage of Emanuel Jaques's death." Of Warner's statement, he wrote: "We don't like the media linking homosexuals with killing...that, it says here, is so much flatulent nonsense. It says here that the Toronto media generally have been responsible in their coverage, sensitive to the rights of the accused, careful not to stimulate antipathy toward the homosexual establishment. Mr. Hislop's part in the case has been adequately reported."[11]

Toronto back at the time was a very different place from what it is today when it came to acceptance of gay and lesbian lifestyles. The timing of the murder, the fact that several of the men charged were homosexuals, and the growth of the city's gay community caused considerable backlash among conservative-minded members of the public. According to Betesh's attorney Paul Tomlinson:

Homosexuals, for the first time since the late Sixties and early Seventies, were beginning to acknowledge, 'I'm a homosexual, so what?' And the majority of the public back then didn't feel good will towards homosexuals — that's the way it was. And when three men get together — four men, but I don't think one of them shouldn't have been charged — and kill a 12-year-old boy, the public became outraged. The public had a hard time distinguishing between homosexuality, and a pedophile. And for the first time, homosexuals were acknowledging they *were* homosexuals; that they should be given the right to teach, to be

Scoutmasters, to be normal people. But the public were reluctant in saying, 'yes, I don't mind a homosexual teaching my son or daughter.' And it was very apparent. There was no question there was terrible prejudice, and there had been for generations. And then when this happened, there was this, 'see, I told you what would happen' attitude among the general public. They did know the difference between a gay person and a pedophile, for God's sake. So there was that element going on at that time in society that caused this to be bigger than it otherwise would have been. That was that factor.

And then, there was the inescapable issue of where Emanuel's rape and murder took place, on the notorious Yonge Street Strip, an area under fire from the public over the growth of its seemingly unstoppable sex industry. *Maclean's* magazine called Yonge "unarguably the meanest street in the nation," one riddled with petty hoodlums, and pesky hookers, who now feared for their livelihoods as talks loomed of a clean-up. Owners of adult bookstores, porno theatres, and body rub parlours were furious, knowing this action would not only cripple, but kill their businesses. Just weeks after Emanuel's murder, discussions were underway to support a resolution passed by the Canadian Association of Chiefs of Police, urging the Minister of Justice to consider re-implementing the vagrancy section of the Criminal Code dealing with prostitutes, repealed in 1972, and making provisions which would see the prosecution of both male and female prostitutes, which had also been repealed in 1972. In August, newspaper stories began circulating about boys, some as young as 12, working the streets as juvenile prostitutes. Making matters worse, a number of these children had been physically harmed during sadomasochistic encounters with older men, reminiscent of Emanuel Jaques' final hours.

Lawyer Paul Tomlinson maintains the location where the young boy was killed had a great deal to do with public opinion about the defendants, in particular his client.

"Yonge Street was known as the world's longest road, and it was the heart of Toronto. People who knew of Toronto may have only known of one thing, and that was Yonge Street, they'd heard about it so often. And back in the Sixties, Yonge Street had become a center for nightclubs, massage parlors, body rubs, adult entertainment movies, all that kind of thing, and it was basically a disgrace, there is no question. So the Yonge Street of old — representing the most famous street in Toronto — was not exactly representing Toronto in a favorable light. And this case certainly spurred the clean-up of Yonge Street, because not only had the death taken place on Yonge, but it had taken place in the upstairs apartment of a body rub parlour, and the boy's corpse had been hidden on the roof of this body rub parlour. So put all those factors together, and it caused a lot of press about the case that may otherwise not have been. Yonge Street really had become decrepit, and so has

Queen Street, but they cleaned that up where the Sheraton Centre Hotel stands today, right across from Osgoode Hall, that strip along there. It was all low-class nightclubs, and things like that. But Yonge Street still remained. And then the third factor was a question of psychopaths, and whether they should be classified in certain cases as a disease of the mind, that it caused them not to appreciate the nature of their case. There was a factor that may not have caused the press to get so involved, but it was certainly a factor, because all three of them were psychopaths. Betesh, in my mind, no question. He had probably suffered from schizophrenia as a child, which is often a forerunner to psychopathy, but psychopathy had definitely developed in Betesh; in my mind, there was no question that he was a first-class psychopath."

Although Betesh, one of the four men charged with Emanuel's murder, had some arms-length connection to Toronto's gay community through CHAT, it was almost impossible for some residents to distinguish that the crime was carried out by a group who actually had very little to do with Toronto's law-abiding homosexual community. The other three men who would also stand trial —Woods, Kribs, and Gruener — were basically a few very short steps above homelessness, and at various times in the months to come would deny they were homosexual, despite evidence proving otherwise.

If 1977 was, as Anita Bryant loudly proclaimed, the year for society to "save" children from homosexual predators, it was also the year of gays and lesbians making themselves more widely known by fighting for equal rights, and against discrimination based on sexual orientation. That year, the first gay demonstration took place in Atlantic Canada, triggered by the Canadian Broadcasting Corporation's decision to refuse airing gay public service announcements on CBC Radio. That March, Windsor, Ontario, became the third city in Canada to pass a resolution prohibiting discrimination against homosexual city employees. In April, nine women in the Canadian Armed Forces were dismissed because they were lesbians, creating an uproar. And following Emanuel's murder, gay community leaders in Toronto held a press conference "to deplore press coverage of [the] Jaques murder which implicates [the] entire gay community."

Controversy over the sexuality of Emanuel's killers did not cease after the trial of the men charged with his murder, and remains to this day. In her book *AIDS Activist: Michael Lynch and the Politics of Community*, Ann Silversides wrote:

The murder was widely referred to in the press as a homosexual killing, and a kind of fear and loathing descended on the city. According to Ed Jackson, a founding member of the *Body Politic* collective, the event was particularly frightening because it was difficult if not impossible to make the sharp distinction that the murder had been carried out by a group with little connection to the local gay community. Just three weeks before the murder, a report had recommended that sexual orientation be included in the Ontario Human Rights Code. That recommendation quickly 'went out the window' in the wake of the Jaques killing. The attitude seemed to be, 'If we give them more freedoms and rights, this is the kind of thing that will result,' Jackson told a federal inquiry.[12]

Throughout the summer of 1977 and during the trial in early 1978, controversies raged on. Demands for the immediate reinstatement of capital punishment in Canada were heard, with politicians including York Alderman Ben Nobleman asking Members of Parliament to debate the issue when Parliament met in the fall. Angry and disgusted at Emanuel's death, newspaper surveys of Ontario residents revealed overwhelming support for bringing back the noose — the only means of judicial execution in the country from 1867 to 1976 — particularly for sex offenders and child killers, including the men charged with Emanuel's murder. Somewhat surprisingly, at the same time approximately 92 to 95 per cent of the province's population was not opposed to crackdowns on prostitution but making it legal, so paid sexual services could be monitored and controlled by the government as opposed to the lack of regulation and enforcement which led to the unrestricted growth of the sex trade in Toronto.

The press, like politicians and police, was not immune to criticism. Unlike any case in Canadian history, coverage of the shoeshine boy murder was exceptionally graphic, both at the time of Emanuel's murder, and spiking in 1978 during the trial, when details were published of his sexual assault, drowning, and the discovery of his remains. Testimony from witnesses would reveal he was not the first boy who had been photographed and brutalized by the men, which fueled further outrage. For many, the facts surrounding how Emanuel died were simply too horrifying to stomach. Only years later would media coverage of the Jaques trial be surpassed by reports about the abductions, drugging, rapes, and murders perpetrated by husband-and-wife team Paul Bernardo and Karla Homolka in the early 1990s. As proved to be the case with the murders of Homolka's sister, Tammy, 15, along with Leslie Mahaffy, 14, and Kristen French, 15, not everyone appreciated reading or hearing about how Emanuel died.

Incensed subscribers flooded The *Globe and Mail*, The *Toronto Star*, and The *Toronto Sun* with letters to the editor expressing their disgust over articles they published. The week after Emanuel's sex slaying, *Star* senior editor Borden Spears addressed the controversy in an article headlined, "Bounds of taste strained in coverage of boy's death." In the piece, he explained how the *Star* has a policy manual for writers and editors, which dedicated six pages to the treatment of crime news, explained how stories like the shoeshine boy murder presented challenges.

Article from the Toronto Sun published when Emanuel's naked body was found, noting the location above a Yonge Street body rub (author collection)

"Brutal details of the crime were literally described," wrote Spears. "A radio commentator referred to the suspects, who had not yet been arraigned, as 'garbage.' Such phrases as 'homosexual orgy' tended to inflame public passions. Hysteria was demonstrated in letters to the editor and comments by politicians, parents and clergymen. Motive was clearly suggested. Is there a prospective juror among the adult population of Toronto who could rid his mind of all this when he sits in judgement on the facts produced in court?" Although Emanuel's mother consented to be interviewed on television, Spears stated the bounds of taste were 'severely stretched' when the highly emotional segment with Maria Jaques was broadcast.[13]

On the same page as Spears' piece was an editorial entitled "We never learn," which lamented mankind's tendency to react *after* the fact to problems which could have been addressed long before a tragedy, namely the shoeshine boy murder. Targeting the steady rise of the sex industry along the Dundas-Gerrard stretch of Yonge Street, the editorial deemed the strip "a magnet for criminals" and, without naming individuals, was highly critical of city and provincial politicians for failing to heed calls from citizens, police, and downtown business owners to clean-up the area. "Nothing effective was being done to curb it, at the political level, until the ghastly murder of shoeshine boy Emanuel Jaques," stated the editorial. "Now Queen's Park and Metro are scrambling to produce regulations with teeth in them to eliminate the public nuisance and menace on Yonge St. We're are capable of acting on hindsight after a tragedy or disaster. But will we ever learn to act on foresight?"

Although the position taken by the city and the province to accelerate clean-up efforts after the murder were applauded by many, others remained critical, claiming politicians, police and the press were responsible for creating a "moral panic." Those deemed undesirable — namely gays, prostitutes, body rub workers, and porno shop owners — disapproved of efforts to remove them from the strip, a place which, despite its seediness, was a place they called home. Emanuel's death changed that permanently. Another factor was the desirability of the area to investors who, it seemed, had been waiting for a dramatic change to happen. For years, Toronto real estate prices had been on the rise; once construction of the Eaton Centre was announced in the Sixties, Yonge's sex industry had to go.

A view of the roof of 245 Yonge Street, looking west at the newly-constructed Eaton Centre (Courtesy Toronto Police)

"...indoor forms of prostitution, particularly massage parlours, became problematized in Toronto and other Canadian cities as a result of economic shifts, urban development, policing practices, and local state interests. Economic interests and local state interests worked to develop the idea that these forms of prostitution constituted an urban social problem, a process exacerbated by media participation in the organization of a moral panic. In the wake of the murder of a young boy in Toronto, public support for the elimination of these places was galvanized. Police were therefore mandated to act, and local business interests were addressed as Yonge Street was cleared of its indoor sex trade."[14]

Sex shop owners, who had seen their businesses grow largely unchallenged by the authorities, were anxious following the murder. Many fought back, including Joe Martin Sr. of Jochatira Entertainment Ltd. The owner of Charlie's Angel, the body rub parlour above which Emanuel had been killed, Martin operated six other similar adult establishments along Yonge Street including Lady Luck, Pleasureland, and Caesar's Spa. He knew the men charged with the killing, and would let the massive and intimidating Kribs — who worked with the eccentric Woods as a bouncer — sleep overnight in the building. The perpetually slow Werner Gruener was assigned laundry duty, washing and bringing fresh sheets and towels to the girls working in the parlour, a job he got because the manager felt sorry for him.

Few average citizens, however, were expressing any sympathy for Toronto's downtown sex industry, and welcomed its demise. Adult book stores, X-rated movie houses, and body rubs were viewed as disgraceful, and roadblocks to improving the downtown core.

In an effort to stop any plans to quash the industry, Martin created The Freedom, Progress and Justice Society Platform to combat the "persecution" of sex-based businesses on the strip. Stepping-up their efforts to remove prostitutes and body rubs from Yonge Street, police raids resulted in 114 charges being laid before the end of August of 1977. While sympathetic over the murder, owners of these establishments maintained Emanuel's sex slaying had nothing to do with them, and it was being "wrongly pinned on the adult entertainment industry." Martin soon accused politicians of exploiting the crime for their own benefit — a "perverse attempt to exploit this tragedy" — and if the raids continued, he would produce a list of politicians who he claimed had used the sexual services at his establishments. Threatening to sue Attorney-General McMurtry, Toronto's Police Chief Adamson and others for $7 million, Martin also tried to deflect attention away from Charlie's Angels by stating Emanuel's naked body was not discovered by police on *his* roof, but that of a tailor shop, six feet away.

Chapter Five: "Hanging is for murderers!"
-Unidentified woman screaming at the funeral of Emanuel Jaques

Although extremely unlikely, repeated calls for the reinstatement of the death penalty remained, many of them coming from Toronto's Portuguese community. In the days and weeks following the Jaques murder, protestors demanded the ultimate punishment for murder be brought back. Some, like young father Bill McDowell, stood outside Charlie's Angels, his face covered by an ominous black hangman's hood as he held a sign reading: "How many more Emanuel's will die? Bring back capital punishment now," and urging passers-by to contact their Member of Parliament over the issue. Hundreds of others demonstrated in Ottawa, carrying pro-death penalty signs and shouting, "Kill them! Kill them!" saying it would save the nation the cost of a trial.

Signs were displayed in both English and Portuguese during the protest following the arrest of the men charged with Emanuel's murder. Many in attendance called for the closure of the Yonge Street Strip's sex industry, while others demanded death for the men responsible for the young boy's abduction, rape, and death. (Courtesy York University Libraries, Clara Thomas Archives & Special Collections, Domingos Marques fonds, ASC17414)

To summarize the position of Toronto's Portuguese community's position, the *Comunidade* newspaper published an editorial soon after the killing in its English-language supplement, entitled "Media Responsible for Overreaction."

As was announced by the Canadian media, a group of about 12,000 people from the Portuguese community in Toronto marched through the streets of Toronto on August the 8th, protesting the death of Emanuel Jaques who was found wrapped in a green garbage bag on the roof of a Yonge Street sex shop on August 1st. This tragedy shocked the whole of Toronto and Canada. We, the members of the Portuguese community in Toronto were not the only people who were horrified at the circumstances surrounding the death of Emanuel Jaques. Politicians such as the Premier of Ontario, William Davis, the Mayor of Toronto, David Crombie and others strongly reacted against the murder. We had many telephone calls from Portuguese and even more from Canadians, telling us to put pressure on the authorities in order that the whole issue of Yonge Street be solved.

From the very beginning the whole story was overly exaggerated and exploited by the Canadian media which purposely incited the public to react, and react they did through various demonstrations under a highly emotional climate. The road was therefore paved for thousands of people to show up at the demonstration of August the 8th, organized by Jose Rafael of the Portuguese Radio Club.

It is our belief however, that the majority of those who participated in the demonstration did so out of simpathy [sic] for the family of Emanuel Jaques and out of concern for their own childrens [sic] safety. We firmly believe that those people were there for these reasons and not because "they are people thirsty for blood," for revenge or to have capital punishment reinstated in our system.

To demonstrate against something one does not like is a very natural phenomenon in a democratic society like ours. There were however, Portuguese and Canadians alike who were shocked with the strong and violent tone of the demonstration. We had telephone calls from many Canadians, some of them insulting the community and the Portuguese in general, in a very uncivilized manner, and people of the stature of Gordon Sinclair ridiculing the Portuguese who live in Canada because of such a demonstration. To him and other individuals such as Mr. Larry Bondy who had the courage or little sense of insulting us on the telephone, we would like to tell them that Toronto has 80,000 Portuguese-Canadians (and they are legally here, Mr. Bondy!) who are an integral part of the Canadian society, that a large number of them are Canadian citizens with the entire right to have a saying in the destiny of this country, that they all have children who were born here and will die here and nobody can prohibit them from expressing their opinion!

There is a possibility that once more the Toronto media, misled by the leaders of the demonstration, made the public believe that such a demonstration had the support of all Portuguese organizations in Toronto, including clubs, social centers, churches and the Portuguese media. Or that all participants wanted revenge and blood as a few placards showed. If that was the impression it was not the reality because 90% of the Portuguese organizations did not officially support the demonstration nor did they agree with the uncivilized behavior of a few individuals.

In our view, which we believe is shared by many thousands of Portuguese Canadians scattered across this country, capital punishment will not solve the problem of crime in any society and it is an uncivilized way of punishing criminals who many times are the victims of the socio-political and economic system. Prostitution, exploitation of sex and violence is unfortunately permitted in many societies through television, magazines and other business enterprises in many disguised forms. Yonge Street is just a small example of this type of sex exploitation which leads into many criminal activities.

We believe that the media and its unscrupulous manipulation of crime, politicians and some individuals involved in the demonstration of August the 8th are the ones responsible for the stir up of the Emanuel Jaques' case causing emotions to run high."[15]

At the same time as some were touting capital punishment as an option for dealing with child killers and pedophiles, others were proposing another radical alternative: castration. Czech-born sexologist Dr. Kurt Freund of the Clarke Institute and an associate professor at the University of Toronto's psychiatry department stated the only cure to protect children from sexual predators was castration, or, as he called it, "testicular enucleation," referring to surgically removing a mass — in this case, the testes — without cutting into, or dissecting them.

Widely recognized for developing phallometry (also known as Penile plethysmography, or PPG), this technique measured blood flow to the penis to determine degree of sexual arousal. Highly controversial while practicing in Europe, and later, after fleeing from Czechoslovakia to Canada during the Prague Spring of 1968, Freund stated in an interview with The *Globe and Mail* he had been testing the 'erotic preferences' on a number of men in Toronto for eight years, and came to the conclusion that surgical castration was the *only* cure against dangerous sexual predators.

"Nine months after the operation [he] will never do it again," stated Freund. "There is no point sending him from jail to jail when castration will make him happy." When asked about the side effects of the surgery, Freund stated additional hormone treatment was necessary to quash any remaining vestiges of a sex drive. Since the male no longer had his testicles and was unable to produce testosterone, he would develop feminine characteristics, like a higher voice, and weight gain. "What's a little fat compared to spending the rest of one's life in jail?" added the doctor, who had studied homosexuality for over two decades.

Hesitant to draw public attention to his research, except among his fellow doctors, Freund said a "castration committee" was needed, including a psychiatrist, sexologist, general physician, and other necessary medical disciplines "to question the motives of volunteers 'who might be acting under a lot of social pressures.'"

Among his other highly questionable comments, the doctor said he was disturbed by the public perception of 'androphiles' — homosexuals who he said were distinct from pedophiles, along with sadists and masochists. "Because of the majority opinion, the homosexual is an underprivileged person in our society. Merely being homosexual is dangerous in the same way that being Jewish is dangerous in an anti-Semitic society."[16]

*****

The Controversial *Men Loving Boys Loving Men* Article.

Set against the backdrop of a nation outraged over Emanuel's murder, Toronto's gay community felt it was under siege by the public and the press, who continually referred to his death as the consequence of a "homosexual orgy." Fearing for their own children, parents kept kids close to home. In Toronto, police stepped-up patrols of Yonge Street. And in Vancouver, officers were dispatched to get young male prostitutes out of the downtown core, not wanting another shoeshine boy-type killing on their hands.

One of the best-known homosexual publications covering the Jaques story at the time was *The Body Politic*. Founded in 1971, the monthly magazine played an instrumental role in the development of Canada's lesbian, gay, bisexual, and transgendered communities. Published by Pink Triangle Press, *The Body Politic* was often controversial, drawing the wrath of mainstream daily newspapers, The *Toronto Sun* in particular. Early in the publication's history, both The *Globe and Mail* and The *Toronto Star* refused to publish a classified ad marketing subscriptions to the magazine, which was seen as discriminatory.

Stories about gay-centric topics, such as the homosexual movement in Germany, gays in rock bands — highlighting androgynous musicians like David Bowie and Lou Reed — reviews of books and films, interviews, editorials, letters to the editor, and gay events regularly ran in *The Body Politic*. At its peak, circulation reached about 9,000 per issue, delivered to readers across Canada, the United States, and parts of Europe. Highly provocative articles about emotionally-charged topics such as obscenity laws, the unsolved murders of three gay men in Toronto, and the magazine being visited by the Police Morality Squad following the full-page publication of a 'Harold Hedd' cartoon depicting fellatio, were not unusual. Still, the biggest controversy facing the publication was about to come.

The city was in the midst of its crackdown on the sex industry, and countless newspaper articles ran about the shoeshine boy in anticipation of the upcoming trial of the men charged with his murder. Anti-gay sentiment was literally everywhere, and newspapers such as the *Toronto Sun* unabashedly published pieces critical of homosexuals with headlines like "The Limp Wrist Lobby" (November 2, 1977).

On November 21, 1977, less than four months after Emanuel's murder, *The Body Politic* printed a lengthy feature by Gerald Hannon, a longtime writer for the magazine. In the December 1977/January 1978 issue of *The Body Politic* was Hannon's article entitled "Men Loving Boys Loving Men." At over 6,000 words, the piece profiled the lives of three adult males who professed the pleasures of having relationships and sex with much younger men and boys. Even today, decades after its publication, the story remains highly controversial.

Listed in the magazine's table of contents as "Men loving boys," the article is described as follows: "Three men who love boys talk about their lives. And in the process, destroy some of the myths about pedophilia that had been used against the whole gay community. As the *Save Our*

Children people push the "molestation tactic," the sane, provocative article makes for must reading."

Prefacing the article, the publication's Collective ran a one-page piece explaining their rationale for "Men Loving Boys Loving Men," which stated: "1977 has been the Year of the Children. The year of the children Anita Bryant wanted to 'save,' of the children lesbian mothers lost. The year of the one child who died in a body rub parlour on Yonge Street. We have been sensitized. There is some irony in this. In the lives of most gay people, children are conspicuous only by their absence. But they are not unimportant to us. We have begun to realize, for one thing, that many gay men and lesbians are parents themselves. Their battles for custody of their children have given them new visibility."

Stating "all of us have been branded as every child's potential 'molester,'" the forward went on to say Hannon's article — the latest in a series on youth sexuality — would introduce readers to homosexuals referred to as "child molesters," "chicken hawks," "dirty old men," "pansies," "lezzies," and "queers," and, in the months following Emanuel's murder, "child killers."

Rather than attempt to deflect from the anticipated backlash, the preface addressed it head-on:

'Men Loving Boys Loving Men' it is not printed here without awareness of the potential consequences. The decision to run the article was not taken lightly nor without debate within the

Collective. We have had it on hand, typeset and laid out, for nearly six months, but we have hesitated, sensitive to the feeling that 'the climate was not right' after the anti-gay media barrage which followed Emanuel Jaques' death in August.

We know now that the 'climate' will never be 'right.' The Jaques trial is yet to come, and when that is over there will undoubtedly be something else we could point to if we wanted an excuse to move with the tide. The tide must be resisted, the discussion must be opened up.

We know that people who are more concerned with 'respectability' than with rights will groan at our 'irresponsibility' are likely to react as though they had just found a delectably rotten plum in a Christmas cake from a bakery they've never much liked. The issue might well be splashed sensationally across the tabloids (especially on days when there isn't much real news), lines may be quoted out of context and juicy bits read over the air to satisfy prurient interest. Columnists like the *Toronto Sun's* Claire Hoy will be delirious. We know about these things because they have happened to us — to all of us — before.

We also know this because we are aware of how desperate the enemies of gay liberation are. They are willing to hurl the bodies and minds of the very children they are trying to 'save' into the fray.

The Body Politic, for instance, recently received a curious series of telephone calls. The voice at the other end of the line was that of a young boy, perhaps nine or ten years old. He asked on one occasion to speak to the author of this article (who, as we noted, has written on youth sexuality before), asked where he might buy *TBP*, asked finally where he could go to have sex. At least once the prompting voice of an adult male was audible in the background. The sound of a tape recorder was not, but could be assumed. It is illegal even to advise people under the age of 18 (and gay people under 21) to have sex.

We can only speculate about the character of someone who would rather manipulate a child into an act of fraud than have him know anything real about the lives of men who love men and women who love women. But the characters of three people whom this man with a tape recorder must fear so much, three 'child molesters,' three men who love boys, are here to be examined.
We leave it to you.
The Collective"[17]

Hannon's article focuses on a number of men, Simon, Peter, Don, and Barry. The first, Simon, is a 33-year-old primary school teacher active with the volunteer organization Big Brothers, along with a number of other social service agencies dealing with children. Working as a teacher in four schools for a decade, Simon is described as having "formed sexual, loving relationships with boys in each of those four schools in each of the service organizations in which he is a member, including Big Brothers. He has never been caught." Simon's young lover, David, is 12. He writes poetry to Simon. The article goes on to describe sexual activity between the two, along with more mundane day-to-day pleasures, such as watching television together.

Another older male profiled in the article is Peter, 48, a wealthy Torontonian, fit and attractive. The article details how Peter uses a number of methods to attract boys, such as impressing them with his fancy car, or feats of athleticism, like diving. Sometimes he meets them in movie theatres, and initiates courtships, which includes driving around the city, going to restaurants, and conversation. "Peter has a special interest in the detritus of heterosexual relationships, the unwanted or unloved boys, the boys from homes where the father is dead or has deserted," states Hannon's piece. "'It seems the more disadvantaged the child, the more he needs some stable, mature human being. And they're looking for love as well. Typically, they are not very articulate and not very well educated and I think I am often a positive influence.'" Although Peter cited his preferred age bracket as 12 to 14, he said he was willing to experiment: the youngest boy he was with was seven.

Don, the third adult man, is 40, but "could look younger if he lost ten or fifteen pounds." Unlike Simon and Peter, Don is heterosexual, married, with a 19-year-old-son. And then there is Barry, described as a chatterer, "five foot five and rather impish."

Describing sex acts with underage boys in detail, Hannon's article ignited a huge firestorm in the mainstream media, with newspapers like the *Toronto Sun* attacking the author for recklessly promoting the abuse of children. Reaction from the public and authorities was aggressive and immediate. The office of *The Body Politic* was raided by police, who seized a dozen boxes of materials, including distribution and advertising lists, classified ad records, financial statements, letters to the editor, and, most distressing of all, the magazine's subscription list, including names and addresses. Charges were laid against owners Pink Triangle Press, and the author, Gerald Hannon, for publishing obscene material and "use of the mails to distribute immoral, indecent or scurrilous material."

Readers of *The Body Politic* were fiercely divided over the Men Loving Boys Loving Men article. While some praised Hannon for addressing the issue of sexuality between older and younger males, others believed it set back homosexual rights and the gay liberation movement many years. One of those opposed to the publication of the feature was Brent Hawkes. Serving as Senior Pastor at the Metropolitan Community Church of Toronto, which was open to gay, lesbian, bisexual, heterosexual and transgendered individuals, Hawkes championed the rights of the LGBT community. Interviewed by Dick Beddoes, columnist for The *Globe and Mail*, Hawkes was tense not only about potential fallout from the article, but anti-gay activist Anita Bryant coming to Toronto at the time, and concerned some gays would meet her with violence. The day after Bryant's scheduled visit was also the start of the trial of the four men charged with Emanuel's murder.[18]

Conceding the death of the shoeshine boy put considerable pressure on the city's homosexual community, Hawkes shared his opinion of Men Loving Boys, calling the timing of its release stupid. "It was published at a time when Toronto gays are under particular fire. Many gays are complaining about it," said the Pastor, adding he had already received about 40 phone calls concerning the article. "It made gays out to be child molesters, which most are not. It simply made it too easy for our opponents to campaign against us."[19]

Likewise, not all subscribers to *The Body Politic* were enthusiastic about its publication. Generating more letters to the editor than any other issue in its history, many were critical of police, stated they overreacted by raiding the magazine's office. Some readers added, "We can't drop the issue of youth sexuality, it is too important a component of our sexist society. And we can't soft peddle it for 'pragmatic' reasons." The reaction of others was, "By publishing the article in question (which you admitted you agonized over for several months), you've demonstrated an immaturity and irresponsibility that is shocking to me," adding the magazine, through its actions, "caused exposure of your readership to the authorities."

One of the few anonymous letters *The Body Politic* chose to print stated that by running the article, the magazine created a backlash against *all* gays. The author of the letter sided with the *Toronto Sun's* Claire Hoy in no uncertain terms: "Claire Hoy is right. There IS a lot about homosexuality that is repulsive and retarded....It may surprise you to know that most of us prefer to keep a low profile about our sexual preferences, and don't need nosy idiots like you to harm us. Why don't you just shut up?"[20]

Many in Toronto's lesbian community were also upset over the publication of the Men Loving Boys article, its position on romanticising love between adults and children, and the imbalance on many levels — including physical, emotional, financial, and sexual — between children and adults. At a formal meeting to discuss the issue, members of LOOT, the Lesbian Organization of Toronto, recalled their own painful girlhood experiences of unwanted sexual advances at the hands of straight adult males. The organization wanted to make it absolutely clear adult lesbians had no sexual interest in children.

By being published when it was, many lesbian feminists argued, 'Men Loving Boys Loving Men' endangered the gay civil rights campaign which at that time seemed to be gaining momentum. Bluntly told, void of nuance, the article worked to feed and reinforce the myth of the homosexual child molester, and thus some lesbian feminists claimed, provided right-wing organizations — Renaissance International, the Catholic Church, Positive Parents, the Western Front (later the League Against Homosexuals) — with fuel for their backlash and served to grease the wheels of Anita Bryant's powerful anti-gay, anti-feminist and "pro-family" machine. More importantly, though, on a deep emotional level, the article evokes shock and disgust among most lesbian (and straight) feminists.[21]

*****

Leading up to the raid on December 30, 1977 by Operation P, a joint Toronto-provincial pornography squad, the *Toronto Sun* ran a series of articles by Hoy, one of them demanding the return of a $1,500 grant earmarked for the publication, another urging police to lay charges based on Men Loving Boys feature. The *Sun*, with its many anti-porn/pro-family value articles, was not reserved in its opinions of the provocative piece, and *The Body Politic*. Titles of articles penned by Hoy left no doubt as to the contents, such as "Morality vs. Perversity" (December 21, 1977), "Our Taxes Help Homosexuals Promote Abuse of Children) (December 22, 1977), and "Kids, Not Rights, Is Their Craving" (December 25, 1977). In one column, Hoy went so far as to say tax dollars "are helping to promote the abuse of children." *The Body Politic* was described as a rag, and worst of all, gays as "child rapers." In an article published about a week before Emanuel was abducted and murdered, Hoy wrote he wouldn't want his kids to be taught "the wonders of being a fag," and that "homosexuality, like alcoholism, is to a large extent a psychological problem, a sickness, and should be treated like one."

Gay rights groups and activists were infuriated. If Emanuel's murder granted Toronto authority — in the form of politicians, police, and lawmakers — to clean-up the Yonge Street strip, the city's homosexual community was viewed by many as guilty by association, and would be targeted. The police raid of *The Body Politic* was followed by charges being laid in January of 1978. Almost a year later, on December 9, 1978, Toronto Police raided The Barracks bathhouse. This was followed by a number of other raids, including the Hot Tub Club in 1979, culminating in the highly controversial bathhouse raids on February 5, 1981, which saw 289 men being charged and membership lists seized, despite changes to the law much earlier in 1969, decriminalizing sex acts between consenting adults in private.[22]

For Toronto's gay community, the repercussions of the Jaques murder would be felt for years. The fact Emanuel was lured away by Saul Betesh, a gay man, painted a picture of the entire community as vicious sexual predators. As Gary Kinsman wrote in his book, *The Regulation of Desire: Sexuality in Canada*:

Through its selective representation of reality, the media plays a clear ideological role. The mass media relies on accredited sources, and thus the perspective of agencies of social regulation are part of the formation of "objective" news accounts.

Such media practices served to neutralize opposition and to create a public consensus for the clean-up campaign.

The sex industry, prostitutes, and particularly homosexuals, were presented as 'folk devils.' Coverage of the 'homosexual murder' served to focus hostility against the whole gay community. Demonstrations by the Portuguese community, of which Jaques had been a member, influenced by the media, called for cleaning up Yonge Street, for granting more power to the police, and for capital punishment for homosexuals. The media portrayed the child molester or child murderer as a homosexual stranger to be found lurking in seedy parts of the city. 'The relationship between homosexual behaviour, pedophilia, and murderous acts became a cluster of images that cemented in the public mind.'

The moral panic thus created would have a lasting effect, defining the political terrain for discussions of the character of the city, Yonge Street, sexual permissiveness, prostitution and homosexuality for years to come.

By focusing on an unusually violent crime, the media obscured the common occurrence of sexual abuse and violence against children and young people in the family setting — which clearly points to the application of the public/private distinction in social regulation. Sexual violence in the private sphere does not attract the same police or media attention (although it may attract the attention of social workers) even though the violence may exceed that of the Jaques case. The provincial government, for instance, prevented the release of a study of fifty-four child abuse deaths in Ontario during that same year, 1977.

The Jaques case, and the 'clean up Yonge Street' campaign signalled a shift in the Toronto social climate for lesbians and gay men. The 'clean up' campaign provided fertile ground for the growth of sentiments against the visibility of the gay ghetto, particularly in the Yonge Street area. The Jaques murder has reappeared as ammunition in right-wing propaganda. It also resurfaced in mass media coverage of the 1981 bath raids and male prostitution on Yonge Street.[23]

The horror of the Jaques murder, combined with several of the men on trial for his death being gay, along with Anita Bryant's ongoing anti-homosexual campaign, Hannon's Men Loving Boys article, and anti-homosexual media coverage continued to fuel misconceptions about the city's gay community. To further underscore his death, the boy's body — found above a body rub on one of the most vilified streets in Canada — ensured widespread reporting targeting sexuality both gay and straight, and served to justify why Yonge Street needed to be sanitized once and for all.

Chapter Six: Where the Public and Punk Collide: The Curse and *Shoeshine Boy*

"In disgust, I heaved a record which is supposedly today's music into the fireplace and watched it melt away. Unfortunately, the words and the memories that they conjure up cannot be destroyed."
-Letter to The Hamilton Spectator

Although they existed for less than two years, Toronto-based band The Curse left an indelible impression on the city's musical scene. Arriving when punk rock was on the rise thanks to groups such as The Sex Pistols, The Damned, and The Clash out of England, Canada soon saw male-led bands like The Diodes, Teenage Head, and The Viletones. And while female-fronted punk bands including The Slits hailed from the United Kingdom, The Curse soon became the first North American all-girl punk band.

Formed in 1977, the group's members — Mickey Skin (lead vocals), Patzy Poison (drums), Dr. Bourque (bass), and Trixie Danger (guitar) — didn't imitate the angry punk boys...in many ways, they surpassed them. The Sex Pistols had songs like *God Save the Queen* and *Holidays in the Sun*; The Curse belted out in-your-face tracks like *Eat Me, If it Tastes So Great, Swallow it Yerself!* and the highly controversial song, *Shoeshine Boy*, inspired by the murder of Emanuel Jaques.

"It's amazing how much impact we had, considering how short-lived it was," says lead singer Mickey Skin of the group, which was the first punk band to play Toronto's legendary Horseshoe Tavern, performing a set with the Dutch Mason Blues Band when The Horseshoe was still a country music venue.

Although they had a set list of about 10 songs, The Curse never recorded a full album. Famous for their live shows, The Curse was loud, dirty, angry, anti-establishment and powerful — embodying everything punk stood for. Like many others at the time, the girls in the band knew the Yonge Street strip up and down, the dive bars, the regulars, and all the hangouts.

Soon after the story broke about Emanuel's rape and murder, Trixie Danger wrote Shoeshine Boy. Mickey, who received $500 for her profanity-laden rant on *Raw/War*, a conceptual piece by Amerigo Marras and Bruce Eves — the two principles behind the Centre for Experimental Art and Communication (CEAC) — featured Skin on *Raw*, and members of The Diodes on *War*. The money was used to fund The Curse's only single, a 45 with *Shoeshine Boy* on Side A, and *The Killer Bees* on Side B. The record was produced by a friend of Skin's, the brilliant and tormented Gabor Hegedus. Fleeing with his parents to England in 1956 during the Hungarian Revolution, he later moved to Canada, became involved in the Queen Street West music scene and, under the name BB Gabor, recorded hits including *Nyet Nyet Soviet*

(Soviet Jewellery), and *Metropolitan Life*. "He was an absolutely stellar musician," remembers Skin. "He had perfect pitch. If you could hum it, he could play it. It was amazing, he was a genius, and a great guy, really fun." Tragically, Gabor committed suicide years later, in 1990.

*****

At 2 minutes and 29 blistering seconds, Shoeshine Boy was pure, unapologetic punk. With its throbbing guitar intro, the track remains famous not only for its place in Canadian music history, but its controversial, deeply disturbing, and tragically poignant lyrics. Written and released soon after Emanuel's murder, only 500 copies were ever pressed of the highly collectible record. The first run featured only the name "The Curse" and "Shoeshine Boy/The Killer Bees" in red on the front cover, with a photo of the band on the back. The second issue — released after the band broke up — contained the same two songs, except the front cover was a black and yellow illustration by Steven Davey, titled "Mickey Skin and The Curse."

Back cover band photo of The Curse (Courtesy Mickey Skin)

The Curse's live shows were wild. Playing on the same bill with bands like The Viletones, The Diodes and Teenage Head, the group's antics saw Mickey sporting a fake lobotomy scar on her forehead, yanking hotdogs out of her pants, throwing them on stage, and grinding them to a meaty pink pulp underneath her heels. Likewise, the record release party for Shoeshine Boy was an event to remember. Held in the basement of the Isabella Hotel, the place was packed. "We made a purple Jesus punch — the famous purple Jesus punch — which is Kool-Aid and Alcool, Everclear, strong alcohol, and purple grape Kool-Aid, which was a cheap way to get really messed-up. And in it, we floated tampons, and we made really hard red Jell-O, cut it in cubes, put it in baggies, and then floated that in there too, like blood clots. And I had a water pistol that I was sucking the punch out of, and squirting it on people, who were sucking on the tampons. It was great."

Performing Shoeshine Boy and having the party afterwards, not everyone was impressed with the band, or the song. A reporter from the *Toronto Sun* wrote a dismissive article about the group and *Shoeshine Boy*, stating The Curse was exploiting the tragedy of the Yonge Street murder; the band, however, believed it was actually the *media* — who ran stories almost daily about the homicide — who were the ones taking advantage of the tragedy. "It's a cool song," recalls Skin. "Of Canadian punk lore, it's one of the outstanding songs that's remembered politically, and for the statement we were making."

Sending copies of the record to the four men on trial for the sex slaying, The Curse soon received hate mail, along with a few death threats. Toronto's Portuguese community was livid. With its controversial lyrics, the intent of the song was to shock others by focusing attention on kids who shouldn't have been out on the street in the first place. Lyrics like, 'Shoeshine boy, is that your pay? How'd you earn a hundred dollars today?' were not only provocative, but asked the question many were wondering: *were some of these underage kids turning tricks on the Yonge Street strip? How could they make that much money just shining shoes?* The questions were disturbing, but valid. Just a few weeks after Emanuel's murder in Toronto, police in other large Canadian cities launched crack-downs on juvenile prostitution involving young boys. On Vancouver's then-notorious Davie Street — which would years later become known as the gay Davie Village — at least 200 boys, also known as 'chickens,' were involved in prostitution and drugs, some making $200 a night. A number of them had been beaten during sexual encounters which got out of hand, and became violent.

Shoeshine Boy was The Curse's response to the many stories surrounding the murder. "The bent of the song was a warning, saying 'Come on, people! Pay attention to your kids!' So that was our impetus, and our feeling of why we wanted it out there," explains Skin. "We weren't glorifying or making fun of it. We really felt like we wanted to get a message out, saying 'Look what's happening. How do you think these kids are making a hundred bucks shining shoes?' because obviously, some shoeshine boys were doing this stuff, it was a thing on Yonge Street. People were looking the other way, that's the thing. They had to know what was going on, and they *were* looking the other way. These kids were being totally taken advantage of. At first, the guy says, 'Oh, come on up, we just want to hang out,' or whatever, and the next thing you know, they're either drugging them, or making them drunk. It was bad. Those guys were horrible."

Others familiar with Toronto's music scene at the time echoed The Curse's musical intentions, including Gerald Pas in the book, *Treat Me Like Dirt: An Oral History of Punk in Toronto and Beyond 1977-1981*. "'Shoeshine Boy' was not only expressive and full of energy, it had a social phenomenon. It was talking about something that was applicable to anyone in Toronto who walked down Yonge Street and saw what the fuck was going on there. What was not to like about that? It was everything I wanted in music. It was vital and it was true and it was speaking about something in our society, as opposed to just sort of being in a trance. So for that reason alone I realized what they were doing was of critical importance to our community in Toronto, and subsequently in Canada at the time."[24]

The song was not only powerful, but tapped into the energy of the city at the time. Just as disgusted as others by the murder, Skin was appalled by how the child was sexually tortured before he was drowned, his corpse discarded like trash. Acknowledging that *Shoeshine Boy* put The Curse on the musical map and that she has no regrets about the song, Skin remains disturbed by Emanuel's death, 40 years later. "We were horrified. We were not callous people in that sense," she says. "Even now, it hurts my heart. I mean, it was a horrible thing."

Shoeshine Boy

Hey Ricardo with the big brown eyes
Yes, you're the kind that money can buy
Bring your friends if they're young and sweet
If they've got acne leave 'em on the street
Shoeshine boy, is that your pay?
How'd you earn a hundred dollars today?
Shoeshine boy, is that your pay?
How'd you earn a hundred bucks today?
Emanuel with the curly hair
Why don't you climb on up these dark stairs
Treat you just like one of the boys
Have some fun with a rubber toy
Shoeshine boy, is that your pay?
How'd you earn a hundred dollars today?
Shoeshine boy, is that your pay?
How'd you earn a hundred bucks today?
They'll beat you
Mistreat you
They'll find you
Wrapped in a plastic bag
Hey Pablo, with the light brown skin
They're just home movies, that's no sin
I know your mama, she prays for you
It's good she don't know what you do
Shoeshine boy, is that your pay?
How'd you earn a hundred bucks today?
Shoeshine boy, is that your pay?
How'd you earn a hundred dollars today?
Hey Ricardo was the big brown eyes
You're the kind that money can buy
Bring your friends if they're young and sweet

If they've got acne leave 'em on the street
Shoeshine boy, is that your pay?
How'd you earn a hundred dollars today?
Shoeshine boy, is that your pay?
How'd you earn a hundred bucks today?
Count all your pennies
Add them up right
You just might be
A millionaire by the end of the night
A movie star by the end of the night
A front-page scandal by the end of the night.
(Reproduced with permission)

Chapter Seven: The Trial

For a city repulsed by the death of Emanuel Jaques, worse was yet to come with the trial of the four men charged with his murder. From the outset, there was no doubt the proceedings would be lengthy, and potentially problematic; no one in the public knew just how graphic media coverage would be, particularly testimony regarding the mental state of the defendants, which included psychopathy. In late November of 1977, the anticipated trial date for Saul David Betesh, Robert Wayne Kribs, Josef Woods, and Werner Gruener was delayed due to a backlog of 50 other murder cases set to appear in court. With the four men held in solitary confinement for months, lawyers for the defendants were eager to see the trial start as soon as possible.

Along with the city's daily newspapers, the trial was covered by *The Body Politic*, which remained critical of homophobic journalists who "have attempted to use the murder to engineer 'public sentiment' against the gay movement." Weeks before the start of the trial on Wednesday February 8, 1978, there was considerable speculation about how long it would take. Some legal experts stated six weeks, others eight. A pool of 226 members were on the panel of potential jurors. This was then followed by weeks of *voir dires* to determine admissibility of evidence prior to the beginning of the trial.

In turn, each potential juror was asked a dozen questions, ranging from their knowledge of Yonge Street to whether or not they knew anyone working on the strip. What were their views on body rub parlours, and was the fact several of the men on trial were gay a factor when it came to their ability to formulate an impartial judgement? While the majority of those questioned said the sexuality of the accused would have no impact on their decision-making as a juror, one man freely admitted, "As far as I'm concerned, I can't stand homosexuals," and was promptly excluded.

Narrowing down potential jurors, the selection process saw the court registrar pull 100 names from a wooden drum. All were challenged, with just nine initially being deemed impartial. With police patrolling outside the courtroom on walkie-talkies, the 12-member jury was selected. Many of them were married, some with grandchildren, others with kids younger than 12-year-old Emanuel. Facing lengthy isolation during the trial, the seven man/four woman jury included a kindergarten teacher, a machine operator, a building inspector, a tool and die maker, and an unmarried urology technician. Deciding the fate of the men charged with Emanuel's murder, each juror would receive $10 per day.

Separated for months before the trial, it was also during this time the four accused men saw one another again. Kribs, 29, Woods, 27, and Gruener, 29, had been held in solitary confinement at the Metro East Detention Centre, while 27-year-old Betesh was housed in a Whitby-area prison before being transferred to a west-end detention centre.

Considering the brutality of the young boy's torture and death at the hands of adult men during a "homosexual orgy," how his nude body had been dumped on the roof of a body rub parlour, and the months of overwhelming news coverage, many wondered: *was an unbiased jury even possible?* Widely reported across the nation, there was literally no city, province or territory where news of the murder on the Yonge Street strip did not reach. Receiving extensive coverage in Ottawa and Montreal, stories about the crime and trial were published as far away as Florida's Boca Raton, Portsmouth in New Hampshire, Corsicana Texas, Gadsden in Alabama, and Jefferson City, Missouri.

Prior to the trial, it became apparent there was a likelihood the jury would be sequestered for weeks or longer, as hundreds of pieces of evidence were introduced, and testimony was heard from dozens of witnesses, friends and family members of the victim and the accused, along with police, psychiatrists, and many others. Lawyers for the defendants were Paul Tomlinson representing Betesh, Earl Levy acting for Gruener, George Marron serving for Woods, and Gordon Goldman defending Kribs. Crown Counsel were Frank Armstrong and Peter Rickaby, and Judge Arthur William Maloney would preside over the trial, which for years would remain known as "Toronto's coming of age."

Screening prospective jurors proved to be challenging. Even for the most open-minded individual, there was no imaginable way of escaping the facts of the case, or sympathy for the deceased. Emanuel, a hard-working immigrant child, was lured by an adult male to a grubby apartment above a body rub parlour, then tortured before being killed. With months of daily press coverage, it was extremely unlikely anyone could remain unaware of these details.

For the dozen members of the jury, the trial meant isolation on a rented floor in a downtown hotel, with around-the-clock police security, and no contact with loved ones except through a monitor, and only then in the case of an emergency, with messages being screened. For the duration of the trial, jurors were required to sit as a group, far away from other guests in the hotel restaurant, out of earshot. Most crucial of all, they were forbidden access to newspapers, magazines, radio, or television programs dealing with any aspect of the sensational murder trial. Over the weeks to come, their numbers would drop to 11, as one was dismissed due to a heart condition, with the strain of the trial too much to bear.

For Saskatoon-born Judge Maloney, the trial proved to be the most challenging of his lengthy legal career. In May of 1976, he presided over another particularly gruesome case, that of Harbhajan Singh Math, his brother Harmohinder Math, and sister-in-law, Paramjite Kour Math. Running a scheme where they brought illegal immigrants to Toronto and demanding they pay protection money or face deportation, one woman, Santosh Kumar Bali, 42, was beaten so badly that the coroner determined she likely choked to death on her own tongue. During the murder trial, court heard how Bali's battered body wouldn't fit in his Volkswagen, with the decision made to chop her into pieces with a sickle.

Representing Harmohinder Math, defence attorney Earl Levy — who would later represent Werner Gruener — stated, "There has probably been no more grisly testimony given in the past 25 years in a Canadian courtroom." During the four-week-long trial, jurors heard the horrifying details of Bali's death, her face smashed to a pulp over several hours. Once dead, she was dismembered and beheaded, her torso found in an Etobicoke trash can the previous September, followed by her left leg and foot three days later, dumped behind a North York factory.

Callously bragging about how they had killed many others before, the trial took an even more nauseating twist when jurors were told how Harbhajan Singh Math, in handcuffs, led police to a farmer's field in Thornhill. There, down a muddy path, a leatherette bag was found at the base of a tree trunk behind Holy Cross Cemetery. Inside the bag was the rotting head of Santosh Kumar Bali. One of the homicide officers involved, Sergeant Gerald Stevenson, would be the lead investigator in the Emanuel Jaques case. At the time of the Bali trial, Justice Maloney referred to the murder and dismemberment of the woman as one of the most wretched criminal acts he had ever come across; this was, however, before the trial of the men accused of murdering the shoeshine boy.

Following lengthy discussions about alternative venues, it was ultimately decided the trial would be held where the murder occurred, in Toronto. "We felt that there was not a place that we could go to in Ontario that had not been saturated with the horrors of the case and that the publicity would follow us wherever we went," wrote attorney Earl Levy. "Any place we went to would be considerably less cosmopolitan than Toronto and the fact that three of the accused were homosexuals would be very prejudicial in the minds of a small community. We agreed that our best chance for the fairest trial would be with the jury from Toronto. It was decided to challenge for cause and ask for sequestration of the jury."[25]

By the time the trial commenced, Betesh, Woods, Kribs, and Gruener had been in solitary confinement for six months, far removed from other inmates for their own safety. Housed in separate detention centres in Scarborough and Rexdale, they were driven to an underground garage at the Ontario Supreme Court on University Avenue in Toronto, and ushered under police guard to the sixth floor of the building via a private prisoner elevator. There, they would enter Courtroom 20 through a side door. The largest of all, the room had seating for 300, in anticipation of a massive turnout by the public and the press.

Jurors, who were going to be sequestered for almost two months during the duration of the trial, were about to see the four men charged with Emanuel's murder, and decide their fate.

The lawyers representing the accused had handled other tough cases. Levy for Harmohinder Math and, in 1976, for Clarence Christopher Walker, 17, one of three young Jamaican men charged with the murder of postal worker and part-time Scarborough cab driver Gordon Stoddart, 40. Gordon Goldman, better known to fellow lawyers as 'Gordie,' was retained to represent Kribs, having represented clients on a number of cocaine trafficking, obscenity and prostitution charges, including a female client who agreed to have sex with an undercover officer at Bare Facts, a "nude encounter" establishment on Yonge Street. Representing Woods, lawyer George Marron had earlier acted for a 36-year-old man who paid two young girls, aged six and nine, for performing "perverted" sexual acts for him in January of 1975.

Chapter Eight: Parallels to the Murder of Kirkland Deasley

Defense attorney Paul Tomlinson, who early on believed Saul David Betesh to be a psychopath, earlier represented a client during a trial with numerous, disturbing similarities to the murder of Emanuel Jaques. In March of 1974, Tomlinson acted for John McBeth Finlayson, 37, charged with the sex murder of Kirkland Deasley.

Like Emanuel, Deasley was young, just nine at the time of his death, and as in the shoeshine boy case, the two were sexually assaulted and killed, Deasley by one man, Jaques by several. In both cases, all of the men charged with murder lived transient, hand-to-mouth existences in squalid surroundings. Finlayson, an alcoholic, was more often unemployed than not, moving from one shabby rooming house to another, occasionally working as a baker. The men on trial for Emanuel's murder were drug users, several of them employed as bouncers at body rubs. All the men were attracted to children, both boys and girls, although Werner Gruener would later deny his interest in young females was sexual.

Despite their youth, both Kirkland Deasley and Emanuel Jaques had a great deal in common. Both boys were from the low-income Regent Park area of Toronto, and met their terrible ends in disgusting conditions: Deasley in a room at the dilapidated Ford Hotel at Bay and Dundas, and

Jaques in a grubby apartment above a body rub. Both died in locations less than a 10-minute walk from one another, and both boys were ambitious and enterprising. Much like Emanuel, who was out shining shoes to make money, Grade 4 student Deasley said he was going to use his bundle buggy to "make lots of money" delivering groceries to nearby neighbours. Last seen by his mother Carol Ann the night before his murder, her son said his goal was to raise enough cash to buy a nice present for his father's upcoming 37th birthday.

On July 26th, 1973, Deasley's naked, mutilated body was found face down on the bed of a ninth floor room in the hotel by clerk Nabir Cassir, a day after he was reported missing. As would be the case with Emanuel a few years later, police and the public searched ravines, alleys, and along the Don River for the missing child, to no avail. The young boy had been sexually assaulted by Finlayson and strangled to death, his tiny body covered in bite marks, including five to his face. In order to confirm the injuries were inflicted by Finlayson, a dental cast was taken of his teeth. It was a perfect match.

"Finlayson killed a young boy at the old Ford Hotel," recalls Tomlinson. "It received a terrific amount of press, because of the nature of the incident. It was not a situation where there was a group accused; he alone had perpetrated the offence. That case had generated a lot of publicity, as much probably as the potential case did at the time."

Along with an empty liquor bottle next to the bed in the hotel room, the young boy's clothes and his shopping cart were found containing a bag of vegetables, bread, and cottage cheese. Testimony would reveal the child was carrying groceries from a Parliament Street supermarket when, like Emanuel, he was lured away to his death. Once news of the murder broke, vigilantes began scouring the east end of the city, looking for someone matching Finlayson's description. Much like Woods, Kribs, and Gruener, who fled Toronto by train to Vancouver and were apprehended before reaching their destination, Finlayson was caught while hitchhiking in the Burlington area three days after Deasley's body was found.

With young friends of the murdered boy raising money to purchase a large floral wreath, Deasley, a sports-loving child, was buried in his baseball uniform along with his catching glove, ball, and prized hockey trophy on July 31, 1973. Four years later to the day, Saul Betesh would walk into a downtown police station, and describe how he and others raped and murdered Emanuel Jaques.

During the trial, defence attorney Paul Tomlinson painted an utterly bleak and hopeless portrait of his client. The son of an alcoholic, John McBeth Finlayson was one of those individuals who, it seemed, had everything against him from the beginning. As his client Saul Betesh would concede during the Jaques murder trial he, like Finlayson, knew he was "different," and not right in the head. An alcoholic from age 14, Finlayson was forced to drop out of school by his own violent, paranoid father, who made his son work to buy cheap booze to feed his addiction.

Displaying strong psychopathic tendencies at a young age, Finlayson used alcohol to mask his often erratic, brutal behaviour, alternating between paralyzing nervousness, and outbursts of rage. One time as a teenager, he tried to kill his own sister, strangling her and smashing her skull with a wrench. In 1963, at the age of 27, Finlayson was charged with assault causing bodily harm after choking a four-year-old boy into unconsciousness. Although the child suffered trauma and deep bruises to his neck, he survived the ordeal.

In and out of mental institutions, Finlayson was dismissed from the Lakeshore psychiatric facility in September of 1970. Soon, he attacked others, including a landlady in 1971 with a steak knife. Although he underwent numerous treatments at the Drug Addiction Research Foundation in 1972, all were failures. Like Betesh a few years later, the behaviour of Tomlinson's client Finlayson was almost always erratic. And like Betesh, Finlayson was down-and-out at the time of the murder. While staying at the Ford Hotel, for eight dollars per night, staff noticed his paranoia when he demanded he change rooms four different times over a 10-day period.

Much like the Yonge Street strip during the Seventies, the Ford Hotel had a reputation, but not a good one. Constructed in 1928, a year before the prestigious Royal York Hotel opened, the Ford

Hotel was prominent for decades before it declined into the "Queen of Dumps," a hangout for prostitutes and cheating husbands seeking a one-night stand. It was not uncommon to see women casually strolling barefoot around the lobby dressed only in panties and a bra, or hear stories about fires being set, and people being beaten-up. One time, a man somehow managed to open the elevator doors, and plummet to his death down the shaft. It was here that Finlayson persuaded young Kirkland Deasley into delivering $2.97 worth of groceries to the grimy room where he was staying, much like Betesh would entice Emanuel with the promise of money for moving photographic equipment a few years later. And, like Betesh, Finlayson's mental state would prove to be a critical issue during the trial.

While the Finlayson trial would not receive the same overwhelming amount of attention from the press as the trial of the men charged with the murder of Emanuel Jaques saw a few years later, there was still a great degree of public outpouring for the family of the murdered youngster, including roses being sold to help pay for his funeral. Concerned about a fair trial because of growing anti-Finlayson publicity, Tomlinson moved for a change of venue. The judge was prepared to grant the lawyer's application, but the only jurisdiction it could be sent to was London, Ontario. "The last place I wanted to go was London, the insurance capital of Canada," says Tomlinson. "It's a very right-wing kind of city. I would not have minded

Ottawa or some other place, but not London, so I abandoned my application."

Several psychiatrists were called to testify during the Finlayson trial, among them Dr. Jerry Cooper, who stated there was no doubt the man on trial was deeply disturbed. Finlayson's fantasy life involved cutting-up women and children — in fact, his initial target was not a young boy, but a girl. Another doctor, psychiatrist Fred Jensen with the Clarke Institute of Psychiatry and the Toronto (Don) Jail, argued Finlayson required specialized treatment, which was never administered. "Treatment in penal institutions is inadequate," stated the doctor. "First of all there is no magic cure for people with personality disorders and second a prison, just because of its surroundings, is a difficult atmosphere to be treated in. We need much more medical and psychiatric treatment in prisons. We should have an extension of the psychiatric hospital in the prisons that could do much more intensive examining. But six months doesn't give any doctor much time to work with an inmate, particularly one like Finlayson who concealed his mental disorder under a drinking problem."[26] Serving as Deputy Crown Attorney for York at the time was Peter Rickaby, who would act as Crown Counsel with Frank Armstrong for the trial of the men accused of killing Emanuel Jaques.

Successfully defending his client came with a price for his attorney in the form of threats. Painting a sympathetic portrait of Finlayson as a mentally-disturbed man living a meagre existence, newspapers were playing-up his pathetic life, something the public did not appreciate for the child killer. One day, Tomlinson picked up the phone, and immediately knew it wasn't a run of the mill crank call, but something potentially more serious: the caller told Tomlinson that he knew he had a four-year-old son. Not wanting to tell his wife so as not to frighten her, Tomlinson immediately called his little boy's school, teachers, the police, and made arrangements for someone to be with his son when he went to kindergarten class, and at lunchtime and recess.

Court heard from police that Finlayson himself wanted to be committed, but instead of treatment in a mental hospital, he usually found himself back in jail. A literal Jekyll and Hyde character, he was unable to strike a balance between good and evil. "I'm like two different people," he said. "I love life, but this other person keeps interfering — it's just awful. I know that every time I go on a binge, something terrible happens. I honestly wish this [police] department had shot me. I had to keep walking to think straight. I go to pieces standing still."[27]

In court, Dr. Jensen was asked why Finlayson, a diagnosed psychopath, wasn't treated for his condition. Jensen replied: "The word alone turned staff and hospitals off. A psychopath is not automatically certifiable and usually society is held responsible for the psychiatric problems of a community. Ninety per cent of those we turn into the community are not dangerous and do very well. There will always be the small percentage who will not cope and that means there will possibly be more John Finlaysons running free."

Charged with capital murder — which at the time carried the death penalty, as Parliament's five-year moratorium on capital punishment had lapsed — Finlayson was found not guilty by reason of insanity. He would be sent to a number of mental institutions, first the Penetanguishine Mental Health Centre, then Brockville after a review of his case in 1979. At the conclusion of the eight-day trial in March 1974, Tomlinson said, "It's too bad. It took a terrible, terrible tragedy to bring this man's cries for help to the attention of the authorities."

Disastrously, Finlayson would go on to commit more crimes. In January of 1989, he was out on a "loosened warrant" from the medium-security Brockville Psychiatric Hospital, which meant he was not required to live on hospital premises, and was working full-time. In a drunken state, he asked a 32-year-old woman if he could enter her apartment to use her telephone. She agreed, and he stabbed her in the shoulder. The woman survived and Finlayson, then 52, was charged with aggravated sexual assault. He was found not guilty by reason of insanity, as was the case with the 1973 murder of Kirkland Deasley. According to District Court Judge Paul Cosgrove in Brockville, Finlayson's attack on the woman had "the dissociative motions of an automaton." A controversy soon erupted when it was revealed staff at the Brockville Psychiatric Hospital were aware Finlayson was drinking alcohol just three days before the incident. On January 24, 1989, the assault was raised as an issue of public safety in the House of Commons. It was revealed Finlayson's other convictions included sexually assaulting a five-year-old girl, and a young boy.

While the murder of Kirkland Deasley had many parallels to the death of Emanuel Jaques — both young boys from the same area, out on the streets making money, lured away by a man, raped and murdered in downtown Toronto — the notable differences remained public outrage, and media coverage. While many were incensed at the Deasley murder, it commanded far fewer stories than the death of Emanuel Jaques, which generated full-page articles in newspapers, editorials, opinion pieces, and television and radio segments. Some called for the noose for Finlayson, yet compared to the estimated 15,000-strong march in Toronto at City Hall and Queen's Park, protests outside Charlie's Angels body rub, and gatherings in Ottawa demanding the return of capital punishment, public anger was considerably less. While some were upset newspapers "divulged to readers the sordid and sadistic details of a murderer," wrote one individual to the *Toronto Star*, coverage of Deasley's death was much less sensational than that published during the Jaques trial four years later.

Like the sex slaying of Emanuel Jaques, the killing of Kirkland Deasley took place in downtown

Toronto. The 12-storey Ford Hotel, much like the Yonge Street strip at the same time, had declined into a miserable hell hole of hookers, criminals, transients, suicide and murder, culminating with the nine-year-old's sickening death. Although the Depression-era hotel was demolished soon after the murder, there were no calls to clean-up Bay and Dundas, as there would be for the Yonge Street strip.

Mayor of Toronto during the time of the Deasley murder and the slaying of Emanuel Jaques, David Crombie says that despite both incidents happening in the same city, a number of factors distinguish the tragedies. Deasley's death took place in the Ford Hotel, and was in a sense a standalone event, whereas Yonge Street drew the attention of literally everyone in the city. "There was a difference about Yonge Street in the public mind, as opposed to the Ford Hotel," he says, adding that there had been a number of efforts to deal with Yonge Street by both Metropolitan Toronto, and the City of Toronto long before the 1977 murder of Emanuel. "For almost 20 years, there were a lot of concerns as the street changed, and became more and more one dealing primarily with the sex trade."

Chapter Nine: Troubling Testimony

For the sequestered jury determining the fate of the men charged with Emanuel's murder, the coming weeks would be extremely difficult. They would hear testimony from an array of police officers and homicide detectives, along with psychiatrists testifying on the mental state of the defendants, Saul Betesh in particular.

Very early on in the trial, the jury and defense lawyers Marron, Levy, and Tomlinson were taken aback when Gordon Goldman, who was defending Robert Kribs, said his client wished to change his plea to guilty. Although Kribs still required sentencing, the move on the part of Goldman immediately impacted the other three men on trial, and methods their lawyers would use to represent their clients. When asked by Justice Maloney if his attorney had explained the consequences of entering a guilty plea, 29-year-old Kribs — wearing a flowered shirt and worn-out blue jeans — said yes, adding "I'm ready to accept it." With the court registrar reading the charge out loud, Kribs replied "guilty," and sat down. His co-accused in the prisoners' box appeared as stunned by his plea as everyone else in the courtroom.

Attorneys representing the other three defendants were taken off guard, since Goldman hadn't informed them about their co-accused changing his plea. "During the course of the trial, without any advance notice to me or anything else,

Kribs entered a plea of guilty to first-degree murder, which didn't help my position any," says Tomlinson. "So I had to revamp what I was going to tell the jury. I wasn't upset, but I was a bit disappointed that Gordie would do that without letting me know in advance. Other than that, there was no friction between any of us."

Moving the trial ahead, Justice Maloney stated Kribs' guilty plea "should not be taken in any remote way to affect the case...against the other three men. It should not have any effect on the position of the other three accused." Sentencing for Kribs, said Maloney, would be made later in the trial, "at the appropriate time as I see it."

Over the course of the coming weeks, the jury would hear horrific details about Emanuel's final hours, the attempts to dispose of his body, and more about the mediocre lives of the men charged with his murder. The court also discovered it was not the first time young boys had been lured back to the apartment above the body rub for nude photography sessions.

Crown Attorney Peter Rickaby summarized the evidence in the case from a 16-page document which he slowly read out loud, so jurors could process every word. Cautioning the trial would be shocking, he said the treatment of Emanuel at the hands of his killers amounted to nothing less than a true-life horror story. Among the questions he asked the jurors to consider were: *was there an indecent assault committed on the deceased, Emanuel Jaques? If so, who committed it? Who did anything — or omitted to do anything — for the purpose of aiding the act? Was there forcible confinement? Who should have known bodily harm to the boy was a likely consequence? Was his killing planned, and deliberate? If so, who participated? Was there an attempt to conceal what had been done? Did any of the defendants attempt to flee?*

The day Emanuel disappeared, it was established for the court that he was shining shoes downtown on Yonge Street with his older brother, Luciano, and their friend, Shane McLean. The boys were approached by a man, Saul Betesh, and polished the shoes he was wearing, along with a pair of work boots he brought along in a bag. Chatting and trying to establish a rapport with the boys, he then offered them $35 an hour to move photographic equipment. Suspecting his offer was too good to be true, both Luciano and Shane left Emanuel with Betesh, went to a nearby pay phone to call their mothers for permission, which was denied, and returned to find Emanuel gone.

Although Emanuel and Betesh were nowhere to be found, jurors heard they went to the apartment above Charlie's Angels body rub, further south down Yonge Street. Realizing Betesh's friends were not yet there, the two headed in the direction where Betesh met the boys, to a Howard Johnson's restaurant. It was here Betesh bought Emanuel a hamburger, and where he later believed he could be, and in fact was, identified by a waiter as being the last one seen with the child.

The court heard that the first person to bring Emanuel's disappearance to the attention of police was his older sister, Valdemira, on the morning of Friday, July 29, the day after her brother went missing. With police searching for the boy, Betesh knew he would be recognized, and tracked down. Late on the evening of Saturday, July 30, he went to see George Hislop at the Canadian Homophile Association of Toronto, which resulted in Hislop securing Betesh lawyer Richard Parker, to accompany him to 51 Division police station. From there, Rickaby outlined details leading up to the discovery of Emanuel's body. Along with Betesh telling police the other three defendants were on a CN train out of town, jurors were told officers found a scrap of paper in the apartment with train schedules and prices for Winnipeg, Edmonton, and Vancouver. This soon led to 51 Division sending a telex to Ontario provincial police at Sioux Lookout, where they stopped the train carrying Kribs, Gruener, and Woods at 5:10 a.m., waking the three as they slept in day coaches.

*****

At the police station, Betesh told officers a weird story, trying to persuade them he had an arrangement with radio station CHUM to find young boys to interview for a segment on child prostitution. The court soon heard how Betesh told police exactly where they could find Emanuel — naked, on the roof of the body rub, wrapped in two green garbage bags secured with electrical tape. To further conceal the corpse, it was placed in an old metal air vent, with wood and other debris thrown on top.

The debris-covered rooftop of 245 Yonge Street (Courtesy Toronto Police)

One of the first persons called to testify was Joe Martin, owner-manager of Charlie's Angels, and a number of other adult businesses along the Yonge Street strip. The night before Emanuel was murdered, Martin stated he went to the apartment above the body rub; tiring of their drug use, he told Kribs and Gruener two weeks earlier they would have to vacate the place, but they were still there. Not knowing Emanuel was behind the door, Kribs blocked Martin with his massive frame from entering one of the bedrooms, stating he "had a girl in there," which was why he couldn't go inside.

Describing the personalities of the other men, Martin said Gruener was friendly and quiet, someone who read the Bible constantly. For the court, Martin painted an image of a man soon to turn 30 who acted like a little boy. Riding around the city on a 10-speed bicycle outfitted with streamers, an array of lights, and even a CB radio, Gruener often spent hours lost in his imagination, playing with toy tanks and motorcycles. When asked about defendant Josef Woods, Martin said the bespectacled 27-year-old was unintelligent and strange, an oddball who spoke about shooting laser beams, and reading minds.

Some of the most disturbing revelations during the trial came in mid-February, 1978, when details emerged about Betesh, Kribs, and Emanuel being far from the first boy they propositioned into having sex. There had, in fact, been *many* others. A number of children testified, including one who had been tied to a bed for about six hours months prior to Emanuel's murder, but eventually let go.

Over the coming weeks, a number of teenagers and young boys told the court about their experiences with the men. Some were runaways or street kids from broken homes who said the apartment above Charlie's Angels was a place they could sleep for a few nights. One of the boys was 'David,' a 16-year-old forced to pose for pornographic photos in the dingy apartment less than two weeks before Emanuel was murdered. While in the room naked, the teenager stated Gruener threatened him with a pellet gun while Kribs and Betesh took photos of him, and forced to perform sex acts with Kribs, Woods, and Betesh at knifepoint. The same youngster was also tied to a bed in the apartment, and raped by Betesh. Another 16-year-old, 'Mark,' testified he was photographed masturbating by Kribs, while Gruener again stood nearby with the pellet gun in hand to ensure he did what he was told, or face the consequences.

Among the many pieces of evidence presented during the trial, the jury was shown numerous photos of boys taken before Emanuel's murder, some of them naked, others bound to the bed. Some of the images has been processed beforehand, while others were taken from undeveloped rolls of film seized from the luggage of Kribs, Woods, and Gruener when they were apprehended at Sioux Lookout. For many jurors, the photos were too much to bear. At one point under cross-examination by Gruener's lawyer Earl Levy, 'Mark,' one of the young men who had been sexually assaulted by the men, angrily got up and left the packed courtroom.

The lengthy trial was taking a toll on the attorneys, defendants, and members of the jury, who were sequestered throughout the entire trial, which went on every day of the week, except Sundays. At the time, sequestering a jury for a whole trial was unusual in Canada. One day, defense attorney Tomlinson went to the courtroom early, already packed, with some spectators bringing lunch so they wouldn't lose their seats. The sight disgusted him. "I remember thinking: who would want to spend their Saturday listening to this horrible evidence? And come down and bring your lunch, like it was entertainment?" For Betesh's lawyer, the spectators reminded him of old films about the French Revolution, and Madame Thérèse Defarge, the fictional character in Charles Dickens' novel *A Tale of Two Cities*, who would sit, knitting the names of nobles who should be executed, while others stood around the guillotine, watching beheadings. "Maybe it was a sign of the times, but who would do that?" says Tomlinson. "Who would want to go to watch people's heads be cut off? And I remember thinking the same thing when I walked into the courtroom, people with their sandwiches on a Saturday — who does that? Who wants to go to a horrible trial?"

The jury soon heard testimony from others, including 'Barry,' a year younger than 'Mark.' Meeting Kribs at a downtown diner, he too was sexually assaulted by Woods and Kribs after ingesting alcohol and Valium, a drug used to treat anxiety disorders and alcohol withdrawal. Combining the two substances resulted in extreme disorientation and loss of consciousness for the teenager, who woke up to find himself bound hand and foot. Claiming to have been locked in a closet for three days, he managed to escape after hearing voices in the room talking about killing him. Although he told others about his ordeal, including a Salvation Army Captain, no one was ever arrested.

Along with promises of payment for photos, a hot restaurant meal, and a place to sleep, another way the men lured young boys back to their apartment was through their Citizens' Band radio. Originating after World War II, CB radios were soon adopted mainly by truck drivers as a means of communication to help them map their location, and make them aware of police speed traps. Exploding in popularity in the Seventies when prices dropped, the units were soon found in many cars and homes. Some CB radios had 23 channels, while newer models had 40. While channels nine and 10 were used for emergency and highway travel use, many others were open. Instead of using real names, most CB radio enthusiasts remained anonymous, or used a 'handle.' Two of them were brothers 'Herbie' and 'Danny,' aged just 11 and eight.

The court learned the mother of the two boys had a CB radio, which is how she first became acquainted with Kribs, Woods, and Gruener, who one day went to the woman's house, promising they had a bicycle for her boys back at their apartment. The mother agreed to let them go to 245 Yonge Street, where the brothers were photographed in a bedroom, and sexually assaulted. Gruener, who sat and read his Bible, was asked by Woods to enter the room, and take pictures of the older child holding Woods' penis. These photos were among the many incriminating images produced for the jury. As Gruener's defense attorney Earl Levy later wrote, "This was devastating evidence insofar as Gruener was concerned because of the knowledge it gave him and the inference he was a voyeur. On the stand, Gruener denied it was he who had taken the photographs."[28] Instead of being rewarded with a bicycle, Kribs handed the boys five dollars, along with a pair of running shoes and a kite, and made them promise not to tell their mother what happened. Woods took them back home, and the brothers kept their secret to themselves until police tracked them down for the trial.

Like other children before him, Emanuel had also been photographed in the apartment. What became uncomfortably clear during the course of the trial was that several of the accused men, especially Betesh, had developed a sexual appetite for younger and younger boys. Promises of paying for photography — or in Emanuel's case, moving photographic equipment — was a ruse, a means of getting kids to accompany them to the apartment for series of photos, and often sex.

*****

During the trial, the jury saw not only photos taken of Emanuel and other boys, but numerous images of the exterior of Charlie's Angels, and the interior of the dirty apartment. To better convey the layout of the entire building, a three-dimensional scale model was created of the entire structure at 245 Yonge, including main floor store Orientique, second-storey Charlie's Angels, the rooms on the third floor, and the roof where Emanuel's body was discovered by police. Sections of the model could be removed, enabling jurors to look inside the apartment, where the boy's final hours were spent.

Toronto Police homicide investigators demonstrating the model of 245 Yonge Street, which was used during the Supreme Court trial of the four men. (Courtesy Toronto Police)

Over the weeks to come, the jury would learn exactly what happened to Emanuel from the moment he, brother Luciano and their friend Shane met Saul Betesh on Yonge Street up to the last time they saw him alive. The information was critical for jurors to determine the degree of involvement of the four men charged with his murder, which would prove controversial by the conclusion of the trial.

*****

After eating dinner at Howard Johnson's on Yonge Street, Emanuel walked with Betesh to the apartment above the body rub. When they arrived, Werner Gruener — the only one there at the time — answered the door. Betesh said he had a boy with him, and instructed Gruener to go around to the back door of the building facing a laneway, so he and Emanuel could go upstairs unnoticed by anyone passing by. Heading up the rear metal fire escape, Gruener obligated, opening the door. Clearly seeing Betesh had a minor with him and holding the door open would become an issue in Gruener's defence during the trial. He would state that later that evening, as the boy was being assaulted, he was in the living room at the time sleeping, watching television, or heading out to Howard Johnson's for ice cream, unaware of the horror going on in another room just a few feet away.

The back alley behind the building where Emanuel was led to his death, with the fire staircase removed, July, 2007 (author photo)

By the time they entered the apartment, Josef Woods and Robert Kribs had arrived. Woods occupied one bedroom, while Gruener and Kribs shared another. This information, and the layout of the rooms, was made clear to the jury though photos, drawings, and the model of the building. It also played an important factor in Gruener's defence, particularly relating to what he was able to see and hear that night.

*****

Emanuel was coaxed into posing for photographs, initially clothed, then removing his T-shirt, pants, and underwear until he was nude. Handcuffed and tied to the bed with wire, he was repeatedly brutalized by Betesh and Kribs, who said they would kill him if he didn't keep quiet. At one point, the son of the owner of Charlie's Angels came upstairs with a friend wanting to smoke marijuana, unaware of what was happening behind the closed door, which was blocked by Kribs. Returning a few hours later, the owner's son was stopped again, this time by Gruener, who said nothing was going on. The court heard Woods and Gruener were "stoned on dope" most of the time, and denied knowing what was being done to Emanuel.

An interior view of the stairs from the apartment above Charlie's Angels, looking down towards ground level (Courtesy Toronto Police)

Hearing specifics of Emanuel's ordeal, many in the courtroom visibly recoiled in disgust. Less than 100 pounds, under five feet tall and bound to the bed, there was absolutely nothing the boy could do to fight back. Attacked with a sex toy at one point, he began screaming. To keep him quiet, Gruener mixed Valium in a glass of orange drink crystals and water. Still conscious, the decision was made to give Emanuel a second pill to knock him out, but this time Gruener and Betesh would cook the medication. Attempts to administer it intravenously failed, as they clumsily struggled to find a vein in his arm, causing more agony. Earlier, the men discussed taking Emanuel with them on the train to Vancouver, as Kribs had done with another boy before, but this idea was quickly abandoned. Too many questions would be raised, and police would be on the lookout for the missing child. At one point Woods, dubbed 'The Mad Scientist' for his wacky inventions and outlandish claims, believed he could hypnotize Emanuel, as he had unsuccessfully tried to do with another boy they sexually molested. Another suggestion was to leave Emanuel in a park, but they realized there was a chance he could go to the police, and they would be arrested.

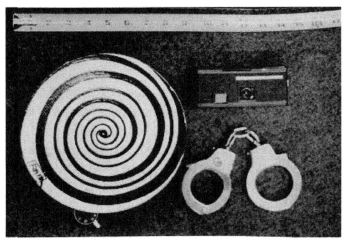

Additional evidence shown to jurors during the trial: one of "Mad Scientist" Josef Woods' hypnotic inventions, a pair of handcuffs, and a camera used to photograph young boys (Courtesy Toronto Police)

The decision was made: he had to die.

Tragically, attempts to kill the child only prolonged his suffering. Among the pieces of evidence shown to the jury was a gold and red bungee cord with metal hook ends. Betesh removed the cord from the back of a bicycle in the apartment, then attempted to strangle Emanuel to death over two or three agonizing minutes. Kribs and Woods were in the room during Emanuel's ordeal, with Gruener allegedly guarding the door from the hallway. At one point, Woods brought a pillow to put over the boy's face, so Betesh wouldn't have to look at him. When strangling him failed, the choice was made to drown the youngster.

The bungee cord Saul Betesh used to try to strangle Emanuel to death before the boy was drowned in a kitchen sink (Courtesy Toronto Police)

Bleeding from his injuries, bruised, arms riddled with puncture wounds, Emanuel was fading in and out of consciousness when Betesh and Woods dragged him off the bed, and carried him to the kitchen sink, which they filled with water. Turning him upside-down, Kribs grabbed him by both legs as Betesh held his head under water. Gruener testified he was asleep during much of this time, and said he believed they were going to let the boy go.

Once Emanuel was dead, Woods and Kribs wrapped his body in curtains before stuffing it into two green garbage bags, secured with black electrical tape. Betesh rifled through the dead boy's clothes, stealing Emanuel's shoeshine money — three, one-dollar bills — stating "The kid was dead and he didn't need it anymore." In a sickening attempt at humour, Woods cracked jokes about Emanuel wanting a shampoo, and suggested "putting him in a trunk and mailing it to Anita Bryant," the American activist who was promoting her Save Our Children campaign to protect youngsters from homosexuals.

Now that he was dead, the question remained: what to do with the body. One suggestion was taking it next door where construction was taking place, in the hope that workers wouldn't realize it was there, and entomb it in concrete. This was too risky, in case they were spotted. In the meantime, the remains were carried downstairs and hidden under the rear stairwell as the men went to Howard Johnson's for breakfast the next morning, discussing what to do next. The decision was made to wait until Midnight, and bury the remains. On the afternoon of July 29, Betesh, Woods and Gruener went to a hardware store, and bought a shovel; instead of paying attention, Gruener was more interested in looking at 10-speed bicycles on sale.

*****

Later that night, Betesh and Kribs tried digging a hole in a nearby lot, but the ground was much too hard and compacted. Abandoning the idea, the corpse was then carried to the rooftop, where it was shoved into an air vent.

The old rooftop air vent above Charlie's Angels, where Emanuel's killers hid his body (Courtesy Toronto Police)

Now afraid of getting arrested for the murder, arrangements were made by Kribs for himself, Woods, and Gruener to leave Toronto for Vancouver on a train, with Betesh saying he would meet them at a later date. Since the train was full that Friday, the three had to take the next one, leaving on Saturday, July 30, at 11:30 p.m.

With the trio on their way out west — and a police search in progress for the missing boy, who was still presumed alive — Betesh realized he could likely be recognized as the last one seen with Emanuel, likely by staff at the Howard Johnson's restaurant where they ate dinner. Soon after, he contacted George Hislop from the Canadian Homophile Association of Toronto, with Hislop advising him to turn himself in to police. That

Sunday evening, Betesh and his then-attorney went to 51 Division police station, where he unraveled his story. Offering to take police to the roof of the apartment and point out where they would find Emanuel, he also implicated Kribs, Woods, and Gruener in the murder, saying they were on a train to Vancouver. Alerting Ontario Provincial Police, the three were taken off the train about 1,100 miles from Toronto.

For Toronto police officers who went to Sioux Lookout to bring the suspects back to the city, the return flight was one of the strangest of their lives. Staff-Sergeant Gerald Stevenson, the homicide officer earlier led by Betesh to the rooftop, testified how he cut the taped trash bags and aqua-colored vinyl drape and "revealed the face of Emanuel Jaques." During the return flight, Stevenson observed the three men, and took notes documenting their behaviour. Gruener sat on the airplane in absent-minded silence reading his pocket-sized Bible, seemingly unaware he was under arrested for murder, save for his wrists handcuffed together. Robert Kribs, the lanky, quick-tempered bouncer, was chatty, speaking openly about being gay, stating Betesh and Woods were also homosexuals. His comments about co-accused Gruener and children were unnerving, as he said Gruener "liked" little girls, "and also liked to watch when they had little boys in sexual activity."

Kribs' comment would result in a number of discrepancies in Stevenson's evidence at trial, where Gruener testified he "liked" to play with little girls and watch them play with one another, but not in a sexual way. On behalf of his client, Werner Gruener, lawyer Earl Levy later wrote:

Since there was no evidence that Gruener took part in the actual killing it was the Crown's theory that he was guilty of first-degree murder by virtue of Section 21(2) of the criminal code coupled with the relevant murder sections, particularly Sections 213 and 214. In the circumstances of this case, therefore, it was incumbent upon the prosecution to prove that Gruener knew or ought to have known that carrying out either one of these common purposes, bodily harm (leading to Emanuel Jaques' death) would be a probable consequence. This evidence was important for the Crown because, if believed, it would show that Gruener knew what his co-accused were doing with young boys and that they were prepared to use force or commit forcible confinement for their purposes. [Crown Counsel] Frank Armstrong very ably argued the striking similarity of each piece of similar fact evidence and how that evidence went to a course of conduct which led Gruener to know what was going on and that Gruener should have foreseen what would occur on the night in question.[29]

Spending hours with his client in preparation for his defence, Levy recalled Gruener's odd behaviour in an article he wrote for a legal newsletter, and years later, for a chapter in the book, *Tough Cases*. Moments of levity were very few during the grim trial, except for one which involved his client, who still remains memorable decades later. In his article for the newsletter, under the subheading 'Gruener's Peculiarities,' Levy wrote at length about his client:

> Talking to Werner Gruener was like swimming through a pool of peanut butter. Although quite friendly, he never volunteered an answer. When he did answer it was as brief as possible, after which he would lapse into a dreamy silence until asked another question. Notwithstanding he belonged to the Children of God sect and was never without his Bible, he saw nothing wrong in working in a body rub parlour, or living with homosexuals. It was quite clear that he himself was not a homosexual. Although he looked somewhat like Rasputin and acted like Mortimer Snerd [a dummy used by legendary ventriloquist Charlie McCarthy], he was likeable. It was obvious that if he was not to be swallowed up in the sea of horrifying evidence that would be heard by the jury, he would have to be separated in the evidence from his friends. To this end his employers, Joe Martin [Sr.] and Joe Martin, Jr. were interviewed. I was aware they were going to be called as Crown witnesses. These were the only people who really knew him since he had worked for them for the past four years. There were no others who knew him well, except his co-accused. Even his parents had not seen him in about five years. It was arranged that Gruener be seen by Dr. Goldsmith, a psychologist, and Dr. Atcheson, a psychiatrist. I also asked the Crown for permission

to examine Gruener's luggage at the police property department. The luggage had been seized when Gruener was arrested in Sioux Lookout. The contents were not part of the Crown's case but I felt that I might gain further insight into Gruener by examining his worldly belongings. Frank Armstrong came with me for this purpose.

*****

The Martins were very helpful. They told me of how Gruener was always reading his Bible, would even talk about it to some of the customers at the body rub parlour. He was a good employee, honest and well-liked by those who worked around him. He had a collection of toy tanks that he liked to play with and at times was seen to drive his bicycle in the early hours of the morning down Yonge Street pretending he was a soldier. There were times that he would hand out his Children of God pamphlets to passing pedestrians on Yonge Street.

A few of the dozens of founder Moses David's Children of God cult pamphlets found in the murder apartment (Courtesy Toronto Police)

He liked to wear his Davey Crockett coonskin cap even in the heat of the summer.

Nicknamed "three wheeler," his bicycle had to be seen to be believed. It has streamers and a coonskin tail and all sorts of gadgets including a CB radio on the handlebars. The Martins felt that they and the girls who worked in the body rub parlour were Gruener's only family and that he enjoyed being told what to do by the girls because it was an indication that they had taken an interest in him. Their evidence was that Gruener had lived at 245 Yonge Street for four years and that Woods and Kribs were new-found friends who moved in about two months before Emanuel was killed.

The psychiatric evidence was important. Insanity was not a defence, but I felt it necessary to explain how Gruener could be so detached from events on the night in question that he could go to sleep. This is not a normal reaction of a normal person under the circumstances. Gruener tested out at low-average intelligence. Dr. Atcheson's conclusions were that Gruener suffered from a personality disorder which was a borderline type, that he periodically demonstrated psychotic symptoms at which time his contact with reality was inappropriate and inadequate. There was no evidence of deviant sexual behaviour. After trying to ascertain a chronological account of the events of the night in question, it was Dr. Atcheson's clinical impression that although Gruener was present much of the time he was in the type of disassociated state that the doctor observed periodically during his examination. That is, he was in a world of his own and almost completely withdrawn from the reality of the situation. He did not feel however that Gruener was certifiable in that he did not present a risk to himself or others. Dr. Atcheson felt that Werner Gruener was a lonely person who sought out the Children of God sect for that reason. It was of course an explanation why he was friendly with his co-accused after they found each other through their mutual interest in CB radios and bicycle riding.

      Visually speaking, if ever there was anything capable of setting Gruener apart from his co-accused it was the treasure found in his suitcase at the police property department. When one of the police officers from Sioux Lookout was called by the Crown to testify, I requested in cross-examination that Gruener's suitcase which she had seized be opened. I of course knew what was there — a picture from the *Toronto Sun* of Gruener sitting on that strange bike of his with ear-phones on his head and a caption underneath reading that Werner Gruener, an international cyclist was on his way from Vancouver to Florida and had stopped off in Toronto (an indication of the fantasy world in which he lived and a certain childlike quality), two Bibles (one Bible was also found on him when he was arrested and which he read continuously whilst in custody at the Sioux and during the course of the police interrogation by the homicide squad), a group of religious drawings which he made, a pile of religious literature, a collection of wallet size photographs of movie stars, a card indicating he was a member in good standing in a Rocket Club.

There was also a receipt from American Express showing he had bought two hundred dollars' worth of American Express travellers cheques about a week before he took the train to Vancouver. This was important evidence insofar as the question of flight was concerned. Crown testimony from the C.N.R. stated that the accused had paid for their tickets with American Express cheques. It was Gruener's testimony, consistent with part of the statement he gave to the police, that he had left Toronto, not as some indication of consciousness of guilt, but that it had been a pre-planned trip. This evidence was corroborated by the Martins who testified that Gruener had told them about a month prior to Emanuel's death that he was going out West the time that he in fact did leave.

There was no doubt in Levy's mind whatsoever that Gruener, who was referred to him by another lawyer through Legal Aid, was extremely peculiar the first time they met, soon after he was apprehended by police. "It was very difficult getting through to him. It wasn't that he was uncooperative, or he felt he wasn't making any sense," says Levy, remembering how confused his client was when he asked him to review two documents in court, and gave an answer which had absolutely nothing to do with Levy's question. "He [Gruener] totally misunderstood what to do, because in his answer, he was looking at something entirely different in one of the documents, totally unrelated to the question. The incident meshed with the message that we were getting from the psychiatrist about how he reacts, how he disassociates entirely. That was a point I made, and I think it must have affected the jury to some extent as far as giving actual live corroboration to what the psychiatrist was saying. And it wasn't the kind of thing that was put on by him; I mean, he appeared very genuine on the stand, with pregnant pauses during the course of my examination and the cross-examination of the Crown. So that seemed to stick with me."

During the trial, Levy asked Supreme Court Justice Maloney to instruct the jury to find his client not guilty of first-degree murder which, under the Criminal Code of Canada, would see the German-boy man face life in prison with no possibility of parole for 25 years. Arguing that although Gruener was in the apartment the night Emanuel was raped and killed, he was sleeping, and was not a party to the boy's forcible confinement, sexual abuse, or death. Levy also stated it was Gruener who came up with suggestions which would have seen Emanuel survive, namely leaving him in a park where he could be found, taking him with them on the train to Vancouver, or drugging him. Stating there was evidence Gruener left the room when the decision was made to kill Emanuel, Levy added there was no evidence implicating Gruener in Emanuel's forcible confinement. Justice Maloney refused Levy's request to instruct the jury to find Gruener not guilty of first-degree murder, and denied another request for a separate trial. While Levy argued on behalf of his client, Maloney ruled there was still some evidence Gruener was involved in the scheme to lure Emanuel to the apartment "for purposes of sexually assaulting him," and Gruener should have been aware there was a chance the boy could be harmed.

However, there was no way to get around the statement from Gruener that he "liked little girls." The accused man and his lawyer denied the interest was sexual, but observational, as he enjoyed watching them at play. Considering Gruener's odd, disconnected personality and temperament, this seemed plausible. His peculiar comment, and the behaviour of his co-accused, was not lost on the press, including *The Body Politic*, who wrote: "With the exception of Gruener, who is said to be sexually attracted to girls, the accusers are probably gay men. All appear to be extremely troubled individuals."[30]

Arguing his client was unaware bodily harm would come to Emanuel, that he was not part of the sexual assault, and that Gruener did not know the boy was dead until Ontario Provincial Police officers boarded the train in Sioux Lookout, Levy told the court: "I emphasize I am not asking you to find Werner Gruener not guilty of second-degree murder; I'm not using a defense of insanity. I am saying Werner Gruener is not guilty of anything, except perhaps in his choice of friends." Court heard that Gruener often became disassociated when confronted with violence or hostility, as a way of detaching himself physically and emotionally from reality to minimize stress. While listening to testimony, Gruener often sat motionless in the prisoner's box, his eyes cast down at the floor, lost in his own thoughts.

Throughout the trial, anyone observing Gruener saw he was quiet and withdrawn, often appearing as though he was daydreaming, or in slow motion. Taking the stand, he spoke so softly he could barely be heard, even in the otherwise silent courtroom. To the jury, spectators and press, he came across as his lawyer described him, seemingly unaware of his surroundings, his mind drifting elsewhere. Although he lived in the third-floor apartment with Kribs and Woods, Gruener said he was unaware they were homosexuals. Although he denied being gay, Gruener admitted that while in jail in 1970 after being charged with breaking and entering, one of his relatively minor charges, he had "involuntary homosexual experiences."

For a 29-year-old man, Gruener had many eccentricities about him that were not only child-like, but genuinely infantile, such as wearing a Davy Crockett raccoon fur hat on his head, and riding his 10-speed bicycle up and down Yonge Street, music blaring from his radio. Described by his lawyer as a man of few words, Gruener usually seemed dazed. The child of religious zealots, he arrived in Canada from Germany at the age of seven, with the family settling down in Dryden, Ontario, before relocating to British Columbia. During the trial, the court heard about Gruener's upbringing, including him dropping out of school in Grade 10, and his mother's mental breakdown while he was in his early teens.

When asked about the night Emanuel was raped and murdered, Gruener maintained his story about being in another room watching television, sleeping, or heading down the street for an hour and a half to buy a pint of butterscotch ice cream. Despite evidence stating Emanuel was crying during the sexual attack, Gruener said he heard no noises. When asked about what to do with the boy's body, Gruener maintained he had no part in hiding it. As for the shovel purchased at the hardware store by co-accused Saul Betesh, Gruener thought it was going to be used to bury some marijuana they wanted to hide, not to dig a hole for the corpse.

One of the most dramatic moments during the trial came when Crown Attorney Peter Rickaby asked Gruener — who carried a copy of the Bible with him at all times — to read a specific passage from the King James Version, Matthew 18:6, relating to children. "But whoso shall offend one of these little ones which believe in me, it were better for him that a millstone were hanged about his neck, and that he were drowned in the depth of the sea," he said out loud. For the jury, the line was prophetic. Continuing his line of questioning, Rickaby ask Gruener how he could possibly be unaware Emanuel was dead until he was told so by the OPP. "I assumed the boy had been sent home," he said in a gentle voice.

On March 10, 1978, the trial of the four men charged with the murder entered its final stage. Lawyer Earl Levy was responsible for the most fitting line of the entire trial, calling it "A forced march through a sewer." Not only compelling, his statement summarized the ordeal jurors had to endure for weeks on end, and was symbolic of just how badly the Young Street strip had eroded over the years. Despite the opening of the then-new Eaton Centre at Yonge and Dundas, just across the street on the east side was the "sewer," a stretch full of X-rated movie theatres, prostitutes, and body rubs. Indeed, it was here a young boy was murdered, stated Levy, but his client Werner Gruener was not responsible; in fact, anything co-accused Saul Betesh said implicating his client in the crime should be ignored. Betesh, argued Levy, was a pathological liar, a man without conscience who delighted in attention, using the courtroom as a "soapbox for his last hurrah."

Jaques jury hears summations   10/3/78 GM
Trial a 'forced march through sewer': Levy

Newspaper headline quoting Werner Gruener's attorney, Earl Levy, who famously summed up the trial and all its gruesome testimony as "A forced march through a sewer" (author collection)

The trial was a highly emotional one for everyone involved, including his client. Fearing violence, police officers used metal detectors on everyone entering the courtroom. Yet despite this rage, feelings of anger and revulsion would not bring Emanuel back to life. Levy's concern was that "the stench from the sewer would come up and involve" Gruener, making him guilty by association. Betesh was not someone to be trusted, he said, particularly when it came to how readily he implicated Gruener in the murder. Levy argued his client had suffered enough, and that he should be acquitted.

Crown Attorney Rickaby, however, had a very different opinion of Werner Gruener. Although he may not have taken part in the brutal sexual attacks, Gruener opened the back door to allow Betesh and the child to enter the apartment. Likewise, he knew Emanuel was in one of the bedrooms, and he was involved in providing Valium in an attempt to drug the boy. How was it possible Gruener did not hear the child's agonized cries from the other room while he was watching television or eating ice cream? argued Rickaby. And why didn't Gruener, who was there when the other three men were discussing what to do with Emanuel, speak up? Despite these questions, Levy did not waver in his belief, challenging retractions made by Betesh who earlier testified lying to police about Gruener's involvement in hiding the body.

George Marron, the attorney representing Josef Woods, asked for his client to be found guilty of second-degree murder, not first. Robert Kribs, who changed his plea early on in the trial to guilty, still required sentencing. Saul Betesh and his lawyer, Paul Tomlinson, maintained his plea of not guilty by reason of insanity. At one point, Crown Prosecutor Frank Armstrong said Betesh told police and others things may have gone differently for the young boy, and they might not have killed him, if Canada still had capital punishment, and there was a possibility they could be executed for the crime.

During the trial, Betesh seemed thrilled by the attention he received. Freely admitting he lied to the police, one of the most shocking moments came when Betesh trivialized the life of the boy he raped and murdered. "What was Emanuel Jaques?" he said, dismissively shrugging his shoulders. "I wasn't thinking of Emanuel Jaques, except possibly before and possibly after. I suppose he was part of my fantasies," his expression morphing into a grin. The courtroom was aghast. Throughout the trial, the one thing — in fact, the *only* thing — Betesh maintained was his lack of remorse, never once apologizing for the cruel murder, or demonstrating any conscience or culpability for his role. When asked by Tomlinson if there was anything else he wanted to say, Betesh nonchalantly responded, "Nothing I can think of," concluding his direct testimony.

While the jury would hear a great deal about Betesh from psychiatrists, police, and people who knew him, his flippant comments about Emanuel's very existence underscored his true self. Examining Betesh twice after he was arrested, psychiatrist Dr. Andrew Malcolm quoted sections regarding what Betesh told him about the vicious attack on the child. At one point, while Kribs was raping Emanuel, Betesh pulled out a swagger stick — essentially a shortened cane used by military officers to direct drills and military manoeuvres — and began clubbing the boy on his legs and back, inflicting as much pain as possible. Many in court were disgusted by earlier comments he made about the thrill he felt using a bungee cord to strangle Emanuel, using words like "sexual excitement" and "power" as the boy gasped and struggled to breathe.

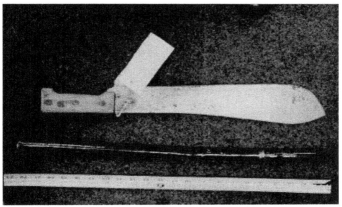

A machete and Saul Betesh's "swagger stick," a short wooden cane, presented as evidence during the trial of the four accused men (Courtesy Toronto Police)

With a volatile personality, Betesh was capable of instantly cutting-off emotions from others, even people he considered friends. Freely admitting he was furious with Woods, Kribs, and Gruener when they left for Vancouver without him after the murder, Betesh proudly said he lied to police, wanting to get even with his co-accused, and "screw them good." His co-accused, Josef Woods plead guilty to second-degree murder, but maintained he was not guilty of first-degree murder, stating he didn't take part in the child's forcible confinement or sexual attacks.

In many ways, Betesh's wild contradictions supported Gruener's defence, who he said was not even aware Emanuel had been drowned in the kitchen sink of the apartment, and who actually believed Betesh purchased a shovel with the intent of using it to bury dope, not the child's remains. Although Gruener was not involved in the murder or sexual abuse of the child, he did watch over the door, according to Betesh, and assisted in hiding the body. Claiming not to remember certain incidents and statements, Betesh refuted the three-page statement he gave to Sergeant Paton Weir shortly after he entered 51 Division police station months earlier. "I don't remember saying anything. And if I don't remember, I don't think it happened," said Betesh, who also signed a second formal statement — practically identical to his initial statement — in the presence of Richard Parker, the lawyer who accompanied him to the station. "I don't deny telling them things, I said 'em all. But I was making up a lot of it."

Chapter Ten: Saul David Betesh: From Heaven to Hell

For the jurors, spectators, throng of television and print reporters, Crown and defence attorneys, much of the incendiary testimony during the trial came not only from police and psychiatrists, but the mother, father, and sister of Saul Betesh. For twenty-seven difficult and troubling years, since the day they brought their newborn baby to their Toronto home, Lillian and James Betesh did everything possible to ensure the physical, mental, emotional, social and moral well-being of their deeply disturbed, angry, and destructive son, from costly therapists to religious lessons, and private schools in Canada and the United States, to no avail.

Sometimes breaking out into sobs on the witness stand, and even forcing Judge Maloney to call a recess, Betesh's elderly mother had to be escorted from court. Stories were told about the once-beautiful little Saul, and the shocking, terrifying behavior that saw his parents forced to bolt their bedroom door from the inside to protect themselves from their only son. Hearing from members of the Betesh family, it became clear James and Lillian Betesh did not create a problem: they adopted one.

Unable to have children of their own after six years of marriage, the Beteshs adopted a girl through an agency, naming her Diane. A decade passed and, on July 20, 1950, a 16-year-old girl in Montreal gave birth to a baby she did not wish to keep. Knowing they wanted another child, a physician they knew informed them of the newborn. For Lillian, a boy made their family complete; for James, the owner of Empire Linens, a successful wholesale importing business in Toronto, the prospect of a son meant he would have an heir to the family fortune, and the company he worked years to build would continue after he was gone. Adopted six days after birth, the child was named Saul David Betesh by James, in honour of his own father.

Delighted at the time with their infant son, there was no possible way the couple could know the utter devastation their decision to adopt would have on their lives, emotionally, physically, professionally, and financially. Over the months and years to come, the business James Betesh built disintegrated bit by bit. The family would move from their stately Forest Hills home to much more modest dwellings, as they devoted tremendous amounts of time and money to pay for psychiatrists, psychologists and institutions to help their troubled son, and themselves.

Unlike his co-defendants Woods, Kribs, and Gruener, who came from working-class backgrounds, young Saul Betesh was surrounded by wealth, opportunities, and everything he could ever wish for laid at his feet, except a sound mind.

For the jurors, lawyers, and the media, the psyche of Saul David Betesh was laid open for all to see, as his lawyer, Paul Tomlinson, presented a myriad of psychiatric and institutional reports, making it clear Saul's mental state — one brimming with paranoia, narcissism, rage, a complete lack of empathy, and utter indifference to the suffering of others, including his mother, father and sister — made for remarkable headlines not only in Toronto, but across North America.

In Montreal, the *Gazette* ran 'Portrait of a killer: homosexual 'chicken-hawk' went to hell from life of love and luxury, says sister,' a full-page article with a photo of Betesh and the brief yet accurate caption, *Saul Betesh: He had no feelings*.[31] The story, based on the masses of testimony from the family, doctors, and others who knew Saul, presented an image of a man who could not relate to feelings in others like joy, pain, and sadness, because he did not possess the capabilities to feel emotion. Trying as hard as he could, defence attorney Paul Tomlinson attempted to make the jurors realize his client was a psychopath who would be better served in a mental institution where there was a possibility he could get help, rather than face life in prison.

Over the course of the trial, the court heard of Saul Betesh's life, one which, in a perfect world, should have been overflowing with wealth, happiness, success, strong and stable friendships, and a loving family of his own. Instead, his mental instability worsened over the years, and the once-handsome youngster began looking like a haggard old man by the time he reached his mid-twenties.

Over the years, his anger transformed into the only true love he would ever know, sadism. His opulent childhood surroundings became filthy and foul-smelling rooming houses, or the bedrooms of clients who took advantage of his sexual services as a leather-clad gay male prostitute.

Interior of the filthy apartment above Charlie's Angels, facing Yonge Street (Courtesy Toronto Police)

As a newborn, Saul demonstrated strange, often disturbing behaviour, as stated by his parents and sister. Here was a family who wanted the best for their new son, from pampering to nutrition, the finest clothes, and pricey private schools. This was, after all, what he deserved: a future bright with promise. Although Saul Betesh started off on much more stable footing than his three co-defendants, over the years they all ended-up in the same dark place.

To the dismay of his new family, Saul's decline was not rapid, it was *immediate*. In the post-World War II era of the 1950s, where charming and wholesome television characters like Ozzie and Harriet Nelson and sitcoms *I Love Lucy*, and *Leave it to Beaver* were the norm, parents expected their children to grow up to be average, law-abiding folk, with jobs, wives or husbands, kids, mortgages and a family dog. Terms like sociopath and psychopathy, from 'psych' (soul or mind), and 'pathy' (suffering or disease) existed, but along with words like 'homosexual' or 'sadist,' they were infrequently used in decent company. And although his parents did everything within their abilities to help their young son achieve normalcy, nothing worked.

When he was less than six months old, baby Saul developed a bowel infection, sometimes caused by babies putting unclean objects contaminated with bacteria or parasites into their little mouths. As a result, his pacifier and bottle were taken away, immediately resulting in him furiously struggling to break free whenever he was held. His sister, just 10 at the time, was especially upset by this, as she wanted to coddle her new brother, who completely rejected all physical contact from her and his parents. Soon, this was followed by even more unusual behaviour. While children develop at different rates, they achieve certain milestones along the way. One is crawling, which usually starts between six and 10 months of age. When Saul began to crawl, it was always *backwards*, never forwards, which disturbed his parents, who began questioning what was wrong with their adopted son.

Other signs that their child was different soon emerged. One of the most distressing was when Saul was learning to walk. Pushing his crib across the bedroom, the boy would start smashing his head against the wall, blood running down his forehead, chunks of plaster tumbling to the floor. While he displayed some positive developmental qualities, like being able to hold a cup and drink by himself at an early age, his negative behaviour far outweighed the good. In children, overwhelmingly males, setting fires can be associated with other conduct disorders, usually referred to as antisocial behaviours. Saul didn't just like fire, he was both fearless of it. At just three and a half years of age, he began setting fires in garages using newspaper for kindling, and even once in a neighbour's den. Word soon spread in the close-knit, affluent Forest Hills neighbourhood that the young Betesh boy was 'different,' which made him an outcast among other children and their understandably protective parents.

Instead of improving, the boy's behaviour grew worse as he aged. While it is not unusual for children to act out when they are angry, hurt, or afraid, youngsters usually outgrow their fears and certain behaviours, or find coping mechanisms to deal with them. The court heard young Saul often refused to nap. Was he afraid to sleep, and so terrified of the patterned curtains in his bedroom and a tree branch occasionally tapping the window? Changing the window coverings and lopping off a tree limb did nothing to calm the young boy, who was also a frequent bed-wetter. "You have to understand Saul never had a normal life, so unfortunately there aren't too many good things to say about him," testified his sister about her little brother, who received everything he could have ever wanted, including a live-in nanny, who would also suffer at his hands. One day, while she slept on the sofa, the young boy deliberately poured toxic nail polish remover into her ear. He was not yet four years of age.

Enrolled in kindergarten, Saul's impulsive and violent behaviour, once confined mainly to the Betesh household, was now on public display. Earning a reputation as a school bully, biting and punching other kids, breaking their toys, and even slashing skipping ropes with a straight razor he stole from his father, he was expelled for attacking another child with a hockey stick. At home, the angry outbursts increased. Around the same time as he was barred from school, Saul cornered his terrified sister — then in her early teens — in the breakfast room, and began throwing steak knives at her, fully intending to cause her physical harm. The only way she could get out of the situation was to call her boyfriend for help.

During the trial, it was revealed Saul saw his first psychiatrist at age five. His mother, growing increasingly emotional on the witness stand, was fearful of even taking him to see a doctor, telling the court driving with him in the same car was unpredictable, even dangerous. "It was almost as if he knew he was doing something detrimental. If it was no, he would do it....It was as if he'd hurt you deliberately," she said. It was also around this time the family's financial fortunes began to flounder. Despite the success of Empire Linens, privately-funded psychiatric treatment for their young son was extremely costly.

For Lillian and James Betesh, concerns over their son's mental and physical state grew much worse. Following his removal from kindergarten, Saul's parents sent him to an exclusive, all-boys private school in Toronto, where they believed he would receive a proper education, guidance, and hopefully, much-needed discipline. This time, however, Saul was the victim. Coming home one day, Lillian saw what appeared to be bite marks and bruises on her son's boy. Confronting the school's principal, she was shocked to hear confirmation Saul had been sexually abused by one of the male teachers, something he stated two decades later while on trial for the first-degree murder of Emanuel Jaques. "When I went to

Crescent School, I remember being sexually assaulted by one of the male teachers, who squeezed my testicles and had oral sex," he stated to the court in a voice that was so monotone he might as well have been ordering a breakfast special in a diner. The teacher, who molested at least one other young male student, was fired, and the parents involved were asked not to discuss what happened to their sons.

Returning to the public school system, Saul immediately began tormenting other students, and was soon removed by his parents and sent to a private reform school in the United States. It was also around this time the family moved to a more modest dwelling, and James Betesh privately sold Empire Linens, the company he had worked so hard to grow over the years.

Throughout the trial, Saul Betesh appeared more pleased than upset with others discussing his behaviour, which included attacking his father with a rake, and shoving his mother down a flight of stairs, breaking her finger. Hoping a dog would help his troubled son become more like a normal child, James Betesh soon had to re-home the pet, which he claimed Saul "molested."

Although he was on trial along with Woods, Gruener, and Kribs for one of the most horrific crimes imaginable — the abduction, torture, rape, and brutal murder of a child — this was The Saul Betesh Show, the zenith of his narcissistic, lying, and unsympathetic existence. As stated in the *Globe and Mail* by journalist Marina Strauss, "If Mr.

Betesh ended up the high-profile character of the trial, it was probably because the 27-year-old wanted it that way. He was the one who went to police after he had been seen last with Emanuel on July 28. He was the one who spilled the whole story in shockingly vivid detail. Mr. Betesh craved attention. He craved power, a feeling of self-importance. He admits it, impassively, without shame. And anyone who has had close contact with the man is quick to point it out."[32]

With headlines like 'Doctor once ordered Betesh committed to mental hospital,' the accused's entire past was subject to scrutiny by jurors, the press and the public. Shifra Nussbaum, a caseworker with the Jewish Family and Child Services, met Saul when he was just 14. She told the court how much delight he took pitting his parents against one another, and seeing them argue over him. No longer knowing what to do with their son, Mr. and Mrs. Betesh had a temporary reprieve when Nussbaum and the agency arranged to send Saul to a private reform school in Pennsylvania, where he remained until June, 1966. Returning to Canada, Toronto psychiatrist Dr. Angus Hood ordered Saul committed to the Lakeshore Psychiatric Hospital later that year. The order also included that Saul — due to his violent behaviour — be accompanied by Metro Police to the facility. However, his commitment never took place. Other arrangements had been made at the time, and the teenager was instead sent to the Browndale (Ontario) Ltd. Centre for emotionally disturbed children. In court, reports from professionals at the Browndale facility — where Saul remained from age 17 to 19 — were produced, all painting a picture of a very disturbed individual.

"I learned about his background, and the terrible behavior that he had manifested, even as a child, right back to two or three years of age," says Tomlinson, "things like pouring nail polish into the maid's year while she was asleep, and trying to rewire the home to electrocute his parents. He threw knives at his sister. He had been expelled from kindergarten, went to a number of schools, and his family sent him to a place in Pennsylvania. Saul's mother tried having him committed. That didn't happen, unfortunately, because it may well be that we'd never have had this tragedy if he had been committed. But I didn't dislike him. I learned that it was mental illness, and I learned that he was a psychopath."

The child, full of anger against his parents, sister and school mates was transforming into a strong, vicious young man. At one point, he kicked a staff member at the Centre so hard that the worker was forced to retire, which made Betesh feel not guilt, but "partly relieved." Remaining true to his Jewish roots, Saul often mixed reality with fantasy; even his friends couldn't differentiate between his truth and his lies. The man he attacked was, he believed, an Egyptian, and this was during the Six-Day War, being fought by Israel and neighbouring Arab states Egypt (then the United

Arab Republic), Syria, and Jordan. In Betesh's mind, this battle justified the assault. Less than a decade later, he would proudly display "wounds" to his body, claiming he suffered them while battling in Israel, which was an outright fabrication.

In Browndale, Saul was subjected to numerous reports by psychiatrists, social workers, and psychologists, all indicating a highly delusional mind. Always full of himself and believing he was better than others, one of his fantasies was to go to Israel, and fight for his homeland (despite never having been there). In true Saul Betesh fashion, however, he envisioned himself as less of a soldier than a mercenary. To him, the glory was not financial gain, but power, and the thrill of controlling the fate of others. He convinced himself he was going to join the Air Force as soon as he turned 18, fly to Israel, and become a fighter pilot (despite having no training or military experience whatsoever), so he could drop bombs on railways and small businesses, "basically things that make the country work," he said. This would finally give him a license to kill.

Testifying during the trial was Browndale's Executive Assistant Director, Barry Reisman, who confirmed Betesh had military fantasies, along with dreams of being part of a gang with "connections with the underworld," involved in violence and drugs. As part of his lengthy folder amassed while at the Browndale Centre from 1967 to 1969, a number of poems written by Saul were introduced, including one entitled "Misery," which was read to the court: "I know that others bear my grief/Grief worse, more biting/Life is utterly futile/HATE, BITTERNESS, CORRUPTION/Never joy or love/But/Emptiness forever/By my soul/Life is misery when I make it so."

Following his time at Browndale, Betesh was somehow able to secure a full-time job at Canada Post as a mail handler, a position he held until 1974. Despite being considered a good employee, he was convicted of possessing $800 worth of goods stolen from the mail, which saw him serve 90 days in jail. While employed, he was also seen committing an unspecified 'homosexual act' at the post office. On the picket line during the first of a series of postal strikes that year, he was charged with assault when he sprayed a noxious substance. However, charges against all federal government workers involved in the strike — held over protection against technological change in the post office — were dropped, including those involving Betesh. Ignoring recommendations of seeking psychiatric help, the same lawyer who represented him regarding mail theft and his antics during the postal strike dropped him as a client.

Viewing himself as a person who "one day might be something," years of treatment from psychiatrists, social workers, and being sent to costly boarding schools for emotionally disturbed children did not help Betesh. Seeing psychiatrists at the C.M. Hinks Treatment Centre an estimated 50 times since the tender age of five did little for the benefit of his mental health. One report from 1971 stated he had a great capacity to harm others through his "charm and manipulative powers." And as much as Saul was incapable of facing his own reality, he was extremely dismissive and critical of others, including his mother and father, referring to them in one report as "two emotionally disordered parents." He never once expressed gratitude towards them for the years they dedicated to him, their only son, or the fortune they spent on doctors, private schools, and individualized psychiatric treatment.

Of James and Lillian Betesh, Saul was not only emotionally indifferent, but often hostile, particularly to his mother. Viewing her as overbearing, he resented feeling like he and his adopted sister were put on display when visitors came to their house, testifying they were "the showpiece of the family...I was going to take over daddy's business. I was mother's pride and joy."

Jaques defendant was vicious as child, sobbing mother says

Newspaper headline (author collection)

In the Betesh household, Saul's anger, never-ending lies and boasts, and crazed behaviour was obvious to everyone. He did, however, keep one thing to himself: that he felt attracted to other boys. By his own admission, Saul was unable to accept he was gay until about age 20. His father, however, believed his boy was homosexual by the way he started dressing, which was much more flamboyant than before.

Lean, handsome and superficially charming — attributes he used to his advantage — Betesh soon realized there was a market for someone like him on the streets of Toronto, so he began prostituting himself. Frequenting the city's bathhouses in the downtown gay ghetto, customers were never in short supply. It didn't take long for him to realize that although turning quick tricks was profitable, full-on sadomasochistic sex was downright lucrative, netting him as much as $60 per hour in the mid-Seventies. For Betesh, S&M was also a powerful release. For the first time, he could let his sexual imaginings take over with a willing, paying partner.

Telling the court "my fantasies were strong on the sadist side, my actions were pretty much on the masochistic side," Betesh accepted his role as the giver and/or the receiver of pain and humiliation for sexual gratification with the same enthusiasm as a university graduate getting his first real job. Instead of buying a new suit, shirt, shoes and a tie, Saul went out and purchased a head-to-toe leather outfit to better advertise his assets, namely his body, and make him feel powerful. "I was really into sex, and I liked it," he told his defence attorney, Tomlinson. "It was a job. I like sex, I got paid for it. It's like being a computer programmer." During his years as a male prostitute, Betesh freely admitted his sexual activities ranged from 16-year-old boys to senior citizens of about 80. However, his own urges were for much younger children.

Around the same time as he began prostituting himself, Betesh's once-handsome looks began to fade dramatically, which coincides with the last times Leslie Brown saw him at Mr. Gameways' Ark, dressed like a pimp and looking painfully gaunt. For Saul, it was the confluence of his declining mental state, physical health, and growing obsession with prepubescent boys.

Betesh tells jury about sado-masochist lifestyle

Newspaper headline (author collection)

In the 1970s, Yonge Street was not only home to much of the city's sex industry, but numerous arcades and places where patrons could purchase or play a variety of strategy, war and fantasy games far beyond the buzzers of pinball machines or driving simulations like Road Racer. Often attracting a slightly older crowd in their twenties, it wasn't unusual to see players deep in thought over a game of chess sometime lasting hours, or the elaborate tabletop role-playing game Dungeons & Dragons, which became enormously popular.

Operating a wholesale distribution company at the time, Brown was the original importer of Dungeons & Dragons into Canada, later opening a retail store called The Four Horsemen, the first in Toronto to sell the enormously popular board game, Trivial Pursuit. His biggest competitor at the time was Mr. Gameways' Ark, which expanded into a large location on Yonge Street in the late Seventies. The basement was set-up for plastic model kits, the ground floor designated for toys, and the second floor for games. There was also a third floor which wasn't accessed from inside the main building, but a stairwell at the back of the building. A games club was started, where groups of players engaged in backgammon, chess — including Canadian chess master Lawrence Day — and family-type gamers who played Risk or Acquire.

"So that's where all of these people mixed," says Brown of the club, which operated for several years until the mid-Seventies, when Mr. Gameways' could no longer afford to run it. At that point, a number of individuals were approached to manage the club, including Brown. Investing a modest amount, Brown and two others ran the operation. Opening the doors two or three nights a week, a fee was charged to gamers, who often stayed for hours, buying chocolate bars, pop and potato chips. Soon, the backgammon contingent disappeared, leaving behind the chess players, family gamers, and others into Dungeons & Dragons, and games produced by Avalon Hill, which specialized in military simulation and strategic board games.

"These aren't like your Monopoly-type games," says Brown of the club's military simulation and Dungeons & Dragons games. Many were extremely large, using small cardboard counters to represent military units. Especially popular were games like Terrible Swift Sword, a huge tactical simulation of the Battle of Gettysburg. These games were intense, and on such a grand scale that they took weeks, sometimes months, to complete.

As one of the operators of the club, Brown soon became familiar with many of the regular players before Mr. Gameways' took it back over in 1976, including the men who would soon be charged with the murder of Emanuel Jaques. When he first came to the club, Saul Betesh played chess, and soon got into military simulation games. "He was never sort of a main character among the small, intensive group of military gamers," states Brown. "For about a year or two, he would come in two to three times a week, play some of the military simulation games, and go out with us."

In a very short time, Brown and his friends became aware of Betesh's bravado and wild exaggerations. Claiming to have been part of the Israeli forces and involved in the Six Day War of 1967, Betesh went on to state with absolute conviction that he was an agent in the Shin Bet, Israel's internal security service, similar to being in the FBI or Britain's MI5. "Nobody really believed him," says Brown of Betesh, who usually came into the club by himself. "It was more tongue-in-cheek,

'Sure, Saul.' But he used to come in and brag all the time about his military prowess."

Along with Betesh, Werner Gruener and Josef Woods would sometimes come to the games club. Gruener, most often than not, would sit quietly and read his Bible. On other occasions, Woods was accompanied by Robert 'Stretch' Kribs, who always brought some young teenage boy along with him. This became something of a running joke among the club regulars. Appearing to be about 14 or 15, the young men were never the same person, with Kribs fawning over them, telling others "This is my son." Patrons soon began wondering exactly how many 'sons' he had. The younger men accompanying him would sit by Kribs' side, play games like Risk or Acquire, and leave together; however, they never seemed as if they didn't want to be there with him. "We were suspicious of the type of relationship that a man of his age would be having with a teenager — at least I was — and we sort of suspected that there was something going on there, but there was never any indication there was any duress involved," remarks Brown. "It really wasn't our business to get involved."

While the young men seemed passive, the massive Kribs was anything but calm. Extremely volatile, Kribs' fury was immediate: if something didn't go his way, he would slam his fists on the games table and swear so loudly that others would stop playing to see what the trouble was. A number of times Brown had to approach Kribs, and tell him to calm down, or he would have to leave.

"Kribs was a mean-spirited guy, with a very explosive temper, and quite intelligent and conniving," says Brown. "Betesh was a guy who said anything that came to his mouth — he'd say he'd done this, or done that — and everybody would just sort of laugh it off. Nobody really believed it." One time, Brown was driving with Betesh down Front Street, and Betesh suddenly said, 'That's my dad's linen store.'" The comment was surprising, since Betesh never invited others to his house, and rarely talked about his family. When asked about practically anything, Betesh usually said he couldn't comment, because he was a secret Israeli agent. "Anything he ever said, we took with a grain of salt."

Whenever Betesh came into the club, he dressed ordinarily, wearing a shirt, blue jeans, and running shoes, occasionally with a construction helmet. Disappearing for a year before the closing of the games club around 1976, Betesh's appearance and personality dramatically changed when he began showing up again. Losing weight, he had developed blisters, which some members speculated were the result of using drugs. His regular clothes were replaced by "funny-looking" suits and velvet brocade. One time, Betesh came into the club sporting a purple fedora, shirt wide open revealing his chest, and gold chains around his neck. "He became weird," says Brown. "He started to show up wearing pimp clothes, and mauve or pink suits with fedoras. And he'd never dressed like that before, wearing stuff that didn't stick out."

Sometimes, he would be accompanied to the club by an extremely shy girl who sat and read, who Betesh claimed he dated. Whenever he came, which was less frequently, others were laughing at him, and telling him he looked like a pimp. "I'm sure he wasn't happy, because everyone was giving him a hard time. He told us he was running a couple of girls. Again, we didn't know what to believe with him, because it was a different story every time you saw him," states Brown. The last time he remembers Betesh was when a number of friends met for dinner at a Bloor Street restaurant after the games club closed. Betesh came in with an anorexic-looking young woman with acne, who he introduced as "one of his girls." Although Brown doesn't recall Betesh displaying any anger, he recalls his change of behaviour during the 'pimp phase,' which also saw his personal hygiene decline, especially his teeth, which were yellowing.

"His behavior certainly changed. Betesh stopped frequenting the club, and his attire changed. His complete demeanor changed, his relationship with the people in the club changed, and then he stopped coming, whereas previously he had been coming maybe two or three nights a week, hanging around with everybody, and going out for coffee afterwards. He just vanished. In the couple of times that he did show up, he was wearing these funny suits and hats. We just sort of laughed at him."

An inveterate liar, bombastic, and especially strange when he started acting like a pimp, Brown remembers Betesh's rapid decline. Months passed, and the next time he heard anything about Betesh was at the time of Emanuel's murder when it was reported in the press, and he saw him on TV with two police detectives. He was shocked. Despite Betesh's eccentric behaviour, he never suspected he was capable of committing such an atrocious crime. Like many others, Brown followed the trial.

"The murder itself was horrific, and the details were even more horrific," he says. "The credit I gave Saul was that he came forward, and gave himself up. I never really felt that he had the personality for doing that. I think Kribs, 'Stretch,' was the real leader in the whole thing, and I think he [Betesh] may have been badly influenced by him. Kribs had the type of personality where you thought he could be a murderer, because he had a short fuse and everything. He had a violent nature. He had beaten a few people up that I know of. And I sort of suspect that he was the ringleader of the whole thing, and that Saul sort of went along with it. Maybe that's just me, that I don't want to think so badly of the guy, because obviously he was involved in it. I don't think he was the ringleader or the guy who made the decisions. For instance, the decision to kill the kid, I can almost guarantee that was Kribs. He was a nasty piece of work."

In court, Betesh's sister Diane — who maintained on-and-off contact with her brother, who was living a semi-transient life — stated: "He went from heaven to hell. From luxury to filth. He did it to himself. It was his own form of self-punishment." Occasionally visiting his aging parents, Saul's mother testified the last time she saw him as a free man was the day after Emanuel Jaques was brutally tortured, raped, and drowned by her own son, something she only became aware of after his widely-publicized arrest. In the years since they adopted the boy, their hearts full of optimism, the Beteshes spent a fortune on Saul. Moving several times over the years, they were no longer in their Forest Hills home, or a more modest residence in North Toronto, but in an apartment overlooking a schoolyard, where their adult son joined them for dinner.

Trying to instill in Saul the importance of basic personal hygiene as a youngster, from remembering to wash his face to combing his hair, cleanliness was always a struggle. As a child, resistance to soap and water was difficult to enforce; as an adult, it was impossible, particularly now since he was no longer living under the same roof. Even the landlady at the boarding house on Irwin Avenue where Saul rented a room for $55 a week, who described herself in court as "Saul's second mother," constantly chased after him to shower. She recalled numerous occasions where she implored him to brush his teeth and launder his clothes, particularly after entering his room, and nearly being knocked over by the stench of stale sheets and body odour.

Opening the door of their apartment, Lillian, 63, and James, 68, were taken aback at just how much their once-beautiful adopted son had declined. Standing in front of them was a 27-year-old man, his unkempt hair greasy, face covered with acne, and clothes looking like they hadn't been washed in months, if ever. Scrawny and haggard-looking, what bothered his mother the most was his discoloured teeth, some of them already turning brown. As the three sat down to eat, his mother looked up at him and said, "Saul, if I didn't know you were my son I wouldn't believe it. You have such evil written all over your face: you were so handsome." His response was simply, "I'm still your boy." Telling the story in court, Lillian burst into tears, resulting in Judge Maloney calling a recess as the woman, overcome by emotion, was escorted from the room.

During the course of the trial, jurors heard from Betesh's parents, sister, brother-in-law, former landlady, and other witnesses testifying to his behaviour leading up to the murder. His attitude towards the human race was conflicted, and often indifferent, except when it came to women, of whom he was especially critical. Never outwardly professing affection for anyone, including his own mother, the few females he felt any kindness towards included his one-time landlady, and an unnamed younger woman. While their relationship was never a sexual one, she would accompany him to discos and gay nightclubs, where Saul would introduce her as his "wife." Although it was obvious to everyone Saul was homosexual, no one bothered to contradict him, as there was simply no point.

Prone to exaggeration at best and outright lies at worst, even those who knew Betesh were unable to keep his stories straight, and determine what he was *really* doing for a livelihood. In 1975, he briefly moved-in with his sister and brother-in-law, a construction worker, and enrolled in the Ironworkers Union. Soon, he was working sporadically on projects including the CN Tower — which remained the world's tallest free-standing structure for three decades — and the Toronto Eaton Centre, located directly across from the scene of the murder. To hear Saul tell it, he wasn't just an apprentice on the project: he was also one of the key builders, architectural advisors, and even had a hand in "Olga," the gigantic 10-ton S-64 Sikorsky industrial helicopter, as it lifted 44 pieces of the Tower's crowning antenna into place on April 2, 1975. For Canadians, this made the 1,815 foot-five-inch structure an engineering marvel, recognized by the *Guinness Book of World Records*. Naturally, Betesh wanted to claim credit any way he could for the structure and its success.

A construction worker by day, Saul fancied himself an aspiring go-go dancer by night in the city's gay clubs, entertaining customers, always the centre of attention. Although he took pride being on display in the evenings, he kept his homosexuality distant from his day-to-day work, fearing what other construction workers might do to him if they found out. Betesh's emotional state around this time fluctuated from delirious, manic highs to mind-numbing lows and stretches of depression, even thoughts of suicide. It was during one of these dark periods his sister and her husband took him into their home, where they immediately faced the same challenges as Betesh's parents, namely chasing after Saul to bathe himself, eat properly, brush his teeth, and get up for work on time. Fed-up with her demands, or being asked to leave, Saul was out of the apartment within two months, and once again living in bathhouses and cheap downtown rooming houses.

Testifying in court, one of his former landlady's knew Betesh was prostituting himself and dancing in clubs at night. And yet, she still believed in him, and his potential. When they argued over his lack of personal hygiene, Betesh often wouldn't fight back; instead, he would grind his hips and thrust his pelvis in spontaneous dance, which more often than not made her burst out laughing. "There is good in everyone, even Saul," she stated, citing occasions when he helped with yard work, and made minor repairs to toasters and other small appliances. Another time, she recalled him making Kung Fu chops at a loaf of bread, foreshadowing the same moves he later made for Emanuel, his brother Luciano and friend Shane to gain their trust.

As kind and lighthearted as he could be occasionally to his landlady and other acquaintances, Betesh was just as wicked to members of his own family. The testimony from his parents, sister, and others about his early years, expulsion from schools, inability to hold down jobs for any length of time, and volatile, often violent behaviour stood in stark contrast to the few glimpses of him resembling a somewhat normal human being. Covering the trial for the *Toronto Star*, reporter Christine Blatchford wrote a lengthy piece headlined "Jaques accused has 'no remorse' about his life," which brilliantly summarized the real Saul Betesh.

Appearing indifferent during much of the trial, the only exception came when Betesh responded to questions directed at him from his lawyer, Paul Tomlinson. Smiling for the first time during the entire trial, Betesh described himself as a Christian — in the broadest sense of the word. Of his life, he said he had "no remorse, no misgivings." Of his parents, he freely expressed opinions which left many spectators stunned. "I never really liked anyone," stated Betesh, his voice devoid of emotion. Much of his outright distain was directed at his mother. As for his father — who earlier testified about Saul, stating "everything he touched he destroyed" — he was somewhat indifferent. He tolerated his sister, which, for Saul Betesh, was about as close to actually liking someone as he could possibly get. Others, even his own family, were simply unimportant, and of no consequence. He came first, always.

In court, Betesh wore the same clothes every day, a three-piece brown suit and tie. Sitting calmly, he sported a pageboy haircut, resembling a cross between comic character Prince Valiant, and children's book figure Little Lord Fauntleroy, long bangs in the front, hair swept back and touching his shoulders. Considerably cleaned-up from his normal self, Betesh's respectable image during the trial was at odds with his testimony. At one point, his attorney asked Saul what he thought of *him*. Betesh chuckled. He had no genuine feelings about Tomlinson, the man fighting for his future. Betesh did admit to being upset over a number of things, including his lawyer's failure to provide him with a subscription to *The Body Politic*, and a copy of Dante Alighieri's *Divine Comedy*, an epic poem describing the author's journey through Hell, Purgatory, and ultimately Paradise, or Heaven.

Courtroom sketch of Saul Betesh, who wore the same three-piece brown suit every day during the trial (author collection)

It is not known if Saul was being serious about reading Dante, or making a sarcastic attempt at humour. Most persons on trial for the first-degree murder of a child would at least try to be serious, or show some signs of remorse for the jury: Betesh did none of those things. Instead, he sat in glowing adoration at all the attention he was getting. Few looking at him, presentably dressed as he was in court, would imagine such incredible violence was capable in another human being if they had not heard the testimony for themselves.

Largely viewed as the ringleader in Emanuel's abduction and murder by police during the investigation, Betesh reveled in the attention. During the trial, his attorney referenced reports from psychiatrists about Betesh written over the years, along with others from group homes for disturbed children he attended. To prepare for his jury address, Tomlinson spent hours writing out 56 double-spaced legal-sized pages in pencil, where he discussed evaluations of his client, and comments about Betesh's state of mind from those who knew him best throughout his life, including the family who adopted him, his sister, and later his landlady, police, and doctors who examined him.

"I don't like to read a jury address," says Tomlinson, who committed as much of the document to memory as possible. At the core of his address was his client's psychopathy. At the time, one only needed to suffer from five or six traits to be deemed to have severe psychopathy, including lack of responsibility, an inability to form meaningful relationships, chronic antisocial behaviour, and emotional immaturity, all of which Betesh exhibited not only at the time of his arrest and during the trial, but since birth.

"That's what a psychopath has," comments Tomlinson. "The concept of empathy, or the concept of remorse, doesn't develop in the brain. And doctors told me that remorse is something that a true psychopath *doesn't* exhibit, and doesn't feel." Delivering his jury address on January 9, 1978, Tomlinson painted a pathetic portrait of his client's existence up until that day, when the jury would determine his guilt or innocence. The jury, stated Tomlinson, was entrusted with "the awesome responsibility of determining the guilt of Saul Betesh on a charge of first-degree murder, or his guilt on the included defences of second-degree murder, of manslaughter, or a verdict of not guilty by reason of insanity."[33]

"He [Betesh] is charged with Murder — the unlawful killing of another person in circumstances that the Crown alleges amount to first-degree murder. So he is charged with the most serious crime in the catalogue of criminality that he could be compelled to face in a criminal court. What is the issue in respect of Betesh — the issue is responsibility — mental illness," stated Tomlinson, who also addressed the guilty plea initiated by Robert Kribs near the beginning of the trial, stating this had nothing to do with the remaining accused, including his client, and that each one of the defendants must be deliberated on individually, as advised by Judge Maloney. Kribs, said Tomlinson, admitted that *he alone* had the necessary *intent* to murder, and he alone planned the death of Emanuel, who outlined the section of Canada's Criminal Code dealing with murder, emphasizing that without intent to kill, there is no murder, and that first-degree murder is planned and deliberate.

With the jury listening intently, Tomlinson anticipated the Crown arguing Betesh picked-up Emanuel that Thursday afternoon in July of 1977 with the view of killing him, planned in advance.

However, independent testimony — other than the statement from Betesh himself — said his intended conquest that day was *not* Emanuel, but his friend Shane, who was also shining shoes on the street corner at the same time. Instead of Shane, Emanuel volunteered to go with Betesh, who promised payment for moving photographic equipment. At the time, argued Tomlinson, Betesh's intent was not murder, but having sex with a young boy.

During the lengthy trial, disturbing exhibits were presented to court, including crime scene photos and images of nude boys. Rather than attempt to deflect attention away from these pictures, Tomlinson addressed them directly. "I have to anticipate what the Crown will say to you," he said. "I have no doubt he will once again lead you step-by-step through the whole night with Emanuel Jaques. I anticipate this for they have filed as exhibits every conceivable thing they could find in that apartment to shock you, to terrorize you, to make you feel hate toward the accused." Although the crime was sick and tragic, Tomlinson said it was not murder. The foundation of the Crown's case against Betesh came from statements made *by* Betesh to the police, with his attorney asking the jury to carefully consider the statements, including the one Betesh made about holding Emanuel's head underwater in the kitchen sink until he drowned.

The sink in the apartment above the body rub, where Emanuel was held upside-down and drowned (Courtesy Toronto Police)

Throughout the trial, jurors heard about Betesh's many strange characteristics, especially his wild exaggerations, and inability to tell the truth most of the time. "Because one of the traits of Saul Betesh is that he is a pathological liar — and pathological means nothing more than due to disease — he doesn't wilfully lie, create lies — his lies are created for him by his psychopathy — they're pathological," stated Tomlinson. Arrogant and boastful, Betesh admitted at one point to the crime of running a homosexual ring of young boys, which was not the case. This example, and many others, served to undermine Betesh's credibility, even against himself; often, he didn't know, or care, that he was a pathological liar, or give a second thought to the consequences. "Credibility is an important factor in a criminal trial, in normal circumstances, but the symptoms of the very disease under consideration is lying (pathological lying caused by that disease) then it is not only difficult to use the statements that flow from the sickness — but I submit that the weight to be attached to any of them is of little or no consequence," said Tomlinson. He cited numerous examples.

Suffering from severe psychopathy and sadomasochistic fantasies, Betesh was often unrestrained, with even the most trivial incident sending him into wild-eyed screaming fits. With behaviour often bordering on theatrical, Betesh loved to be at the epicentre of drama, which, in his case, included narcissism and continually manipulating others to do as he wished.

A provocateur since infancy, Betesh took pleasure in shocking others, even telling police he was the one most responsible for Emanuel's fate. This type of outlandish behaviour, said Tomlinson, was made so others would take notice of him. Quoting Dr. Andrew Malcolm, Tomlinson stated his client enjoyed the attention he was getting, and asked the jury to give weight to those comments, saying they were "the statements of a person who is histrionic, loves publicity, a pathological liar seeking centre stage." Dr. Malcolm, who also interviewed Betesh's co-accused Josef Woods, stated both men were mentally disturbed, but not legally insane. This, despite Betesh admitting one of his fantasies was owning a house where he could torture boys to death.

Tomlinson then quoted excerpts from various psychiatric interviews with Betesh, conducted by a number of doctors. Diseases of the mind, he said, render someone incapable of realizing the nature of an act, and knowing it is wrong. He said there was no doubt Betesh was a psychopath, citing numerous examples, including lacking a moral code, chronic antisocial behaviour, no impulse control, and emotional immaturity. While at the Browndale Centre for emotionally disturbed children, staff treated Saul as though he was a child, when in fact he was 18 years old at the time.

Throughout the trial, others testified about Betesh's erratic behaviour, habitual lies, and frequent, uncontrollable outbursts. Self-centered, and unable to face the consequences of his own actions, Tomlinson focused on his client's inability to experience guilt, even over Emanuel's death, stating, "We cannot hate him for that, there is something undeveloped in his makeup and that is the ability to show compassion — lacking appropriate feelings for the boy is a feature of his illness — remember him telling police he took the three dollars afterwards because he didn't need it anymore. You decide the extent of his disease of the mind."

Driven by wild impulses, those who knew Betesh spoke of his poor judgement, utter lack of ambition, spotty work history and unpredictable temper. Briefly living with his sister and brother-in-law, Saul was emotionally unstable, soon leaving their residence. Consistent with his psyche was a persistent unwillingness to better himself in any way; at one point, Saul was offered a free condominium. Living in a cheap rooming house at the time, he refused the offer. When asked why he turned it down, he stated he didn't want the responsibility.

Tomlinson recounted for the jury his client's lifelong history of mental illness, including evidence of childhood schizophrenia, from smashing his head against his bedroom wall to setting fires, and Betesh's inability to allow others to get close to him. "This is something far more serious than the hyperactive or even autistic child — this was mental illness," stated Tomlinson. His parents, desperate and fearing for the sanity of their adopted son and themselves, took Saul to see his first psychiatrist in 1955, at a time when seeking help for youngsters was extremely unusual. "There was something obviously wrong with the mind of the child. A normal five-year-old does not threaten others with razors, throw steak knives at a sister, set fire in neighbours' houses and pour nail polish remover in the maid's ear while she's asleep.

The mental illness, has not been concocted, it is all documented in the social agency's records, the notes of the Mental Health Centre, and the doctor reports...mental illness has plagued this human being since infancy." As a child, reasoned Tomlinson, was it even possible that Betesh had the capacity to appreciate his actions? As an adult, was he still incapable of knowing right from wrong.

Always different, perpetually strange, young Saul was expelled from kindergarten, and bounced from one school to another. An outcast, he was without friends because other children were terrified of his violent behaviour, inability to play like a normal toddler, or do anything other than be vicious and frighteningly unstable. As Tomlinson spoke passionately in defence of his client, it was impossible to ignore the crucial tipping point in the scales of Betesh's existence, which came in 1965 at the age of 14. "There starts the bizarre reign of events that ends with Saul Betesh facing first-degree murder," stated his lawyer.

Mentally and physically exhausted by the time their adopted son was a young teenager, the

Beteshes devoted much of their once-significant, and now rapidly dwindling, wealth to Saul through exhaustive treatment, private schools, and other efforts, as they were also prisoners of their child's mental illness. In desperation, Saul's father James approached Juvenile Court authorities, while his mother Lillian spoke to the police, who *talked her out of having her son committed.* Instead of being sent to a mental health facility as they begged, the parents were instead referred to the Jewish Family and Child Services by Juvenile Court, "to an agency that then reports say show *them* as being emotionally disturbed," stated Tomlinson, calling it a "horrible twist of fate."

Doctor once ordered Betesh committed to mental hospital

Newspaper headline (author collection)

A once-affluent linen merchant family who envisioned Saul taking over the family business, his parents were now on the brink of financial ruin, because of the child to whom they had given much of their lives. Overwhelmed, anxious and unable to deal with their son any longer, James Betesh signed over his life insurance policies to an agency so they could pay to send their unstable son to a special school in Pennsylvania. "The chance for commitment is lost as the school for emotionally disturbed boys is hastily arranged," stated Tomlinson in his jury address. "The Beteshes were not medical people but they could see the mental illness and were prepared to commit their own son."

Returning to Toronto from Pennsylvania in June of 1966, the Beteshes were shocked at their son's behaviour, which was just as uncontrollable and vicious as when he left. In court, Tomlinson quoted part of a report prepared by Dr. Angus Hood of the Toronto Mental Health Clinic, who had earlier recommended committal for Saul, stating he "...is being resistant and assaultive to parents, is unable to attend school or socialize, is tampering with electrical circuits with unrealistic (scientific) experiments — *is unrelated to reality.*"

During his address to the jury, Tomlinson argued his client should not have been sent to the private reform school in the United States, or later to the Browndale Centre for emotionally disturbed children, but to a psychiatric hospital for treatment. Acting and behaving like an ill-tempered child, Betesh was treated like one between the ages of 16 to 18. By the time he left these costly group homes, he was approaching 20 years of age. With no medical follow-up and away from control mechanisms, his life continued to collapse on itself. It was also around this time Betesh admitted he was homosexual, with fantasies of violent sadomasochistic sex soon taking over his mind.

His mental health deteriorating, Betesh soon began ignoring, or simply not caring, about other areas of his life. When he held a job, it usually didn't last very long. With little money, teeth rotting and his personal hygiene practically non-existent, Betesh began living in shabby rooming houses. By 1975, he suffered a complete emotional breakdown. That fall, he went to live with his sister and brother-in-law at their home for a time before being told to leave. His behaviour worsening, Betesh noticeably gained 40 pounds in a brief period, from May to October, 1976.

On many occasions, Betesh would start ranting and raving at other rooming house residents for no apparent reason, the muscles of his neck bulging, face distorted by rage. Others, including workers at the Community Homophile Association of Toronto, spoke about the time he stood in the middle of the CHAT office screaming uncontrollably, pupils dilated. The incident, which lasted several minutes, heard one of the witnesses testifying, "Saul did not seem to appreciate what happened."

On the fringe of Toronto's mainstream gay community, Betesh — in the words of *The Body Politic* — had a reputation "as an exaggerator and dreamer." Gerald Hannon, author of the controversial Men Loving Boys Loving Men article, stated Betesh was a master at bluffing others; at least, that's what he liked to believe. Hannon related the time when Betesh applied for a position selling advertising for the magazine. Although he appeared extremely confident during the course of the interview, stating he could do the job, "he gave us no clear impression that he knew what it involved, or that he had the talents. We didn't hire him," wrote Hannon. It seemed to those who genuinely knew him that Betesh's unsteady grip on reality, and his ability to distinguish between truth and lies even to himself, was worsening.

According to Tomlinson, the gruesome rape and murder of Emanuel Jaques arose from Betesh's mental illness and dark fantasies, which took over the man's mind. His client had "terrific excitement" as he tried to strangle Emanuel to death with a bungee cord. Attempting to take the focus away from Betesh and directing it to his co-accused, Tomlinson said Betesh had no appreciation for the nature and quality of his actions, and that he was not the leader, but assisted Kribs. "We know from Gruener that Woods wanted to hypnotize him [and] that Betesh wanted to take him to the park. Kribs is a self-confessed killer who wanted to do away with the boy."

Near the conclusion of his jury address, Tomlinson stated his client should not be sent to prison, but a maximum-security facility for the criminally insane. Only there could Betesh be taken care of by qualified personnel, "and doctors, who are able to submerge their abhorrence for his crime in order that they can treat him — to find out what caused him to do what was done here." Treatment over incarceration, said Tomlinson, would reveal the causes of his disorder, "and once found in his case and in others like him — it will ultimately help to prevent a repetition of this tragedy in future cases."

Summarizing Betesh's life and history of mental illness, Tomlinson stated his client had no feeling or empathy for others, being denied the capability for those emotions owing to his mind. For Tomlinson, the address presented him with an opportunity to explain his own thoughts about the lengthy trial. "I am willing to confess that representing Saul Betesh has been a long period of great anxiety — a burden which I gladly would have been spared excepting that his is not a cure for hate — he is mentally ill." Speaking of the horror of Betesh's psyche, and how many were affected by his actions, Tomlinson concluded by saying, "The proper verdict for Saul Betesh is one of not guilty by reason of insanity and that is what your verdict should be."

Despite Tomlinson's impassioned defence, and imploring that Betesh should be sent to a psychiatric facility for treatment instead of prison, the overwhelming evidence against his client was too much for the jury to ignore. After a lengthy, often excruciating trial which saw jurors separated from their families, friends, and work for weeks, the verdict on three of the four men — excluding Robert Wayne Kribs, who plead guilty near the beginning of the trial and still required sentencing — was handed-down late on the evening of Friday, March 10, 1978.

The verdicts were read as follows:

Saul David Betesh: guilty of first-degree murder.

Josef Woods: guilty of second-degree murder.
Werner Gruener: acquitted, ordered released.

Many in the courtroom gasped. Homicide detectives who worked on the shoeshine boy case for months were visibly furious. Staff Sergeant Gerald Stevenson and Sergeant Robert McLean who spearheaded the investigation loudly criticized not only the verdict, but the attorneys for both the prosecution and the defence. Stating Crown Attorney Peter Rickaby and prosecutor Frank Armstrong were responsible for "blowing the trial," Rickaby was called gutless for failing to have Gruener arrested and prosecuted on a lesser charge. To the detectives and many others, it seemed inconceivable that Gruener — despite his claims of sleeping, watching television, or being out of the apartment buying ice cream during Emanuel's rape and murder — would walk out of court a free man for the first time since his arrest seven months earlier. After all, he was the one who opened the back door of the apartment for Betesh and Emanuel. Knowing other youngsters had been photographed and molested, how could he fail to realize harm could come to the boy?

As part of his preparation to defend Gruener, Levy visited the scene of the murder to gain a better understanding of the apartment layout. He was surprised, because he initially thought there was more open space, instead of individual rooms. "What I was happy about was that some things could have been going on that he couldn't have seen, because he was staying in his room," he says.

At one point after the verdict was read, McLean and Stevenson turned to Levy, one of them saying, "I hope you sleep well tonight, Earl. I know I will." Their words would come back to haunt them months later following a complaint from the attorney, and a subsequent investigation into their conduct. Surrounded by TV cameras and newspaper reporters Gruener, smiling for one of the first times during the trial, described himself as friendly, and not someone would hold a grudge when asked what it was like spending months in jail. Gruener said reading his Bible and writing poetry helped him to maintain his faith. When asked what he would do next, he mentioned possibly going back to Frankfurt where he was born, or return to the Children of God sect. Other options included heading out to Vancouver, possibly to open up his own body rub business, and write his life story, which later proved to generate no interest whatsoever from publishers. Of one thing he was certain: he wanted his 10-speed bicycle back.

Moments later, Gruener was led by Levy and his assistant, law student Simon Scheiderman, to a small room away from the crowd. Later emerging from the University Avenue courthouse, he was again questioned by reporters. "I think I'll phone my mother," was his reply. Exhausted by the lengthy trial, Levy said, "I'm checking into the Clarke Institute (of Psychiatry) for a month, and you can quote me." Heading to his attorney's car, one of the police officers called out to Gruener, "No hard feelings," with him mumbling "No'" in response, as he got into the vehicle.

Decades after the lengthy trial, Levy recalls the anger directed towards him and his client, a free man after spending months behind bars. Receiving numerous threatening phone calls during the trial, including one made to his home, which his wife answered, Levy was forced to get police protection for the safety of his family.

"When the trial was over, we had a big concern about him [Gruener] leaving the court," says Levy, "so I arranged to smuggle him out of the courthouse. There is a tunnel under the courthouse on University Avenue that leads to Osgoode Hall, which fronts onto Queen Street. We were followed [by the press]. I wanted to get him out of the city, and made arrangements with a court reporter. She was going to have him stay at her house overnight, she wanted to interview him, that was the arrangement made. And then we had also arranged to get him the following morning out of Toronto."

Police detectives, angry over the acquittal, said it was not over. Peter Rickaby stated the next morning the prosecution would pursue an appeal of Gruener's acquittal, and likely Woods' second-degree murder conviction, which was being considered by Attorney General Roy McMurtry. Acquittal meant Gruener was free to do as he wished, including travel, and police were worried:

the instant Gruener left Toronto, he would disappear, likely forever. Stating that an appeal could only result in a new trial — and not his acquittal being reversed, or a first-degree murder conviction — Levy said Gruener was under no obligation to return.

Days later, both Kribs — who had earlier entered a guilty plea and been convicted of first-degree murder — would be sentenced, along with Betesh, who said he was going to starve himself to death if he wasn't immediately sent to a mental health care institution, which would prove not to be the last such threat he would make to harm himself. For Justice Maloney, the final word on the three convicted men and Gruener was still to come. Calling Betesh a great danger to society and someone very likely to commit other "sexual-sadistic acts" in the future, Maloney heard from his lawyer, Paul Tomlinson, who argued during the trial that his client was not guilty by reason of insanity, and should be taken to the Penetanguishine Mental Health Centre for a 60-day psychiatric assessment prior to sentencing.

During and after the trial, many involved were criticized for comments they made, not the least of which was Justice Maloney. Toronto's gay community, still reeling from Anita Bryant's anti-homosexual Save Our Children campaign, the controversial Men Loving Boys Loving Men article, and the constant media references to Emanuel dying after a "homosexual orgy," objected to a statement made by Maloney at the conclusion of the trial. During Betesh's sentencing, the Judge remarked: "There are those who would seek legal protection for homosexuals in the Human Rights Code. You make me wonder if they are not misguided. I wonder if there shouldn't be legislation to protect the people you seek to entice," referring to the killer's sexual appetite for young boys.

Justice Maloney was not alone, as others also suggested links between the murder, and amendments to Canada's Human Rights Code, including some conservative politicians, and the head of the commission. As gay and lesbian activist Tom Warner would later write, "In a comment that shocked and infuriated lesbians and gays, Dorothea Crittenden, the chairman of the commission told a newspaper reporter that, because of the Jaques case, the time was not right for adding sexual orientation to the code."[34]

Others also took offence to Maloney's comments including Toronto-based pastor and advocate for the city's LGBT community, Brent Hawkes. Highly critical of the publication of the Men Loving Boys article, Hawkes was horrified by Maloney's words. "It's a very unfortunate thing for a judge to try and make some kind of a connection between a certain crime and a group of individuals in the community as a whole," said Hawkes. At the time, there was a proposed legislative amendment by the Ontario Human Rights Commission, which would protect individuals from discrimination based on sexual orientation, and which would, in no way, sanction homosexuals involved in criminal behaviour.

Additionally, the gay media was resentful and fearful of any repercussions stemming from the judge's comments. *The Body Politic* echoed Hawke's concerns, publishing an article at the conclusion of the trial. "Gay people and their supporters have feared the testimony given by the convicted men could be used to support reactionary demands for regressive social legislation which would return the death penalty and 'protect' children from the 'homosexual lifestyle.' In particular, it is feared that the sexual tastes of Betesh and Kribs could be used to support the scare tactics of people like Anita Bryant."[35] Spokesmen for two other groups championing homosexual rights in the province, including The Coalition for Gay Rights in Ontario, were equally outraged by the judge's remarks. In a joint statement, the Coalition wrote, "For Judge Maloney to suggest that the amendment would protect rapists or murderers shows an appalling ignorance of human rights law."

Many of the Judge's comments for the three men convicted of murdering Emanuel Jaques were stark, as he stated they should not expect to be released from prison during their lifetimes. Kribs, Betesh, and Woods were brought into court individually for sentencing. Standing before the judge, dressed in the same flower-patterned shirt and denim suit he wore during the entire trial, lanky Robert Kribs was asked if he had anything to say prior to sentencing. His request was for psychiatric treatment before he would be released from prison, "If I ever get out." Maloney agreed, yet steadfastly refused requests made by defence attorneys that would result in their clients heading to the Penetanguishene Mental Health Centre instead of prison.

Maloney's remarks to Kribs were essentially the same as those made to Betesh and Woods: don't expect to be a free man — ever. "I would like to make one thing perfectly clear," said the judge. "Life means life. It is not probable you will be out in 25 years. It is not even likely you will be out in 25 years." Maloney did, however, say he would write a letter to penitentiary authorities on behalf of the three men requesting everything possible be done to serve their best interests, and those of the community.

The next to appear in the prisoner's box for sentencing was Saul Betesh. Considered by many as the group's leader, it was Betesh who lured Emanuel back to the apartment, and remained one of the key persons involved in the boy's sadistic murder. Standing before the Judge, he was dressed in the same three-piece suit he wore at trial. "With your bare hands, you strangled this poor little fellow, and you deserve the sentence," said Maloney, adding Betesh should not expect to receive parole after serving the mandatory 25 years behind bars, and he would be "making a recommendation to that effect."

The last to appear before the judge was Josef Woods. When asked if he had anything to say, he stammered in response: "Well, uh, I suppose when I chose not to become involved in what was going on [the rape and death of Emanuel] I made the right decision...." Maloney told Woods how fortunate he was to have been convicted of second-degree murder, adding "You were found not guilty of first-degree murder, but that doesn't mean you're innocent." Soon after, the judge would make a similar comment about Werner Gruener who was acquitted; to Maloney, that didn't mean he was blameless, expressing that he wished Canada had a verdict of "not proven" as an alternative to conviction or outright acquittal, as existed in Scotland.

Of Gruener, who read his Bible and preached peace and love — yet somehow justified working at body rubs including the Pleasure Palace and Charlie's Angels — Maloney was particularly incensed at what he saw as his insincerity, referring to him as "that diabolical hypocrite with a Bible in one hand and taking money from a body rub parlour with the other hand walked out of here a free man." Many leaving the courtroom nodded in agreement with Maloney's comments, some stating punishment for rape and murder of children must be much more severe. Noticeably absent from court on the day of sentencing was Valdemira, Emanuel's 17-year-old sister, who attended most of the trial accompanied by an aunt or priest, who were also not present.

Controversy over Gruener's acquittal and Woods being found guilty of the lesser charge of second-degree murder raged long after the trial was over, along with blame over how the prosecution handled the case, and the slow response to cleaning-up Yonge Street before Emanuel was abducted and killed. Phillip Givens, a former Toronto mayor and then-Chairman of the Metropolitan Toronto Police Commission, was upset with the Attorney General's office, saying it was uncooperative, and refused to take any police crackdown on Yonge Street's sex industry seriously until *after* the shoeshine boy was dead. "Our problem was we couldn't get anyone to take us seriously," stated Givens. "That's what the terrible Jaques murder did. It focused attention on the terrible depravity that exists."

Weeks after the conclusion of the trial, Stevenson and McLean were reprimanded for the comments they made to the Crown prosecutors about "blowing the trial," and remarks to Earl Levy following his client's acquittal. The two detectives, however, were far less concerned about being chastised for their comments than they were about tracking-down Werner Gruener before he vanished, and serving him with an appeal.

Chapter Eleven: The Campaign to Clean-Up Yonge Street

"I hope Mayor (David) Crombie rots in his socks."
-Unidentified 18-year-old female prostitute commenting to the *Globe and Mail*

Within days of the murder of Emanuel Jaques, Toronto's public — especially parents concerned for the safety of their children — and many business owners were demanding something be done to clean-up the Yonge Street strip. Although it was not the first attempt at dismantling the sex industry from the area, the boy's death accelerated efforts which were applauded by some, and denigrated by others.

For years, the business of sin on Yonge Street was regarded by many as an inconvenient eyesore. Some steered clear of the Dundas and Yonge area entirely, while others simply ignored what the street had become. Every few years, newspaper stories appeared about the strip, most invariably calling it 'run-down,' 'seedy,' or any other number of adjectives. In April of 1975, just over two years before the gruesome murder, the *Globe and Mail* published a full-page article entitled 'From dirt road to dirty movies, Nothing stays the same on Yonge St. Strip.' Chronicling the street's then 180-year-old history, the piece profiled a number of local haunts, including the Bermuda Bar just north of Dundas, and the Brown Derby. Some of those interviewed stated the street had gone downhill fast, with the reporter noting a big blonde woman soliciting her services from a doorway in broad daylight, which, "Even for the porno-pix Strip and its regulars, that was going a little too far."

The landmarks were all still there, stores like Sam the Record Man, and Classy Formal Wear. So was the sign proclaiming, 'Yonge Street is Fun Street.' Further south were the smoke-filled old-time dingy bars with their regular clientele, next to places with dancing girls flashing exposed breasts, their nipples covered by pasties to get around by-laws governing nudity. The article referenced how economics was changing the street, and made one of the greatest understatements of all time: "Fly-by-night porn shops and body rubs apparently can make money."

*****

Despite its explosive growth of the sex trade and the street's steady decline, Yonge remained a popular destination for locals and tourists alike. Perception of the strip back in 1977 varied considerably, depending on who you asked. To its detractors, Yonge — the longest Street in the world at the time — was often described by its critics as loud, tacky, sleazy, and dirty; to its supporters, it was exciting, cheap, and unpredictable, which made it a hell of a lot of fun.

Even after the much-anticipated arrival of the enormous Eaton Centre at Young and Dundas extending all the way south to Queen, Yonge remained a shopping paradise, with smaller stores selling everything from camera equipment to clothes, sneakers, music, jewellery, and a great deal more.

In the Seventies, Yonge Street was the place to be. Back then, many were embracing the raw power of the street, its characters, and countless bars and hangouts. One of them was Colin Brunton. In his early twenties, Brunton embraced all that Toronto had to offer, from driving cabs to making handbills for the Horseshoe Tavern. Working as assistant manager at the .99 Roxy on the Danforth — alongside musician Nash the Slash — and later as the manager at downtown's New Yorker theatre, he developed a strong interest in art, film, and counterculture, particularly the Punk Rock movement.

"We knew so many freaks on that street from working at the New Yorker," says Brunton. "One of the guys we talked to was Crad Kilodney, who stood at Yonge and Charles and sold his self-published books."[36] While on Yonge Street, Brunton and his friends would play pinball at the Funland Arcade, a staple of the strip. One day at the arcade, they were approached by someone from the Children of God, hoping to entice them into their cult. Decades later, Brunton is still amazed at the man's powers of persuasion. "None of us were religious at all, and the next thing we know, we're on Yonge Street, *praying* with this guy! And then he left, and said something like, 'The base is just around the corner,' and it was the Children of God. After he left, we said, 'How did that happen?' We were pretty street-smart...how did we get suckered into praying on Yonge Street?"

Along with its assortment of street vendors, musicians, and teenagers out for a good time, there were the shoeshine boys. Late one evening, Brunton was downtown to see a Blues performer in the summer of 1977 at the Colonial Tavern, then one of the best-known jazz venues in the city. Outside the building, he was approached by one of the kids to make money: Emanuel Jaques, about a month before he was abducted and murdered.

"By that point, I was 22 in 1977," says Brunton. "So I'm there, and this kid comes up and he goes, 'Hey, mister! I bet you a buck I can tell you where you got your shoes,' and I knew immediately it was a scam, but I thought, 'OK, I've got to find out what the joke is here', and I said, 'Sure,' and he said, 'On your feet! You've got your shoes on your feet!' And I said, 'You got me, man,' and I gave him his dollar. It seemed like he'd been around, and he was one of these kids that you'd see around Yonge Street at that time. It was a dirty street, and I remember thinking it was kind of weird, because people didn't live near there — there weren't any houses nearby, and where were this guy's parents? You could tell he could get into mischief. He didn't seem like a bad kid at all, he just had a glint in his eye, he had that little spark like you thought, 'This kid is a street-wise hustler.' To him, small-framed and slight Emanuel looked like he was no more than 10 years old, if that, and Brunton couldn't shake the thought of a child out on the street so late at night, in one of the dirtiest parts of town.

"You did get a sense that, not 'this kid's up to no good,' but 'this kid's going to do anything, he's going to scrape bucks together.' To see a 10 or 11-year-old kid out on Yonge Street wasn't that out of place, but it was a little odd. 'Who are your parents? Do you really have to make a dollar?' But he did have his glint in his eye, and it's not like you're thinking 'this kid's an entrepreneur, but he'll do anything for money,' like odd jobs."

For Brunton, who went on to an acclaimed career as a film and television producer and director, it would be the last time he saw Emanuel Jaques alive. The next time he heard anything about the boy was after the murder, the trial of his killers, and the purge of Yonge Street's body rubs. "I remember that it triggered the cleanup," he says. "It was scandalous, that whole thing. That was the final straw, 'now it's getting cleaned up, enough of that.' Not that I went to strip clubs or body rub parlours, but part of me liked that about Toronto."[37]

Although many enjoyed Yonge Street's unique character, calls to scrub the strip of its "filth" over the years were quashed following the murder of Emanuel Jaques. One of those who knew the Street very well was George Rust-D'Eye. Called to the Bar of Ontario in 1971, Rust-D'Eye remains today one of Canada's best-known and most respected municipal lawyers. With an interest in administrative law, he started working in Metro's legal department in 1973, a position he held until 1989. Renowned for his expertise, he continues to provide legal assistance to governmental institutions, municipal councils, local boards, private sector clients, and candidates for municipal office. In 2007, he was awarded the Ontario Bar Association's Award of Excellence in Municipal Law.

Along with a passion for law, Rust-D'Eye is a heritage specialist. He recalls being given a copy of the landmark book by Eric Arthur, *Toronto: No Mean City*, around the time he began working for the city. An avid photographer, Rust-D'Eye went on a mission to document all the existing buildings in Arthur's book, and began building his own collection of work recording Toronto's history. His interest proved to be extremely beneficial when it came to chronicling the rapid rise of the downtown sex industry. Over the years, he walked to work daily from his home down Yonge Street to City Hall on Queen Street West, including the period when the body rub parlours were increasing, primarily from 1973 to 1977. "So I used to actually see all of the body rub parlours as I walked downtown, and all the activity," says Rust-D'Eye. "The Yonge Street strip was quite wild in those days. The panhandlers, the Hare Krishnas…there were a lot of seedy people." Carrying a camera, he took pictures of the city as it transitioned over the years.

Historically, many of the buildings along Yonge Street's east side were houses, going back to the 1870s and 1880s. A century later, they were largely unrecognizable as ever having been homes.

A number of structures were demolished over the decades and replaced with new ones, while others had their fronts refaced. Some of the street's strip clubs and body rubs were covered with vitreous, a type of opaque glass, and gaudy chrome accents. And in the early to mid-Seventies, the number of these adult establishments grew.

Experienced in prosecuting liquor offences as a Metro solicitor, Rust-D'Eye states municipal governments were responsible for enforcing violations at the time. In the Seventies, the province of Ontario assumed responsibility for the liquor code, and Rust-D'Eye's legal attention soon turned to body rub parlours which would later become the topic of his Master's thesis.

Toronto's sex industry had developed a strong foothold for years, not just on Yonge Street, but Yorkville and places like the Mynah Bird, which boasted musicians like Rick James and Neil Young. Featured on TV programs hosted by Johnny Carson, Merv Griffin, and Mike Douglas in the Sixties, the Mynah Bird advertised 'Topless go-go girls,' with owner Colin Kerr offering the police morality squad a peek at shows back in August of 1966. Although officers declined the invitation, the press didn't, and reporters crammed into a tiny room for the event. Inside, a masked female was dancing in a metal cage illuminated by a black light, the room filling with rolling clouds from a dry ice machine. As the *Globe and Mail* wrote at the time, there was so much smoke it was nearly impossible to tell if the 21-year-old Swedish woman was actually topless.

In the months to come, this act was followed by 'the world's first topless folksinger,' along with silent nude films of large-breasted women in a soapy tub, and other strange ways to drum-up business.

Elsewhere in the city, other establishments were pushing the boundaries of nudity, and Toronto's tolerance. At the corner of Dundas and Spadina, there was the Victory, a theatre featuring burlesque and exotic dancers, which was often raided by morality officers. Over time, nipple-obscuring pasties vanished, and gimmicks like strobe lights to obscure dancers' breasts were introduced. Places on Yonge Street like the Zanzibar, starting off as nightclub featuring jazz and blues artists, began transforming into the 'Zanzibar A-Go'Go' with rock and roll music and topless girls before becoming a strip club in the Seventies. By 1971, the Zanzibar was joined by Starvin' Marvin's Burlesque Palace, Les Girls, and Lori Lane's Le Strip, which was the first to offer total nudity. "Each of these things was considered to be tremendously sinful and dirty," says Rust-D'Eye. "No self-respecting person would go to Lori Lane's Le Strip, or Starvin' Marvins, or Le Girls. That was where the sleazeballs hung out, that was their reputation."

That same year, in an effort to boost the area's sagging reputation, the Yonge Street pedestrian mall was introduced. Other streets had been considered for a designated walking area, including Yorkville, Bay, and Elizabeth, but Yonge was selected because it was well-known, and readily accessible from subway stations. Running from May 30th to June 5th in its inaugural year, the summer-only mall saw sections of Yonge closed to vehicular traffic, and filled with street musicians, open-air cafes, and small vendors to appeal to families and tourists. Running annually from 1971, the mall closed for good three years later, when merchant approval dropped significantly. Although the mall's first year saw it run for six days, and 11 weeks in 1972 and 1973 — with it being extended from three blocks to almost a mile — it was only open for eight weeks in 1974.

By the last year of the urban pedestrian experiment, panhandlers and vagrants congregated to the area, and started harassing people for money. Some began referring to the area as a gathering place for degenerates. Fights broke out, arrests soared, and many parents walking with their children were infuriated when religious groups and body rub parlours handed out pamphlets along the street, like Delilah's Den at 356 Yonge — promising everything from nude encounters to naked card games — and Neptune's Health Spa at 331 Yonge, providing topless and nude body rubs, nude photography, Finnish sauna, and needlepoint showers. In an attempt to make the Yonge Street mall a permanent fixture, City Council retained a number of planners and architects in the spring of 1974, named The City People. Conducting a feasibility study, the group discovered there had been too many issues involving noise complaints, violence, drug pushers, hookers and street people lying about. Sputtering to a stop in 1974, many welcomed the demise of the urban experiment; some, including the *Globe and Mail*, cynically stating, "Dumping a few tawdry trees and some dirty benches on a street does not constitute a mall."

One of the reasons for the downfall of the Yonge Street pedestrian mall ended-up being a factor touted for its initial success, namely easy access from Toronto's transit system. "The subway played a very major role in the whole thing, whereas previously Yonge was a shopping street with fairly low-rise buildings on both sides; this was before the building of the Eaton Centre, when people used to shop and walk down Yonge Street," says Rust-D'Eye. "And with the subway of course, it took people *past* the shops of Yonge Street and down to Eaton's and Simpsons, and it was considered the big shopping centre of the city, and people no longer — at least, much less — walked and shopped on Yonge Street, because the subway would carry them past all the shops down to Queen Street."

In the early Seventies, the rising number of body rub parlours became increasingly obvious. By 1971-72, there were 16 sex shops billing themselves as 'relaxation' or 'pleasure palaces.' By 1973, the number had grown to 36, most of them along Yonge. The nomenclature for strippers at the time was 'massagits' and 'massage parlours,' although they were not registered massagists under the Drugless Practitioners Act, and provided sexual services to men. In that year, Metro sought powers from the province of Ontario to prohibit body rub parlours. Rust-D'Eye, who had a history of successfully prosecuting numerous cases under the liquor license act, was legal counsel for the Metro licensing commission and the Metro legislation and licensing committee, both subparts of Metro, which were the most involved.

Drafting most of the Metro body rub parlour bylaws and much of the provincial legislation, Rust-D'Eye remembers going back and forth to Queen's Park to meet with provincial officials to decide what the province and Metro were going to do about body rub parlours and their various outgrowths. One of the challenges at the time was the ambiguity of the businesses, as they often went under different names on their signs. Some billed themselves as nude encounters, others as pleasure palaces. The province, at the time, refused to pass the legislation that Metro wanted to control body rub parlours, believing it was criminal legislation. Rust-D'Eye suggested the city use its zoning powers to force these places into industrial areas, where there was no market for them.

"Once again, you can't prohibit them, but you can zone them out of existence — that was the idea," he says. "But once again of course, a law like that is of no use unless someone enforces it. And until the big splash in the middle of the 1970s — when people realized this was a serious problem for the city and we'd better do something about it

— it was just considered something that went on downtown, and 'sure, there are always prostitutes,' and 'sure, Jarvis Street is full of prostitutes,' and the fact they are on Yonge Street was no big deal."

Still, the numbers of body rub parlours continued to swell downtown, to 83 by 1974, and 115 by 1975. Prices at the time were $20 to $30 dollars for half an hour, and $40 to $50 for a full hour, with the rubber receiving a 25 per cent cut for her services.

"The idea was to get a naked man and a naked woman in a room together in private, where they could do what they wanted, and it was usually charged for on a time basis," comments Rust-D'Eye, who said enforcement of these establishments was sporadic. "Yonge Street became known as kind of a sleaze strip. There has always been prostitution in the city of various kinds. People knew that it existed, and until the proliferation of body rub parlours, people didn't really realize what a serious moral dilemma this posed for the city."

One of the issues at the time remained: who ultimately had power over enforcement? The federal government had criminal power, whereas the provincial government had power over planning, zoning, and regulation of local businesses. Says Rust-D'Eye:

I gave legal opinions to Metro; Metro itself didn't have the legal power to prohibit sin, in effect, in the city. Only Parliament had the power to pass criminal legislation. And prohibiting the operation of a business on moral grounds was considered something entirely within the jurisdiction of Parliament, and not something the provinces could touch. And once again, the municipal government, Metro, was entirely under the control of the province, and unless the province basically authorized Metro to do something, it couldn't do it. Under municipal law, municipalities can only do what the province specifically allows them to do, they are creations of the province. And in those days, municipalities had to have specific powers. Now, municipalities for instance are allowed to license, regulate, and govern basically any business they want. And there are still some specific provisions, both in the City of Toronto Act — most of which I drafted for the province — and the Municipal Act, dealing with adult entertainment parlours. And adult entertainment parlours include what was formerly called body rub parlours. So the legislation is all still there. There are some specific provisions dealing with them, like the power to limit numbers.

With a steady clientele and plenty of money to be made, owners of body rub parlours and their workers had no intention of leaving the Yonge Street strip. Some opened for a brief time, closed, and soon re-appeared in other buildings. As an assistant solicitor in the Metropolitan Toronto legal department, Rust-D'Eye frequently dealt with the Ministry of Municipal Affairs, asking what they were going to do about the situation. Many sex-related businesses were located at half addresses, like 393½, or 393A Yonge Street, on the second floors of buildings for a number of reasons. Landlords had a hard time renting second-storey spaces to retailers, since potential customers usually didn't want to trudge up a flight of stairs. He remembers photographing many of these places, including Charlie's Angels, with its hand-lettered wording above the door, stating, "Come to world of love, your happiness may depend on it."

A number of attempts were made to curtail the city's many body rub parlours in the mid-Seventies, beginning with provincial legislation introduced on July 8, 1975, authorizing municipalities to license, regulate, and govern body rub parlours. Not only were the public and politicians tired of Yonge Street's steady decline, owners of respectable businesses were also fed-up, like Peter Clark. President of the Downtown Council, Clark believed the presence of these body rubs were a threat to his three shoe store locations. Clark made representations to police earlier that year on behalf of the Downtown Council about cleaning-up Yonge Street, stating they were "shackled in their attempts to deal with the street's essential 'sleaziness' by 'lax laws.'" This was largely the case, as controls proposed by Mayor David Crombie did not fall within the city's jurisdiction.

On the other side of the clean-up campaign was Arnold Linetsky, President of the Yonge Street Adult Entertainment Association, speaking on behalf of the city's sex industry. There was no love lost between Clark, operating his Yonge Street shoe store next door to Mr. Arnold's, a body rub owned by Linetsky. As representative of the Yonge Street Adult Entertainment Association, Linetsky often gave interviews about the "discrimination" he claimed the city's sex industry faced from the Downtown Council. At the same time, some of the city's newspapers went on a so-called morality crusade, with the *Toronto Star* publishing stories about the strip being a haven for "raunchy movie houses," and suggesting the American Mafia was involved. Another proposal to clean-up the street at the time was an amendment to the Theatres Act, which would expand the province's ability to censor videotape and other films. None seemed to work.

At issue was the 15-part bill, An Act To Amend The Municipal Act; Section 8 dealing specifically with licensing body rub parlours. In her piece for the *Globe and Mail* entitled "Politics and pornography: the Yonge Street cleanup," Christina Newman wrote of the proposed amendment: "No doubt it will be touted from election platforms across Ontario in months to come as *the bill that cleaned up the Yonge Street Strip and saved Toronto for moral turpitude — praise the Lord and Law and order and vote for the Tories if you hate sin* — or words to that effect."[38] Stating that the "cast of characters" involved in the ongoing saga might have leapt off the pages of an Evelyn Waugh novel, Newman referred to politicians involved at the time. Toronto Mayor David Crombie was "a short man seized by a tall ambition"; the government of Ontario Premier William Davis, about to face the electorate and faring poorly in opinion polls, "is beset by basic economic and social problems (inflation, pollution and urban sprawl) which it can't control, and has turned to peripheral law-and-order problems (television violence, pornographic 8 mm. movies and body rub parlours) which it can't control either, but is pretending it can."

The history of Bill 107 actually went back to the winter of 1973, when Crombie, soon after being elected mayor for the first time, made an emboldened speech telling downtown sex merchants to clean-up their act on Yonge Street, or the city would do it for them. Not everyone, from the sex industry to civil libertarians in particular, appreciated Crombie's words and intentions, stating it was these very same body rubs that gave the street its character. Interestingly, Newman wrote, "At Queen's Park nobody is saying exactly why these bills were drafted so quickly after the abuses they seek to correct had been ignored for so long."

On July 9, 1975. Paul Godfrey, who was Chairman of the Municipality of Metropolitan Toronto, launched the Yonge Street clean-up, and the establishment of a body rub parlour committee. "And that was the time when Metro had instructed me to develop a bylaw for licensing, regulating, and governing body rub parlours," says

Rust-D'Eye. "So I created it, and the bylaw was passed on August 26, 1975, as a schedule to the Metro licensing bylaw. It was 19 pages, and permitted 25 body rub parlours, required to be licensed." These bylaws applied to all of Metro, and not just Yonge Street. However, the issue was not being enforced, with a greater emphasis on the licensing of taxi cabs at the time.

Graffiti outside the office of Toronto's Yonge Street Revitalization Project, misspelling Mayor David Crombie's name as "Crumbies." Not everyone wanted Yonge cleaned-up, fearing the legendary street would lose much of its character.(Courtesy George Rust-D'Eye)

"These body rub parlours were kind of an offshoot that nobody really wanted to deal with," stated Rust D'Eye. At the time, newspapers reported the new body rub license laws would possibly require the names and addresses of all customers, including an itemized account of services received. Additionally, the new bylaw might regulate advertising, limiting the number of body rub parlours, restricting them to designated areas, and seeing them inspected by the municipality to ensure they weren't fronts for prostitution. Under the new legislation, body rub parlours were described in very specific terms as places where the human body — or any part of it — was kneaded, manipulated, rubbed, massaged, touched or stimulated by any means, except for medical or therapeutic treatment, by registered masseurs.

Still, many politicians exercised caution, with Godfrey stating the city didn't want to "legislate morals, while others such as Alderman Reid Scott, who had been appointed by Crombie to lead Toronto's part of the cleanup efforts, stated it was necessary for the bylaw to be "treated delicately" when he came to dealing with moral issues. As of August 26, 1975, 25 body rub parlours were permitted. Less than a month later, on September 23, body rub parlour owner Arnold Linetsky made an application to quash the Metro bylaw. Cross-examining him that day, it was at this time Rust-D'Eye became acquainted with Linetsky, and Joseph Martin Sr., who owned Charlie's Angels, the body rub above which Emanuel Jaques would be murdered less than two years later. He remembers Linetsky inviting him to see his establishment, Mr. Arnold's, at 241A Yonge Street, and inspecting it for himself. It was one of the few times he dealt with body rub owners directly, as they usually retained their own lawyers, and very few of the body rub parlours were actually licensed.

Within days, owners of Yonge Street body rub parlours came up with ways to circumvent the new sex laws — which were approved by Metro Council by a vote of 24 to 6 — and protect their livelihoods. Some stated they would open 'nude encounter' parlours, or offer private burlesque shows. Some promised male customers could sit naked next to a woman, also nude, while they watched a half-hour's worth of pornographic films together for $25. Others offered a man, who remained dressed, the opportunity to dance with an unclothed girl for 15 minutes for $20, or just talk to a woman who wasn't wearing any clothes for 20 minutes, also $20. At the time, some girls were refusing to put on any clothes at all, because they could earn bigger tips that way, making up to $300 a week and more. Toronto's 84 body rub parlours were obligated to comply with the new rules within 59 days, or face fines ranging from $1,500 for operators to $3,000 for owner-operators. Additionally, body rubbers were required to pay $50 for a license, submit their photograph to the Commission, and be subject to medical examinations. Licenses for the parlours themselves were not transferable; if the establishment was sold, the new owners would have to apply to the Metro Licensing Commission for a new permit.

For Metro, an enormous challenge was keeping track of these parlours before they vanished. "Of course, many of these places opened and closed regularly," says Rust-D'Eye. "It wasn't like these were long-existing businesses. These places would open on the second floor, they would be in operation for a month or two, and then they would close again and disappear. It wasn't handled on a very businesslike basis."

Although numerous attempts were made to clean-up the sex industry on the Yonge Street strip between 1973 and 1977, none were entirely successful. In June of 1977, shortly before the murder of Emanuel Jaques, the Report of the Special Committee on Places of Amusement was released, urging government to clean-up Yonge Street through legislating bawdy houses, and other prostitution-related businesses. Three Toronto aldermen investigating nude entertainment parlours and pinball arcades called for a Provincial Royal commission into organized crime. Conducted by Allan Sparrow, Susan Fish, and Patrick Sheppard, the Report concluded American organized crime was largely controlling Toronto's adult bookstores, prostitution rings, X-rated movie theatres, nude adult entertainment services, and pinball arcades; at the time, over half of the 2,000 pinball machines in the city were on Yonge Street.

Using information provided by Metro Police and the Ontario Provincial Police, the Report considered the situation urgent, referring to large American cities like New York, Chicago, and Detroit, who were in the process of exercising tighter controls over sex service businesses and pinball arcades. By comparison, the Report concluded Metro Toronto's use of bylaws as a means of control was largely ineffective. Sex-related businesses in Toronto, such as massage parlours, were also having an undesirable effect on residential streets around the Yonge Street Strip, with neighbours complaining about feeling unsafe at night, and female residents even being propositioned for sex by men in passing cars. According to the *Globe and Mail*, organized crime was already controlling body rub parlours. "The special subcommittee of Toronto City Council also has recommended that the province recognize the urgency of Toronto's problem with pinball and nude services and expedite requests for enabling legislation to tighten controls through bylaws and their enforcement."[39]

While many applauded Metro taking a much tougher stance on sex businesses, owners of these establishments promised to keep fighting against any threats to their existence. In July of 1977, Arnold Linetsky filed a lawsuit against the Corporation of the City of Toronto and Aldermen Allan Sparrow, Susan Fish, and Patrick Sheppard — authors of the Report of the Special Committee on Places of Amusement — for $250,000 for libel and slander, stating he had "been seriously injured in his character, credit and reputation and has been brought into public scrutiny, odium and contempt." The previous fall, Linetsky ran for alderman in Ward 6, finishing in last place.

One of the biggest challenges facing Metro all along when it came to curbing body rub parlours was apathy on the part of landlords. Rust-D'Eye states a number of factors were involved in Yonge Street's decline, including the subway (which made it possible to bypass the Strip entirely) on the way to the new Eaton Centre. Attempts to improve the area's respectability, such as the Yonge Street mall, failed to make a lasting impact.

To make room for the Eaton Centre, buildings on the west side of Yonge Street between Dundas and Queen were demolished. Owners, developers, and numbered companies holding properties on the east side of Yonge assumed they were next in line for a new shopping centre, believing their buildings would soon be purchased and torn-down to make room for another new shopping complex. "In effect, they didn't care what happened," says Rust-D'Eye. "They didn't care about the little shops lining the street. The shops operated on the ground floor as retail sales and various things, goods and services, and on the second floor, nobody cared what happened. So the second floors were available for these places to go in on short-term rentals, run their dirty businesses, and get out again."

With body rub parlours opening and closing frequently and keeping a few steps ahead of police, it was easier for them to operate illegally than within the confines of the law. In 1975, only five body rubs applied for licenses; that year, with increasing enforcement, about 300 charges were laid against illegal operators. In 1976, the number of license applications grew to 30, with six being granted; that same year, a number of body rubs began calling themselves 'nude encounters.' In March of 1977, the city enacted zoning bylaws so these establishments would have to move to distant industrial areas of Toronto, with some billing themselves as 'adult physical culture establishments.' By that summer, six licenses had been granted, but there had also been 73 raids, and 397 charges. "I used to give advice to police officers, and of course Metro by-law enforcement officers as to what they could do, and then I would prosecute the charges," says Rust-D'Eye.

On Thursday July 28, 1977 — the same day Emanuel was out shining shoes and disappeared — Toronto City Council officially launched its attack on body rub and sex shops on the Yonge Street Strip. A five-member implementation committee including Mayor Crombie was announced, along with the city endorsing over 100 control recommendations. Draft legislation was poised to give Metro powers to both license and control nude entertainment services and pinball arcades. At the time, Ontario Premier William Davis stated any recommendations requiring provincial action were being "actively pursued by the government," adding he was concerned some legislation would be too restrictive, and prove "inhibiting to bona fide businessmen."

Following a 90-minute debate, and a 19-to-1 vote, Council requested a number of powers.

These included asking the provincial government to create a Royal Commission into organized crime in Ontario; requesting Metro Council to authorize its solicitors to seek court injunctions which would stop unlicensed sex establishments and pinball arcades from operating; asking for powers to phase out nude entertainment services and sex shops from downtown; and permitting nude entertainment, adult movie houses, and pinball arcades to operate only in industrial areas of the city. Attorney-General Roy McMurtry stated earlier in the month he did not believe a Royal commission into organized crime in the province was necessary or justified, based on police briefings.

While the proposed changes were welcomed, some, including Mayor Crombie, accused the Ontario government of unnecessarily taking its time to enact legislation expanding Metro's licensing powers, stating "Our concerns about cleaning up the yawning cesspool on Yonge Street are being lumped together in an administrative review of municipal authority to license chestnut vendors."[40] Named to serve on the implementation committee were Susan Fish, Allan Sparrow, and Patrick Sheppard — authors of the Report of the Special Committee on Places of Amusement — along with Alderman Arthur Eggleton, chosen because of his experience with the city planning Board and Metro Council's legislation and licensing committee.

The city was already being criticized at the time by some politicians and business owners who believed forcing pinball arcades and nude entertainment to relocate to far-off industrial areas was being overly restrictive. Operators of the pinball arcades, some who had offered cubicles for screening adult movies, were forced to remove the viewing rooms, or keep them bolted shut. A number of local politicians, like Alderman Anthony O'Donohue, said all sex shops and other adult services "should be padlocked now because they are a cancer on Yonge Street," criticizing previous city councils for failing to take action about the strip's relentless decline until that point. "It is a tragic position for us to be in that we can't really do something here in this council today," he added, stating Toronto's downtown had been taken over by "weirdos."

At the time, Council also approved motions asking police for stronger enforcement, and being able to lay charges already existing within the Criminal Code against anyone soliciting sexual activities, and criminally charging customers in unlicensed premises. A host of other recommendations were also made. They included: applicants needing to demonstrate to the Metro Licensing Commission why they should be granted a license to operate nude entertainment services or a pinball arcade; a complete financial background checks for all license applicants, and license fees paid at the time of application; the ability for Yonge Street sex establishments to have their finances inspected by the federal Department of Revenue; monthly police inspection of nude service establishments; and prohibiting adult movies in premises already occupied by adult book stores, pinball arcades, and body rub parlours. Additional recommendations relating to police included the use of plainclothes female officers to step-up charges against men soliciting or harassing women downtown, and increasing surveillance and deportation of American pimps and their prostitutes.

    Inconsistent attempts to rid Yonge Street of its growing sex industry over the years did not curtail body shop operators from setting up shop on the strip. Even the sadistic 1973 slaying of young Kirkland Deasley by drifter John McBeth Finlayson at the downtown Ford Hotel, widely known as a hangout for prostitutes, hustlers and transients, did not spark a clean-up. The murder of Emanuel Jaques just four years later proved to be the breaking point for citizens, councillors, businessmen, politicians and police. Fears of a backlash between Toronto taking a forceful legal and moral stance, and the sex industry, were finally quashed. Soon, other major cities across Canada, including Winnipeg, Vancouver, Edmonton and Halifax, stepped-up measures to rid their downtowns of body rub parlours and prostitution.

    For politicians and lawmakers, the gruesome death of Toronto's shoeshine boy provided ample ammunition to shutter the city's body rub parlours permanently. The victim was a child, abducted and brutally raped and murdered on the very same stretch of Yonge Street many wanted cleaned-up for years. To imagine a crime this gruesome taking place in 'Toronto the Good' was simply incomprehensible. Considering the immediate reaction from many, the Portuguese population in particular, failure to act immediately would likely have proven disastrous, as many were calling for a return of capital punishment — with some protesters offering to take matters in their own hands. Some, like 12-year-old Luis Sequeira, gathered over 2,000 signatures on a petition to Premier Davis urging him to make Yonge a safe street for children. "I'll send a copy to the mayor (David Crombie), but the premier has more power," he said. "If the mayor could do anything, he'd have to ask the premier anyway, so I thought I'd start at the top." The youngster also refused to present the petition to Attorney-General McMurtry, stating "I felt Premier Davis could tell the Attorney-General what to do." Among Sequeria's suggestions to Davis: "I told him they could be moved down to the industrial areas and scattered, then they would lose business and soon close. And they could be charged more often, then they would close down."

From the formation of the Downtown Business Association Task Force in 1972 to the creation of the Metropolitan Toronto Executive Committee, Legislation and Licensing Committee in 1975 aiming at making recommendations about body rub parlours, there had been a number of initiatives aimed at limiting their numbers. Although amendments to By-laws were made, and passed by Council — such as the once made to By-law No. 88-69 on August 26, 1975 — over licensing, ingenious owners and operators of body rubs simply changed how they operated, and remained open for business.

Other initiatives soon followed, including the creation of a committee in February of 1977 to report on the rise of nude establishments along Yong Street. That March, the Places of Amusement Offering Nude Services report was released. In May, 42 body rub parlours were investigated by Metropolitan Toronto Police over licensing violations, while in July, less than a month before the death of the shoeshine boy, a police task force was created. Although well-intentioned, none of these initiatives resulted in a drastic clean-up of Yonge Street and its well-established sex industry.

Chapter Twelve: Enter Morris Manning

"Hired gun cleans up sex-n-sin strip"
-Toronto Star, January 16, 1978

Within days of Emanuel's murder, furious protests were held in the Toronto and Ottawa, with many calling for the return of capital punishment. Overnight, newspapers and TV stations were interviewing experts for their insights on 'street danger,' with one social worker warning parents that 12 years old was too young to be working, "especially to be on the street at night." Others, like Inspector Ferne Alexander of the Metro Police youth bureau, said the Jaques case could be used as an extreme example of children taking risks. "If you're going to let your kids earn money, made damn sure you know where and how," she told the *Toronto Star*. Other articles provided safety tips to parents, including setting curfews, the importance of parents investigating a child's job, and youngsters working in their own neighbourhoods.

Subpoena served to Saul Betesh, Robert Kribs, Joseph [sic] Woods and Werner Gruener, charged with Murder, to appear at the Supreme Court of Ontario on January 16, 1978 (Courtesy Toronto Police)

Just one day after Emanuel's body was found, Attorney-General Roy McMurtry, assistant deputy Attorney-General John Hilton, and legal officials from Metro held a meeting to create draft legislation to address Yonge Street's sex trade. That day, Mayor Crombie addressed about 150 protesters who marched from the Jaques' home in Regent Park to City Hall, and acknowledged the urgency of the province acting quickly: "We need to move now, and I promise you we will."

On August 5, 1977 — a day after Emanuel's funeral — the front page of the *Toronto Star* reported "Politicians plot a secret war on sex shops." Refusing to discuss specific details which would give sex merchants the opportunity to create a defence, Metro Chairman Paul Godfrey, spokesman for the special Yonge Street committee, said legal measures "some new and some not so new," would be sent to the Legislature that fall for consideration. It was the second meeting that week discussing Yonge Street clean-up efforts. Afterwards, Mayor Crombie spoke to demonstrators outside City Hall, promising the city was fixed on closing the sex industry, but assuring them it was "not a moral crusade." In just days, police raided body rub parlours, made over 100 arrests, and laid charges of keeping a common bawdy house.

While the move to rid the street of its sin was welcomed, some like director of the Metro Licensing Committee J.H. Neville were critical, stating Metro would have been able to limit Yonge Street's sex industry and pinball arcades if it had implemented earlier recommendations made by the Robarts Royal Commission on Metro. Created under former Premier of Ontario John Robarts, the Commission recommended Metro "be assigned a general power to license trades and businesses in the interest of the community." Recommendations stated that licensing trades and other business activities, and enforcing regulations and standards with respect to their operation was an important regulatory tool of local government. In fact, the 395-page report actually referred to body rub parlours by name.

The power to regulate trades and businesses through licensing can be a useful tool for the community to protect itself from undesirable or injurious activities. Currently, however, the power to license is restricted to those trades and businesses expressly defined in legislation. Therefore, if an activity is not specifically subject to licensing by the legislation a council must seek a legislative amendment before attempting regulation.

Metro's difficulties in attempting to regulate body rub parlours give the clear illustration of the problem. Because body rub parlours were not specifically designated in legislation, Metro was forced to seek an amendment to The Municipal Act to permit it to license them. When legislative authority was granted, Metro was forced to seek an amendment to The Municipal Act permitted to license them. When legislative authority was granted, Metro passed a by-law on the subject. The wording of the by-law proved to contain too many loopholes, the Metropolitan Council at time of writing was still wrestling with the problem.[41]

Others at the time, such as New Democratic member for Scarborough-Ellesmere David Warner, also lent their support to Metro being given power over licensing, stating "The Robarts commission report has verified what I have known for a long time, namely that Metro should be able to set its own bylaws as long as they do not conflict with existing provincial legislation."

Newspaper readers were highly divided over the fate of the Yonge Street strip, calling its assortment of quirky characters — including body rubbers and hookers plying their trade from doorways, homeless persons preaching in the name of Jesus, and older men playing impromptu games of chess on overturned plastic milk crates — lent to the street's unique charm. One letter from South African-Canadian writer and journalist Marq de Villiers was critical of the clean-up efforts outlined by "neo-puritans" Aldermen Sparrow and Fish, accusing them of having no sense of humour. "And the Mayor? If he's read the Sparrow/Fish report he must know there's nothing in it save the preconceptions of its authors. So what's all this rubbish about the Yonge Street cesspool? His constituents clearly don't think it's a cesspool; they go there in their thousands to entertain and be entertained. To 'clean up' something like this is to kill it, to remove the incentive to go there. Or maybe that's what the politicians really want."[42] Letters from others stated any society allowing criminal elements to flourish — as they did on Yonge Street — were misguided, with one writer stating, "Weak-kneed David Crombie and his cohorts worry more about a 45-foot bylaw then the cancer that is plaguing them. Sick."

Others, including the Chairman of The Parish Council, Church of the Holy Trinity in Toronto, feared an angry public backlash. "At the same time we must be very careful not to let our horror at the ghastly act influence our judgement or clarity, so that we become as crazed as the perpetrators. This is not a time for frenzy, prejudice, repression or mob rule. It is terrifying to read some of the exhortations to violence in the press." At the time, some protesters carried signs during demonstrations urging Emanuel's killers to be strung-up, with politicians like conservative Member of Parliament Otto Jelinek (High Park-Humber Valley) calling for a return of capital punishment, asking for the minister to "consider introducing legislation which would make sexually related murders as well as murders of prison guards and police officers punishable by death."

Then, on August 11, 1977, the front cover of Toronto's newspapers featured the headline reading 'Special lawyer ready to pounce on sex industry.' Making the announcement during a press conference at City Hall, Godfrey said well-known lawyer Morris Manning would prosecute Yonge Street sex shop owners and operators for violating nude entertainment bylaws. Yonge Street's body rubs had no clue how swift his measures would prove to be, or effective.

Serving as Chairman of Metro Toronto from 1973 to 1984, Godfrey took on the role at the tender age of 34. Like other government officials, he realized solutions to the Yonge Street sex trade had to be addressed immediately. Calling the Strip "an embarrassment to us as politicians," he recalls seeing young women in front windows of so-called massage parlours, which were really fronts for prostitution.

"We knew that we could not sit back and do nothing at all," says Godfrey. "Doing nothing was the worst alternative out of everything. Yonge Street had become a den of prostitution in the downtown core. It was a scar on the face of the city of Toronto, and Metropolitan Toronto, and I wasn't going to sit back as Chairman to allow things to continue and face another incident like the death of this young boy. So we felt we had to get the best legal advice that we could in changing the face of Yonge Street, and over a period of time we were able to do that. There was no doubt that the boy's capturing and murder really exposed the horrors of Yonge Street. It was not where you'd want families to go to visit. It was not where residents in the adjoining areas enjoyed being. And we, as the elected representatives of the community, didn't have to be told that something drastic had to take place. Once we saw what had happened, there is no issue that was more important than the resolution to what became of Yonge Street. The killing of young Emanuel Jaques was the last straw to taking aggressive action to making something positive happened to change the face of our city."

While politicians at the time agreed immediate action was necessary, both Godfrey and then-Mayor Crombie agree the decline of the famous street took years, but was hastened by the construction of the Eaton Centre. That was a major change, "and therefore caused a different understanding of what might happen to property values," says Crombie. "So there is no doubt that when the Eaton Centre was built, that began a major historic change in that part of Yonge Street." Calling the growth of the sex industry "contagious," Godfrey says the public — no matter where they lived, from North York to Scarborough or in the downtown core — were demanding political leaders act quickly, "and I was not going to let the ball slip through my hands, and that's the reason I pressed the alarm button very quickly, and many of my colleagues in politics joined in the fight to eradicate what was going on there." This urgency resulted in the hiring of Morris Manning.

Graduating from the University of Toronto law school in 1965 and called to the bar of the Province of Ontario in 1967, Manning was the ideal choice to rid Yonge Street of its sleaze. Articling with the province's Department of the Attorney General, the 36-year-old Manning worked in the Criminal Appeals and Special Prosecutions Branch of the Attorney General's Department, arguing cases for the Attorney General in the Ontario Court of Appeal, and the Supreme Court of Canada. A few years earlier, in 1973, he was appointed Senior Crown Counsel, Civil Litigation Constitutional Law and Legal Advisory Services, and would be appointed Queen's Council in 1978.

When news broke of the clean-up, it was reported Manning would be handling injunction proceedings against owners of approximately 50 sex shops along Yonge, from Bloor Street in the north, to Queen Street in the South. Carefully planning his strategy, 60 writs had already been prepared by Manning and Metro's legal staff. To be served by the city's by-law enforcement officers, the writs required sex shop owners and operators to show cause why they should be allowed to continue to operate in the wake of alleged violations of Metro licensing by-laws. Through cooperation with the provincial government, a judge and special court time had already been reserved so Metro could get the writs served the coming week. Part of Metro's strategy was linked to an existing police crackdown on Yonge Street, which saw a task force make 130 arrests, with approximately 330 charges laid since July 11, many of them for soliciting and living off the avails of prostitution. These charges would then be used as evidence to demonstrate violations of Metro's bylaws. This was Paul Godfrey's secret 'game plan,' and it worked. By retaining Manning, who had years of experience in the Attorney General's office, the city was given an edge when it came to a special prosecutor. Sex businesses disobeying injunctions granted by the court meant they could be found in contempt.

"The immediate concerns were in a sense to redouble the efforts that had been going on not only with us, but with Paul Godfrey's office, with the Metropolitan Toronto Police, and the hiring of Morris Manning," says Crombie. "All were efforts to make sure that this was in a sense an event that showed that concerns people had raised over previous years were certainly well-founded. So if there was any concern, it was to understand that the public as well as officials had sort of caught on, and to make sure we did properly. When I say 'properly,' there was a terrific amount of cooperation between the City, Metro — the province had already been working with Metro on some parts of it, on zoning regulations and licensing and all of that — so it had a terrific effect on speeding-up the efforts that were already in play."

Described as "very forceful in a friendly way" by R.M. McLeod, Director of Ontario's Crown Law Office, many applauded Manning's initiatives, including the Downtown Business Council and Art Eggleton, stating Torontonians could soon expect "substantial improvements to Yonge Street." Predictably opposed to any changes to their industry were owners, operators and employees of sex-based businesses. These included Gary Snider, an attorney representing several body rub operators. Daily police raids, along with judges denying bail to female rubbers, was hurting their business, and in some cases making it impossible for them to stay open, said Snider. Throughout it all, Morris Manning remained professionally unapologetic. "I'm delighted they're locking their doors," he said. "It is the result of co-ordinated attacks on a number of fronts." Another strategy saw Metro Council asking the province to ban the sale of alcohol in establishments featuring nude entertainment.

A number of measures were proposed, including the reinstatement of certain vagrancy charges in the Criminal Code, and the power to padlock sex-related businesses failing to abide by the law. Paul Godfrey and Crombie realized appropriate legal solutions were necessary to clean-up the strip, resulting in Godfrey reaching out to the Attorney-General's Department to get advice on what could be done. Contacting John Hilton, a lawyer working as the assistant deputy attorney general, Godfrey said he needed someone with a background in criminal law, regulatory defence law, *and* civil litigation, because a different kind of approach was required to solve the issue of body rub parlours. Hilton recommended Manning for the job. Soon, a meeting was arranged, and Manning — who had already spent a total of about 14 years with the government, including articling as a summer student — gladly accepted the role.

"I always felt it was a special part of my life, and so this was public service of a different kind," says Manning, who left public service the previous year, and was in private practice. With the government from 1973 to 1976, he was head of the Civil Litigation branch, which also handled administrative law, and constitutional law; additionally, he was also Her Majesty's Proctor in Divorce.

In preparation, Manning read every newspaper article he could find about the growing sex industry on Yonge Street before approaching the police, and requested their files on body rubs and other establishments. Although there weren't many, some were small, while others were considerably larger for places with repeat offences. Poring through the pages, he kept asking himself a number of questions, including: *who were the owners, what trouble had they gotten into,* and *what charges were laid?* Receiving complete cooperation from the police, Manning soon discovered a common thread: numerous owners of body rubs had been charged with various breaches of bylaws, including some of keeping a common bawdy house. A number had been convicted, receiving modest fines.

With extensive legal experience in constitutional law cases — including appearing several times in front of his former constitutional law professor Bora Laskin, who was on the Court of Appeal and later served on the Supreme Court of Canada — Manning recalled a reference Laskin made in his constitutional law casebook in a endnote while conducting his research. "So I went back to that, and found a reference to a statute called the Disorderly Houses Act. It went back a long way. And that was a key. I use that act, I took all the boxes, and pulled out three establishments, and then brought an application against all three to shut them down under the Disorderly Houses Act, because the principles had been convicted of keeping a common bawdy house, which was a Criminal Code offence, the municipal response was under the Disorderly Houses Act — you could lock the doors. And that's how it was. We took that application to court, we won, and then we threaten the other two to close their doors, and that's what started the cleanup."

Under the Disorderly Houses Act — originally passed in 1942 as the Gaming and Betting Act before being renamed in 1950 — even building owners were not allowed to enter their own premises, a condition causing widespread controversy. On August 26, 1978, Judge William Lyon ordered the Lady Blue Body Rub Parlour at 368 ½ Yonge Street closed for a year, a move the owner considered nothing less than Draconian. The order to padlock the building could not be appealed. Additionally, the landlord was not permitted to rent or use the premises, and no one could enter the building for the same period of time. In addition to the owner being required to post a $1,000 bond, an application could be made to have the ruling lifted by the registered owner, or another interested person, before a County Court judge by demonstrating good faith governing the purposes for which the premises would be used for.

Investigating a number of legal options, Metro Chairman Paul Godfrey says as far as he was concerned, the sky was the limit when it came to shuttering Yonge Street's many body rubs. The law made sense, as it was already in place, and could be administered. "Usually the wheels of government move quite slowly, but the wheels of government moved quicker during that period of time than I've ever seen it, even to this day."

Although no appeal was permitted under the statute, affected building owners could apply for a reopening order for "limited occupancy" — specific terms set by the court, with the required assurance illegal prostitution activities would not continue. To underscore the severity of the Act, anyone aware of the padlock order entering or using the premises was subject to a jail term ranging from one month to one year.

At the time, the Criminal Code statute pertaining to bawdy houses stated:

193. (I) Everyone who keeps a common bawdy house is guilty of an indictable offence and is liable to imprisonment for two years.

(2) Everyone who

(a) is an inmate of a common bawdy house,

(b) is found, without lawful excuse, in a common bawdy house, or

(c) as owner, landlord, lessor, tenant, occupier, agent or otherwise having charge or control of any place, knowingly permits the place or any part thereof to be let or used for the purposes of a common bawdy house, is guilty of an offence punishable on summary conviction.

(3) Where a person is convicted of an offence under subsection (I), the court shall cause a notice of the conviction to be served upon the owner, landlord or lessor of the place in respect of which the person is convicted or his agent, and the notice shall contain a statement to the effect that it is being served pursuant to this section.

(4) Where a person upon whom the notice is served under subsection (3) fails forthwith to exercise any right he may have to determine the tenancy or right of occupation of the person so convicted, and thereafter any person is convicted of an offence under subsection (I) in respect to the same premises, the person upon whom the notice was served shall be deemed to have committed an offensive under subsection (I) unless he proves that he has taken all reasonable steps to prevent the recurrence of the offence.

With reporters and photographers present, York County Sheriff Philip Ambrose posted the official two-page closing order on the door of Lady Blue; the existing lock was not changed or added to, as it was not required, he said. Accompanied by sheriff's officer Richard Morton and Marc Schiffer from Manning's office, also in attendance were George Rust-D'Eye from Metro's legal department, and the supervisor of enforcement with the Metro Licensing Commission, Desmond Duffin.

The order read:

UPON the application of the municipality of Metropolitan Toronto for an order closing the premises known as Lady Blue Body Rub and known as 368 ½ Yonge Street, being part of the premises known municipally as 368 Yonge Street, in the City of Toronto, in the Judicial District of York, against its use for all purposes for one year, upon reading the affidavit of Marc E. Schiffer, filed, and the exhibits therein referred to, and in the presence of and upon hearing from counsel for the applicant and counsel for the registered owners of the above-named premises, Stanely [sic] F.S. Mang and Shirley H.C. Lu Mang (joint tenants).

1. IT IS ORDERED that the premises referred to in the application as 368 ½ Yonge Street...be closed for a period of one year from today's date for any or all purposes pursuant to...the Disorderly Houses Act.

As soon as the order was posted, a crowd rushed forward to read it. Some were disappointed, mumbling complaints about Yonge becoming "dull," while others were loudly praising the end of "another one of these whorehouses."

Under the Disorderly Houses Act, closing these premises was permitted if there had been a conviction within the previous three months of keeping a common bawdy house on the premises, or being an inmate in a bawdy house. At Lady Blue, the tenant occupying the property had been convicted of keeping a common bawdy house the week prior, and fined $300 in provincial court; the owner, Stanley Mang, leased the property for five years to the tenant, realized only the month before what it was used for, and terminated the lease, which was costing him $1,300 every month in lost rent.

Through his lawyer Oscar Wong, Mang stated the "recent stigma" over the Yonge Street strip made it hard for his client to find another tenant for the premises. Mang, said the judge, needed to show he was ignorant that his building was being used in contravention of the law. At the time, the closure of Lady Blue was only the second reported use of the provincial statute since 1945. While Wong was preparing an application so the premises could be reopened, prosecutors obtained temporary injunctions against three other adult entertainment operators, prohibiting them from providing unlicensed nude body rub and nude entertainment services anywhere in Metro.

Many at the time were critical of the Disorderly Houses Act, believing it penalized innocent, unsuspecting landlords who simply did not realize their premises were being used for sexual purposes. Lawyer and head of the Canadian Civil Liberties Association Alan Borovoy opposed the order against Mang, stating he was concerned about it being an "exercise in overkill," penalizing those who had nothing to do with illegal sexual activities. Using the Mang case as an example, the *Globe and Mail* published an editorial criticizing the Act, stating "we don't like padlock law, but we like strong-arm tactics by government even less. When the two are combined, as they were combined in Toronto this week, there is little — in fact, there is nothing — to be said in their favour." This opposition by the press did nothing to stop premises from being closed.

Calling the Disorderly Houses Act "quaint," the *Globe* stated it might be unconstitutional, "and Mr. Manning knows it." Although Mang had not been convicted of an offense relating to the use of his premises as a bawdy house, his building was still padlocked. Options available to him included paying taxes on the property he was unable to use or rent, apply to the court for an order reopening the premises subject to conditions, and post a $1,000 bond. Another option, stated the editorial, was to challenge the constitutionality of the Act, with the *Globe* going so far as calling Mang a guinea pig in a test case.

If Metro wants to use the Disorderly Houses Act in its campaign to clean up the bawdy litter of the Yonge Street strip, it should first apply to the courts to determine the constitutional validity of the law and only then — and only if the law of validity is proved beyond question — should Metro invoke the law as a weapon in the campaign. Instead, Metro has simply grabbed the weapon and started firing, perhaps in the hope that no one would notice the weapon might be illegitimate, perhaps in the hope that a challenge of the weapons legitimacy might just fail. A lot of hope, but not much concern for the people standing in the firing line, some of whom might be innocent. We wonder, in any event, if a padlock law of any sort, constitutional or otherwise, is absolutely essential to the laundering of Yonge Street…Let us not throw out concern for the means of the law in our anxiety over its ends."[43]

A few weeks later, the newspaper published another editorial about Mang after County Court Judge Hugh O'Connell suspended the order on his property, unlocking it. And once again, the *Globe* questioned the provincial legislation "that probably violates the Constitution," adding "Mr. Mang is out of the soup, but other landlords, who may be guilty or innocent, cannot be sure where they stand. Let's get the padlock act straightened out so that they, and special prosecutor Morris Manning, Metro's Mr. Cleanup for Yonge Street, know precisely whether it is valid or illegitimate. Questionable laws should be amended, or abandoned."[44] For reasons known only to itself, The *Globe and Mail* wrongly assumed Manning, who had dedicated much of his professional life to the Attorney General's Department, failed to thoroughly investigate the constitutional aspects of the law: he had.

"I researched that before I launched any missiles, because I wanted to avoid that," he says. "What I was doing was looking at a municipal statute or a provincial statute dependent on something that happens in the criminal law field. And the doctrine at the time of paramountcy says, if you got a similar issue and you're handling it in a similar way, and the one act prohibits and the other act allows, the federal act takes precedence — that's the Doctrine of Paramountcy. Where there is merely a municipal reaction to a federal prosecution and conviction, there is no clash between the two, and therefore under the separation of powers, section 91 and 92 — 91 is the federal powers, 92 is the provincial powers — under the separation of powers doctrine, it's only when there is a clash that the federal take precedence; otherwise, the two can stand together."

Utilizing the services of the police, Manning's strategy was brilliant, brutal, and effective. The number of charges skyrocketed from efforts made by Manning. From June to early July of 1977, only 16 charges were laid against 'keepers' and 'inmates' of common bawdy-houses; from later in July until early September 2, the number of charges increased to 224. "Women were literally rounded up and loaded into paddy wagons by police. By November 1977, only four adult entertainment establishments remained on Yonge Street, where there had been forty in July. In December 1978 the last body rub parlour on Yonge Street closed its doors."[45]

"Morris was obviously the right guy at the time," says Godfrey." I think that case gave him more exposure than anything up to that time, and I think that because of the success there, it no doubt put him in the spotlight more for people to hire him afterwards."

At the time, a number of Metro sex shop operators — one of them intending to open an escort service on the Yonge Street strip — were instructed not to breach the court order prohibiting them from operating these services without a municipal license, one of them being Jochatira Entertainment Ltd., controlled by three individuals including the Martins, owners of Charlie's Angels. Breaching the court order would result in significant fines, or jail time. "The reason for the granting of the injunction is because they've shown disrespect for the municipal bylaws," said

Manning in an interview. To be then found guilty of contempt of court by breaching the order would be a most serious matter."

In mid-January, 1978, the *Toronto Star* published an article entitled "Hired gun cleans up sex-n-sin strip" about Manning, which ran the same day as the four men charged with the murder of Emanuel Jaques went on trial. While there were still some body rub parlours on Yonge Street, they were rapidly disappearing as The Disorderly Houses Act was enforced. Freely admitting to being a 'hired gun,' Manning's widespread clean-up of the city's sex industry was balanced by his views on individual freedom and responsibility. Not a believer in censorship, Manning was, however, against those who believed a lack of censorship meant they could do what they wanted on Yonge Street, from posting nude pictures in windows to circulating hate literature.

Initially, Manning proposed four possible strategies to Metro for the clean-up. These included prosecution under the Canadian Criminal Code, licensing of body rubs and other nude service establishments through municipal bylaw, injunctions to prevent properties from being used for prohibited purposes, and the padlock law, requiring property owners to take responsibility for the purposes for which the premises were used. The Disorderly Houses Act proved to be the most powerful weapon in his legal arsenal, along with his exhaustive background in criminal, administrative, constitutional law, and training at the Attorney

General's Department. Many politicians at the time were taking credit for the success of the clean-up, yet Manning says much of it should go to Paul Godfrey for his involvement.

Back in the Seventies, it was impossible not to be aware of just how many sex shops and body rub parlours pockmarked Yonge Street. Police, the public, and many business owners were frustrated with the rapidly expanding sex trade along the strip. Possessing the experience necessary to look at the issue from a multi-disciplined perspective lead to a solution which was both praised, and demonized.

"Because of our divided jurisdictions, with our criminal law in hands of the federal government — and that includes the Criminal Code, the narcotic control act as it was then called, and municipal law, which is dependent on provincial powers — no one was looking at it from all angles to see what could be done," states Manning. "And in those days, there wasn't this coordinated approach to social problems. You didn't get the mayor sitting down with provincial counterparts and the federal government, and so on and so forth. There were very few conferences. There were constitutional conferences forever in this country, but there were very few conferences where provincial and federal government representatives would sit down with the municipal governments; they were just pothole repairers and bylaw enforcement people, very low on the totem pole. So I think an answer might be that no one was looking at it from the perspective of, *what can all of us do together?* Today, it is one big balloon: you press one end, and it comes out the other."

Another issue thwarting earlier efforts to clean-up the strip was the cost. Back when Manning was head of the Civil Litigation branch, a quarter of one per cent of the entire provincial budget was allocated to the justice system, which included the cost of running the court houses, a provincial administration, and salaries of provincial employees in the court houses, including Crown attorneys, and Xeroxing, which was new and expensive at the time. Compared to Health, Education, and Highways, monies allocated for the Justice ministry were minuscule. "I think the answer is there was no interest in cleaning this up, because they didn't want to spend the money," he says. "How much money did they allocate for dealing with the problem before Emanuel Jaques was killed, I have no idea. I doubt it was very much. Someone would have said, 'Wait a minute, the potholes on my street are more important,' and 'I don't go downtown anyway.'" Other areas, such as Scarborough in the East, were growing, and saw increasing numbers of businesses open there rather than downtown Toronto, which steadily declined in the 1970s.

Although many citizens and businesses applauded the efforts on the part of politicians and police to sweep Yonge Street clean of its "sin," not all were pleased, particularly the owners, managers, and employees of body rubs and burlesque theaters, who made their living working in these and other adult-oriented establishments. One of them was Valerie Scott. Nineteen years old at the time of Emanuel's murder, Scott was a dancer at Starvin' Marvin's Burlesque Palace, and Le Strip.

Valerie Scott
A Touch of Class

Valerie Scott in one of her burlesque costumes (Courtesy Valerie Scott)

As a child growing up in Moncton, New Brunswick, Scott stayed at home with her mother on rainy days, watching old Western movies on television. The scenes with the cowboys held little interest for the four-year-old, but the saloon girls — with their confident swagger, quick wit, and elaborate costumes — were fascinating. "I would watch the long, endless parts with the cowboys and wait for the saloon girls, and they were always too short," she says. "I wanted that. By contrast, when they showed the cowboys' wives, they always lived on the outskirts of town in some rundown shack. They were overworked, they looked half-starved, were constantly worried, had squalling babies hanging off of them, and I didn't want that, I wanted to be the saloon girl. The saloon girls didn't look too worried, and sometimes they even owned the saloon — a cowboy couldn't pull any wool over their eyes, and so that's what I wanted to be. And that stayed with me."

Moving to Toronto years later, Scott realized there were dance clubs where she could see her dream of becoming a saloon girl come to life. Admittedly nervous the first time she performed at Le Strip and Starvin' Marvin's, which took on amateurs, Scott would later take lessons in dance, pantomime, and singing (even though she never sang on stage), secured an agent based in New York, and invested thousands of dollars in her first professional costume, an elaborate saloon girl outfit resplendent with Austrian crystal beads. Club owners she worked for included 'Honest Joe' Martin, who she remembers as someone who was easy to deal with, and who paid on time; others would even make cash advances to the performers, and honoured chits that were months old. Times were good, but everything changed in the weeks following Emanuel's murder.

Although she was still dancing, the atmosphere of Yonge Street grew very different, and many of the performers feared for their safety. With four shows per shift, each lasting about 14 to 15 minutes, the girls would go to the Eaton Centre between performances, grab a coffee, or a bite to eat from a nearby restaurant. Since theatre make-up and false eyelashes took a long time to apply, they left it on before heading back for their next show. "Before the murder of Emanuel Jaques, this was fine; after the murder, it wasn't," she says. "People thought we were working on the street or in a massage parlour, even though we were just walking somewhere, it didn't matter."

During the crackdown on the Strip's body rubs, Scott nearly went to jail for something she didn't do. Her boyfriend at the time was an artist, and was hired to paint a sign for one of the clubs, Lady Strawberry. Leaving all his pricey paints and brushes at Lady Strawberry, Scott thought she would do him a favour, and retrieve his art supplies. With her hand literally on the second-floor doorknob, she was about to head inside when the place was raided, and an undercover police officer came running up the stairs. With the girls huddled together into a small reception area by police, there were no clients, since it was around dinnertime. "We all explained that I wasn't working there, but they didn't want to believe it," she says. "The manager explained, as did all the other staff, but they wanted to charge me too." Although she was never charged, Scott remained in Toronto for about four months following Emanuel's murder before taking her act on the road, performing across Canada, the United States, and Puerto Rico every February.

A few years later, at age 24, Scott entered the sex trade. "In those days, you could not be a dancer *and* a sex worker," she says. "If you were, when you went on stage, the other girls rip up your costumes, or piss in your coffee. It wasn't jealousy, because we were dancers, not hookers."[46]

Years after the murder, Scott — today the Legal Co-ordinator at the Sex Professionals of Canada — remains haunted by the young boy's death. "Emanuel was tortured and murdered; dehumanized. I feel like Emanuel was dehumanized all over again by the politicians, and corporate businesses used his murder as a handy tool to enhance their own interests. They did not care to learn anything about the boy. I did not see them reach out to the Jacques family in any meaningful way."[47]

*****

After successfully leading the Yonge Street clean-up, Manning became known for many other landmark cases, including his successful representation of Dr. Henry Morgentaler over the abortion law in the Supreme Court of Canada, and representing the Church of Scientology of Toronto.

Following controversial raids by Metro Toronto Police of The Barracks, a gay Toronto bath house in December of 1978, and again in 1981, Manning represented George Hislop, and other owners charged with keeping a common bawdy house. Raided by 150 police at the same time as other downtown clubs, over 250 men were charged with being found-ins in common bawdy houses, with extensive damage caused by police including cubicle doors being destroyed with sledgehammers and crowbars. Eventually, 315 went to court. At the time, Manning questioned the extreme methods used by police, stating there were other private men's clubs in Toronto with doors that lock. "'Do the police care what goes on inside of them?' asked Manning. 'Do we really have to spend all that money for this kind of situation? Who cares, who really cares except the morality squad? There are killers that haven't been caught in this city, why don't we concentrate on them?' Mr. Manning said doors were broken in at the clubs, windows and glass smashed and paintings ripped off the walls."[48]

Over the years, Manning maintained a high degree of respect for Hislop, who successfully lobbied for the inclusion of gays and lesbians in Canada's Charter of Rights and Freedoms, and survivor pension benefits for homosexuals before he passed away from esophageal cancer in 2005, at the age of 78. Viewed by many as a role model, Hislop was also Canada's first openly gay candidate for public office, when he ran for city councillor in Toronto's 1980 municipal elections, defeated by then-mayor John Sewell.

"George styled himself, and I think rightly so, as a leader, not *the* leader, of the gay community in Toronto," says Manning. "Times were really tough then. The bathhouse raids were scandalous, and took place [four years after the Jaques murder]. The lead officer, I understood he was heard to say, 'This will not be San Francisco North.' I don't know if he said it, but I know they certainly acted it. I had no qualms about taking the case, which another lawyer 'refused' by quoting an outrageously high fee." The Barracks, argued Manning, was a safe haven for consenting adults, as were other clubs raided by police. "George was quite a guy, quite a fighter. A very courageous man, and I like courageous people, and I like acting for people who believe in the motto, 'God helps those who helps themselves.'"

Unlike several of the lawyers representing the four defendants at the time of the Emanuel Jaques murder trial, Manning says he did not receive any threats during the controversial clean-up of Yonge Street, despite opposition from body rub owners and operators. All these years later, the man known as Toronto's "hired gun" does not believe the once-infamous strip will ever return to the sleaze of the Seventies for numerous reasons, ranging from city councillors who are more in tune with the best interests of their constituents, to a greater level of awareness in the police force. "I don't think it'll ever go back, because people don't want to return to those days," states Manning. "Now that being said, I'm not a great believer in using police to waste their time with silliness about consenting acts in a public bar. I think it's a complete waste of time. I'm not in favour of the police doing by-law enforcement."[49]

The years after the clean-up was initiated saw some of the same body rub owners attempt to resurrect their once-lucrative businesses, including Joe Martin Sr., owner of what was Charlie's Angels. In July of 1979, two years after Emanuel's disappearance and death, police and politicians were cracking-down on places where fully-clothed dancers were arranging for sex acts to take place in other locations. Charging a number of establishments with running public baths and places of amusement without licenses, the Metro Licensing Commission saw owners appear in court, facing fines of $1,000, or 30 days in jail. Police were adamant that after all their work to clean up the strip, they would not allow the sex businesses "creeping in again...like a disease," stated one sergeant. Martin said even he was surprised women wearing clothes could make $20 to $30 per half-hour by just talking to lonely men. "I don't hide the fact that the girls make arrangements to meet men the next day in a restaurant, or by telephone," he told the Toronto *Star*. "But nothing is happening inside our place."

Around the same time, an organization called The Downtown Youth Centre was created following Emanuel's murder. Located on Yonge, the Centre had four workers patrolling the area to help teens in need, particularly runaways and those lacking street smarts, which made them easy prey for drug dealers eager for customers and pimps looking for girls and boys to prostitute. According to the *Toronto Star* "Prostitution remains a huge problem on The Strip despite the crackdown on 'massage parlours' after the murder of Emanuel Jaques. Girls used to a strong father image are vulnerable to pimps who step in and take over the protective role. Boys as well as girls are picked up at the fast-food joints, which are popular because they're cheap." Others, including volunteer cadets from the Salvation Army, did Friday night patrols of the Strip, offering to help to those in need.

Throughout the late Seventies and early Eighties, newspaper articles favourable to the clean-up appeared, with headlines like "Yonge St. shedding its sleaze: Blatant pornography's all but gone, stroll of Strip reveals," and "The Strip: It's sinful but safer." While a number of X-rated theatres like The Biltmore and adult magazine and movie house Cinema 2000 remained, much of the hard-core porn had vanished. Pinball arcades and bars still existed, but almost all former body rubs had new tenants, or the premises were left vacant.

In mid-1981, comments made by Toronto Mayor Art Eggleton about a resurgence of street prostitution in the city were labeled "garbage" and "ridiculous" by a number of city councillors, including Pat Sheppard, who chaired the Yonge St. Implementation Committee. Stating he had no information that Yonge had experienced a rise in prostitution, an upset Sheppard was worried about Eggleton's statements, made during a conference to other Canadian mayors in Regina, would only serve to create a climate of fear, and once again make Yonge Street appear undesirable.

The changing face of the Yonge Street Strip: the Oriental Gift and Fashion store at 245 Yonge, with signage for a silver shop where the entrance was to the apartment where Emanuel was killed, July, 2007 (author photo)

A recent photo of the once-infamous Yonge Street Strip, September, 2016 (author photo)

Chapter Thirteen: The Legacy of the Shoeshine Boy

Unable to experience guilt, even over the death, but we cannot hate him for that. There's something undeveloped in his makeup, that is, his inability to show compassion.
-Attorney Paul Tomlinson on his client, Saul Betesh

Long after the trial and sentencing, the killers of Emanuel Jaques continued to make news, especially so-called ringleader Saul Betesh. Always hell-bent on shocking and provoking others, Betesh put himself in the spotlight the moment he went to police after the murder, telling them where the boy's body could be found. His impulsive behaviour demonstrated itself in a number of ways, from protesting conditions behind bars to demands for mental health treatment, his fascination with the ancient Celtic religion Druidism, and his numerous threats of self-injury through starvation and denying himself medication.

By April of 1978, after the conclusion of the sensational murder trial, Betesh announced one of many so-called 'hunger strikes' over the years to come. The first was to protest the lack of psychiatric care for his mental illness while in prison. While being held at the West Toronto Detention Centre awaiting transfer to Kingston Penitentiary, which would be his home for decades, Betesh announced a six-day-long hunger strike. With a habit of writing letters to newspapers to fuel his unquenchable need for attention, Betesh mailed a letter to the *Toronto Star*, stating "The hunger strike that I started at 7:30 a.m. Sunday, April 9, will continue until my death."

During and after the trial, Saul Betesh and his attorney Paul Tomlinson requested the killer receive treatment for psychopathy. After a well-known psychiatrist refused to help him, Betesh attempted to kill himself with an overdose of sleeping pills. It would prove to be one of a number of failed suicide attempts in the years to come (author collection)

Reginald Barrett, the Superintendent of the Toronto facility, said Betesh was protesting the lack of psychiatric treatment being provided for him, adding that the last thing Betesh consumed was a glass of milk a day earlier. Tomlinson stated his client was being sacrificed, as the government was not prepared to spend money on proper treatment for sex offenders and mentally-ill criminals, and the hunger strike, he claimed, was a way of drawing public attention to the lack of psychiatric care.

"Here we have a man who isn't insane in the eyes of the law but is mentally ill," said Tomlinson. "There is no question that he's treatable and curable but I doubt that he will get the necessary treatment at the Kingston Penitentiary because they don't have a proper treatment centre."[50] Officials at Penetanguishene refused to take his client because of his lengthy jail term, and the hospital felt it could use an available hospital bed to treat "three or four other people in that time," instead of just one.

Petitioning on behalf of Betesh, Tomlinson spoke to a number of psychiatrists to try to get his client recognized as a psychopath, and have attempts made to treat him, rather than see him imprisoned. "Many did not want to get involved, because of the high profile of the case," he says. "I gathered that they didn't want to be in the public eye as saying this man was insane. There are bed limits at the Penetanguishene hospital, and psychopaths were people who cannot be easily cured, if at all, which would take years. In that timeframe, the hospital looks at statistics, and believed they could cure 10 patients in the time that they had one patient who is taking up a bed for a long period of time. So there was a reaction among certain doctors about psychopathy, and psychopaths being found not guilty by reason of insanity, for that reason." Assembling a panel of six doctors to review all the materials on Betesh, the psychiatrists reached a joint decision: the killer was not insane, and did not fit the description of insanity as defined in the Criminal Code at the time. "So that left me with the defense of insanity with no doctors to back it up."

Says Tomlinson: I was a big believer that a person who was a psychopath had a disease of the mind that would prevent him from being found guilty of a crime, and that's why I went to the lengths I did to try and find doctors who would agree with my position. When I put that panel together, I was putting all my eggs in one basket, and of course they came back and said they couldn't find him [insane]. But I have a feeling a lot of that decision amongst those psychiatrists was based on the problems that they were having at Penetanguishene. I don't like to say that sometimes professionals make decisions for other reasons than the right reason— as to whether or not he was insane — but exterior factors. Many of them did not want psychopaths to fill their hospitals, because there was no question they were causing problems. Being psychopaths, they would lie about things, turned nurse against doctor, turn nurse against nurse, patient against patient, and they were causing problems within the psychiatric facilities because of the very nature of their illness, which didn't help the doctors trying to treat them — they could treat five people, or 10 people, in the time it takes to treat this one fellow.

Despite the severity of his crime, and his childish antics, Tomlinson maintains that he did not dislike Saul Betesh. "There was no question that he suffered from, in my mind, a mental disorder, a serious one. And he was histrionic, there was no question about that. He wanted to be the center of attention. But I didn't dislike him, even as I acted for him."

Like most claims made by Betesh, the seriousness of his hunger strike was greatly exaggerated. That same week, an unnamed employee at the Detention Centre stated the increasingly problematic Betesh was not only receiving meals, but eating all of them. Betesh's claims were proven to be bogus, as his plan to 'starve himself' started with drinking orange juice, followed by coffee with milk and sugar, abstaining from food for two days, then eating full-course meals immediately.

There was, however, no denying Betesh's mood was worsening behind bars. During the trial Paul Tomlinson was challenged with finding psychiatrists who would put their professional credentials and reputations on the line, and provide expert opinions his client was a psychopath, which would, if successful, have seen Betesh transferred to a mental health care facility, instead of prison. Unable to garner enough support from the psychiatric community, his client was instead found guilty of first-degree murder.

"I went right to the very end with the defense of not guilty by reason of insanity," says Tomlinson years later. "The only defense open to me was not guilty by reason of insanity, and I persisted in its defense, even though all my cards had been taken away, or any cards I thought I might have."

At the best of times, Betesh's behaviour was erratic and irrational, defying all logic; at worst, it was pure, undiluted rage. For Tomlinson, his client's frequent outbursts and abrupt mood changes were nothing new. At one point during the trial, in February 1978, Betesh passed him two notes during court proceedings, stating his services were no longer needed, providing no explanation. Occasionally, Betesh would ask Tomlinson for a cigarette — at the time, smoking was permitted in jails. His attorney obliged. A few days later, Betesh asked for three cigarettes. "I knew what was coming, as I knew about psychopaths," says Tomlinson, with Betesh soon asking for an entire carton of cigarettes, and a book. "I knew it was coming, I was doing it almost as a test to see if he fit the description of a psychopath. And he fired me for a day, because I wouldn't bring him a carton." Betesh never apologized for his behaviour.

Following his conviction, Betesh sent a letter to a Kingston-based psychiatrist who was regularly called upon by the Canadian Penitentiary Services (CPS) to treat prison inmates, imploring him for help. The written response was wholly unexpected by Betesh and Tomlinson, with the doctor stating: "Your crime is as repugnant to me as it is to many other members of the Canadian public. So long as I have some choice in my priorities for treatment, people like yourself will be very low on my list." This prompted Tomlinson to contact Canadian prison ombudsman Ron Stewart, demanding a formal complaint be made against the doctor.

Despondent and feeling hopeless over the psychiatrist's refusal for treatment, Betesh was suffering from insomnia. Instead of taking the two sleeping pills he was receiving from the prison nightly, he stockpiled them for weeks until he believed he had enough to commit suicide. Unable to wake him one August morning in 1978, guards rushed him to the intensive care unit, where he was revived. It was his second suicide attempt. Sources said that ever since receiving the letter from the psychiatrist denying him treatment, Betesh was depressed and in a "lousy, hopeless mood" when he took the handful of sleeping pills. Despite some like Stephen Lewis, former provincial New Democratic Party leader and an executive of the Canadian Psychiatric Association stating the psychiatrist should be forced to sever all connections with the CPS, charges of professional misconduct against the doctor were dismissed in April of 1979, with a disciplinary committee at The College of Physicians and Surgeons of Ontario stating the comments against Betesh were "tasteless," but did not constitute professional misconduct."

The psychiatrist stated he was pleased with the ruling, but he was not prepared to discuss the "series of complex reasons" why he refused to treat the convicted child killer. Around the same time, the secretary for the Criminal Lawyers' Association of Ontario conceded prisoners were not offered treatment for psychopathic personality, and a considerable number of inmates in Ontario suffered from severe psychopathic personalities.

During this time, it was reported Betesh had been offered a psychiatric assessment, which he refused, and that another psychiatrist was present on an as-required basis. While a four-month long program for sexual offenders was available, it was intended for inmates about to be *released* from prison; as Betesh received a 25 year sentence for first-degree murder, the treatment was not needed, with the director of the CPS regional psychiatric centre, Dr. Roy Brown, stating there was no point in providing the program to Betesh, as he was simply going to return to his cell. "It's better to do it close to the period when they will be released," said Brown. "We're doing this to protect the public as much as anything else."

In March of 1980, Betesh penned a lengthy letter to the *Toronto Star* from his prison cell. Under the headline, 'Convicted murderer calls for the death penalty,' he stated the newspaper had printed letters about the pros and cons of the death penalty for well over a year, many of them written by lawyers, psychologists, prison staff, and church groups, but he could not recall seeing any from someone who actually *knew* if capital punishment would prevent murder. Claiming to speak for himself and six other killers, Betesh wrote, "All of us agree that the death penalty should be in effect for all first-degree murderers (premeditated, cop or prison guard)," adding that the method of death should be non-painful and humane, preferably by lethal injection, and "Hanging or other such forms of execution should not be used."[51]

"We all agree that, in our cases, the death penalty would most likely have made us reconsider what we did," continued Betesh, who went on to state that although it would not stop "spontaneous types caused by arguments or passion," the death penalty would save taxpayers $20,000 a year for each prisoner. "It is more humane than making a person stay in prison knowing he or she will never be released. As a convicted murderer me and my fellow convicts' words will probably go unheard. But who is to know better if such a law will prevent such a crime other than somebody who's been through such an experience?"[52] True to form, at no point in his letter does he, Betesh, mention he was one of the killers responsible for the vicious sex slaying of Emanuel Jaques, guilt over his crime, or sympathy for his victim.

Later in 1980, Betesh was one again in the news, but not in a way he would have imagined. On the morning of August 24 he was found in his prison cell, slashes to his throat. Although not fatal, the wounds required 13 stitches to close. The attacker was Josef Woods, Betesh's co-convicted, who had long-standing issues with Betesh. Testifying he was asleep when he felt something cutting into his neck, Betesh awoke to find Woods standing over him, holding "something shiny" in his hand. Another prisoner, James Stewart, later said Woods told him he wanted a knife to kill Betesh, believing it would lift the "curse on him," but Stewart refused to help. For the attack, Woods 'the mad scientist' received an additional four years in September of 1981 to be served concurrently to his life sentence.

For Saul Betesh, his pattern of lying and wild exaggerations to get attention continues to this day. In May of 1981, he was in the news for yet another hunger strike, this one over his Jewish faith, and its strict dietary laws. Once again, Betesh wrote to the press announcing his intentions to do away with himself. "The prison [Kingston Regional Detention Centre, formerly Kingston Penitentiary] refuses to purchase three prepared kosher meals a day even though the meals are available," he wrote to the *Toronto Star*. "This refusal is a violation of my human rights."

Once again, Betesh's contradictions were on display. Filing a complaint with the prison weeks earlier, officials confirmed their less-than-model prisoner was indeed refusing to eat any meals provided by the institution, yet he was stuffing himself with junk food from the inmate canteen like soda, granola bars and popcorn, which was

Saul's version of self-imposed starvation. Prison officials noted inmates were granted special meals only on "recognized religious high holy days," and were entitled to special foods every day, but this had to be confirmed with a rabbi, or chaplain. At the time, it was unclear if Betesh had made any such request.

Despite declaring he would willingly "suffer health problems" unless he received three kosher meals per day Betesh, who refused to be weighed, appeared in perfect health. At the time, prisoners could not be compelled to take medical attention, except in cases where they became unconscious or unable to refuse help, when measures such as intravenous feeding could be used.

Public relations official Dennis Curtis stated there had never been a serious hunger strike at the penitentiary. "Inmates go on hunger strikes for various reasons from their rate of pay to being segregated. It's their way of drawing some attention," he said, noting that none of the other 264 prisoners at the facility cared about Betesh's protestations. With the gruesome murder of Jaques still in the memory of Canadians, many were anything but sympathetic to the convicted child sex slayer. Flooding newspapers with letters, one man who had earlier supported Betesh's demands for psychiatric care by contacting the Solicitor-General of Canada questioned his motives, stating the killer didn't eat three kosher meals a day when he was a free man. Most said the murderer forfeited any rights he had back in 1977, when he decided to drown Emanuel Jaques in a sink. Others stated he should be grateful Canada no longer had Capital Punishment, and that he should be allowed to starve to death.

After speaking with a rabbi who supplied Betesh with cassette tapes about the Jewish religion, a yarmulke, and a siddur — a Jewish book of daily prayers — the prison stated Betesh would be served one kosher meal per day, which saw him abandon his hunger strike. Rabbi Howard Finkelstein of the Beth Israel Congregation, who also served the religious needs of Kingston's Jewish prisoners, called officials on Betesh's behalf, and made arrangements for a frozen kosher TV meal served to him for lunch, and vegetarian food for dinner. Although unconcerned about Betesh's claim of 'starving himself to death,' the rabbi believed it was his job to support the killer's religious request. "As prison chaplain for Jewish prisoners, I am responsible for meeting the spiritual needs of Jewish inmates — regardless of the nature of their crimes," he told The *Canadian Jewish News*. At the time, Betesh was only one of three or four Jewish inmates at Kingston.

"I try to touch their humanity," said Finkelstein, refusing to answer if, or when, he would visit Betesh again. Rabbi Sheldon Steinberg, director of chaplaincy services for the Ontario Region of the Canadian Jewish Congress, stated prisoners seeking out their Jewish roots were doing so through "a spiritual identification," he said. "Each person has to be regarded as an individual human being. It doesn't mean I condone the crime. As a chaplain I stand for certain values, but my role is not to judge."[53]

The next year, Saul David Betesh was in the news once more when he announced his intention to run for Kingston city council, despite serving a 25-year sentence behind bars. The news enraged many, including the family of Emanuel Jaques. Mel Lastman, Mayor of North York at the time, who had initiated a fundraising effort for the family at the time of the murder, said he had received a number of calls protesting Betesh, including some from friends of the Jaques family. Arguing he had been a resident of Kingston, Betesh said he should be permitted to run in the November 8, 1982 municipal elections. Lastman, and many others, disagreed. "Where is the constitution for the innocent?" he asked incredulously. "It is crazy that a guy who should be strung up, who killed a kid in the most horrible way, is (trying to run) as an elected official. If he does win, what could he do with it? He sits in Kingston (penitentiary) while council meets. We are wasting time with animals like him." Lawyers at the time in Kingston were required to verify Ontario law prohibiting inmates from running or voting in elections.

Requesting nomination papers from Kingston City Hall, Betesh threatened legal action if his demands were denied. Voting rights at the time were subject to "reasonable and justified" restrictions under the Charter of Rights. The issue was put on hold and largely forgotten until August

1984, when Joyceville Institution inmate, Robert Gould, won the right to vote in a federal election for the first time, a decision which was being appealed by the justice minister. Betesh wrote to the chief electoral officer demanding to be enumerated, only to be told he could vote if he pursued his own court case.

Almost a decade after the murder, Betesh was back in the public eye for another hunger strike. This time, he wasn't protesting lack of psychiatric care, but budget cutbacks to educational programs being offered at Kingston penitentiary by Seneca College, and the use of female guards in some areas of the prison. Still in protective custody Betesh, now 36 years old and weary-looking, stated he would phase-in his so-called 'hunger strike' gradually, limiting himself to only two meals per day starting on March 24, 1986, then scaling-back to one meal daily, commencing April 8. If his demands were not met by April 23, Betesh claimed he would refuse all food. By this point, his weight ballooned to 240 pounds, and claims he would starve to death were predictably exaggerated.

Among his numerous complaints, Betesh was protesting cuts to an automated computer data processing program at the prison, the decision by officials to reduce the number of hours for a community college teacher, and the presence of female guards in shower, toilet, and sleeping areas. Representatives from the penitentiary said the two-year-old computer shop was no longer viable, as not enough private contracts for work had been secured. None of these facts seemed to matter to Betesh.

Along with frequently penning letters to newspapers, Betesh also wrote to other publications including *Ahoy!* a magazine dedicated to users of Commodore International computers, focused on the Commodore 64 and Amiga. In one, he offered a solution for increasing the speed of a cursor, signing it simply, 'Saul D. Betesh, Kingston, ONT.' Curiously, his technical advice appeared next to an ad for SEXTEX, a company providing "The nation's leading erotic computer communications network" for a lifetime membership of $12.95 U.S. Years later, still behind bars, Betesh edited *The Acorn*, a publication focused on Druidism.

In 2002, not only Betesh but his co-convicted were once again in the press. Considerably overweight, diabetic, and requiring daily insulin injections, he threatened another hunger strike, believing his religious rights as a Canadian citizen had not been respected for the previous six years. In a two-page typed letter to the warden of Kingston Penitentiary, Betesh stated he was being discriminated against because he was a Druid, and a practicing pagan. In order to practice Druidism, he said candles were required — one each for "the source," God and Goddess — along with incense, "and various smudging/purifying materials," along with access to a natural garden/ritual space to be used to grow herbs and flowers as offerings to his Gods.

Among his demands, Betesh wanted the Correctional Service of Canada to acknowledge his same-sex relationship, a transfer to a facility in British Columbia (along with his partner), being allowed to take a program for sex offenders and violent offenders, up to three "safety" candles in his cell, being allowed to purchase and use incense, and that the federal and provincial governments investigate the activities of the Crescent School in the late 1950s where he was "repeatedly raped by one of there [sic] teachers," and that he be granted Legal Aid so he could pursue compensation, and an apology.

Claiming his rights and freedoms were being ignored, Betesh stated, "These actions will at ALL TIMES be PEACEFUL and NO-VIOLENT [sic] and will include both legal and civil actions and such further actions such as a hunger strike as practiced by Ghandi and other non-violent protestors. In the name of the God and Goddess I hereby give my oath to undertake whatever non-violent actions are required to end the religious and other discrimination that I and other inmates are forced to endure."

While prison officials, guards, and the public had long since grown weary of Betesh's bizarre threats to do harm to himself by this point, 2002 marked not only the 25th anniversary of Emanuel's murder, but the possibility that one of his killers could go free. Robert Kribs, the tall, quick-tempered sadist who pled guilty to the boy's death, went before a three-member panel of the National

Parole Board in a bid to gain his freedom after serving his mandatory life sentence. For the Jaques family, who avoided the media spotlight for years, the possibility one of the men who unconscionably killed Emanuel could actually go free was terrifying.

In an interview with the *Toronto Star*, Emanuel's sister — who faithfully attended the trial of her brother's killers in 1978 — spoke publicly. A mother of two, Valdemira felt it was vital to speak out against the killer's potential parole. "My hope is that he dies in prison," she said. "They should keep him locked up and throw away the key. And after that I hope he rots in hell. He shouldn't even be alive. He took a life. My brother didn't get a second chance at life, why should he?"[54] With the right to speak at the parole hearing for Emanuel's killer, the family declined, unable to tolerate being in the same room with Kribs; instead, they sent a letter to parole board members objecting to his release, "now or in the future."

Many Canadians recoiled at the prospect of Kribs getting out of prison, especially Toronto's Portuguese community. In a two-page letter dated October 4, 2002, Peter Ferreira, the National Vice-President of the Portuguese-Canadian National Congress in Toronto, wrote to the National Parole Board urging them to deny "both full and partial parole to Wayne Robert Kribs," then 54 years old. Serving the approximate 400,000 Canadians of Portuguese origin — an estimated 200,000 of them living in Toronto — the Congress was distressed to learn Kribs might be freed, "one of three men who was convicted in the 1970's of the abduction, gang rape, torture and drowning of the shoeshine boy, Emanuel Jaques."

Referring to the crime as "an especially brutal murder, the likes of which the city had never seen before," Ferreira outlined how Emanuel, shining shoes to raise money to support his family, was sodomized, tortured, murdered, and found dumped on the roof of a massage parlour. The letter read as follows:

At the time, this crime horrified the residents of the City of Toronto, who had never experienced this level of brutality. It was committed in a time long before the arrival of Paul Bernardo and the murder of various other children in the city, under similar circumstances. Emanuel's murder eventually led to the permanent removal of the many sex-trade operations, which were flourishing at the time, on Yonge Street and, as such, permanently change the face of the city.

Yet, this crime particularly traumatized those in the Portuguese-Canadian community. At this time, most Portuguese-Canadians were recent immigrants from traditional, rural origins, for whom this type of savagery was totally unheard of. Many people in our community were left deeply scarred by this murder, and by the newfound sense of vulnerability which it created for all of the residents in this city. Hundreds of these individuals took the day off from work (including some who are presently Directors of our organization) and attended Emanuel's funeral at St. Agnes Church on

Dundas St. and Grace St., in the heart of the Toronto Portuguese neighbourhood.

Portuguese-Canadians are now being forced to, once again, relive the horror of that crime, with the possibility that Mr. Kribs could be paroled to re-enter the community. Most of our constituency, particularly those with young children, feel that this individual will pose a significant risk to their communities, should he be allowed to return. They are particularly fearful that, if allowed loose into our streets, he will begin to prey on yet another generation of its children. This is a particularly sensitive issue, since there are presently in Toronto a number of other unsolved sexual assaults, involving individuals who have attacked children in — and around — local schools.

We therefore strongly beseech the parole board to deny both full and partial parole to Wayne Robert Kribs. Only in this fashion will our community feel that our children are being protected and that justice is being served.[55]

On October 18, 2002, many were relieved when Kribs was denied parole by the Board, informing the killer, "it has concluded your risk to re-offend cannot be managed in the community at this time."

In its four-page pre-release decision sheet, the National Parole Board detailed its reasoning for refusing parole, stating few details of the circumstances of the murder had been provided by Kribs over the years, and describing him and his co-accused luring Emanuel to the apartment, where he was sexually abused "over a protracted period of time," an attack which was "intrusive in nature." Questioning his credibility, the report also referred to Kribs denying his participation in the murder.

"You admit to a lifestyle where you solicited sex from young males in the street in exchange for money, food, or lodging. Having previously prostituted yourself, you did not appear to view these sexual assaults as criminal, despite the fact that they were perpetrated against young children. You referred to your victims as 'hustlers' diminishing them somehow as less important human beings. File information suggests there were two sexual assaults on young male victims, aged eight and eleven, when you were an early teen. You deny that these were sexual assaults and describe them instead as 'sexual games.' As a result of your sexually deviant behaviour you were admitted as a patient to a psychiatric hospital. A conviction for Indecent Assault on a Male is noted in 1974, when again your victim was a minor. The balance of your criminal history dates back to 1966 and consists of property-related offences which took place in many cities across the country, indicating a vagrant lifestyle." The report went on to describe Kribs' distorted thinking, propensity for violence, and lack of empathy for his victims.

His performance deemed satisfactory during incarceration, Kribs completed a number of programs, including one in Cognitive Skills in 1999, and another in Anger and Emotions Management in 1998, both with relatively good reports. In addition, he also fulfilled a Living Without Violence program in 1997, yet file information suggested he attend the program as a former *victim*, not as a perpetrator of violence. Completing two, one-on-one sex offender programs with psychologists in 1988 and again in 1992, results showed he still remained a "grave danger" to society. Making some gains during the second program, the psychologist determined Kribs still tended to embellish facts, further distorting his credibility. Worse still, "Phallometric testing showed deviant sexual arousal to underage males and females, and to male sexual violence." Demonstrating little empathy or cognizance of the impact he was responsible for on his victims, a psychiatrist suggested Kribs required additional programming to address this major criminogenic risk factor.

Working against Kribs' favour was his decade-long unwillingness to participate in the High-Intensity Sex Offender Treatment Program at the Regional Treatment Centre. His refusal was based on location: the sex offender program would have required him to transfer to the Regional Treatment Centre, and he did not want to jeopardize his institutional privileges such as range placement and employment. Likewise, an earlier attempt in 1993 to move him to a lower security institution was unsuccessful, as Kribs was unable to integrate into the general population due to the nature of his crime, and his request to be placed in segregation for his own protection.

In June of 2002, a psychiatric assessment stated Kribs suffered from Anti-Social Personality Disorder and Pedophilia, and that he still presented as significantly psychopathic, and at a high risk for both sexual and violent re-offending, with a psychiatrist concluding Kribs' release into the community "would not be a viable option for many years." Another factor working against Kribs was his lack of family support in the Kingston area, and no offers of employment.[56]

Upon learning Robert Kribs would remain in Kingston Penitentiary, many in Toronto's Portuguese community were pleased. One of them, school trustee Nellie Pedro, had led a letter-writing campaign urging others to oppose the killer's potential parole. Decades after the brutal rape and murder, Kribs still denied he was in the room when Emanuel was drowned in the kitchen sink. When speaking to the three-person parole board, which only took 45 minutes to reach its decision, Kribs appeared resigned to his fate. "I'm guilty of murder. The boy died on my shift. My feeling is that I should spend the rest of my life in prison. As far as I'm concerned, if you do something like that you should never get out. I should die in prison," he said. Many members of the public, who followed the lives of the convicted men for years after the trial, agreed.

"Kribs was a nasty piece of work, and he wouldn't be capable of luring a young boy anywhere," remembers attorney Paul Tomlinson. "A young boy would run away from him, he was scary looking. Whenever I saw Kribs, he always reminded me of pictures of Rasputin. Woods was a psychopath, no question. He was ridiculous, from the point of view of things he did, the rocket that went the wrong way, and some other things, reading tarot cards, silly things. And Werner Gruener? I don't think should have been charged. He was a marijuana user, and basically slept through the whole thing. And the only reason I say that is because all the other accused said that he wasn't involved in anything, that he was high on marijuana and slept through the whole thing, even though he was in the apartment. Which isn't what co-accused normally do. Normally, they are pointing a finger at the other guys saying 'he did it, not me.' Here, they're all saying Werner Gruener didn't do anything."

In July of 2002, newspapers were reporting on Toronto's blistering temperatures, and ways to beat the heat. The July 18 edition of the *Toronto Star* featured interviews with a number of locals. Included in that day's edition was a photo of a man with a scraggly beard and long, unkempt hair lying on the grass in St. James Park, drinking a bottle of donated water. The journalist was likely unaware the person they were speaking to was Werner Gruener, the only one of the men tried for the murder of Emanuel Jaques to walk free. "I really appreciate them coming around," said Gruener, who managed to find a shaded nook in the park. Homeless, Gruener was described by the reporter as being "in the right place at the right time" to receive a cold bottle of Aquafina water, distributed by kind-hearted volunteers to those in need.

*****

In 2003, after spending 25 years behind bars, Josef Woods — also known as Joseph Michael Woodsworth — was transferred from federal prison to a Saskatoon hospital, where he died on April 10. Known as 'The Mad Scientist' of the group, the 58-year-old Woods, who read tarot cards, was heavily involved with the occult, stated the Holy Ghost and clouds spoke to him, and believed himself to possess psychic and hypnotic abilities, had suffered for years from Hepatitis C, spread through blood, contaminated needles, unprotected sex, and other means. After a quarter of a century behind bars, the so-called "Mad Scientist" of the group was dead.

For years, Woods believed himself to be gifted with psychic abilities. A self-taught "inventor," Woods' claimed he used pyramid power to transform cigarettes into marijuana, and his many odd devices saw him cannibalizing a microwave oven to create a weapon to kill pigeons, which annoyed him. Often arguing with Saul Betesh, Woods decided one day that he was going to kill him while he worked on the CN Tower. Fashioning a home-made rocket out of cardboard, he climbed the roof of the apartment on Yonge Street, miles from the Tower, and fired. Instead of finding its target, the rocket sputtered, slamming into the Cadillac driven by journalist and broadcaster Gordon Sinclair.

Seeking release from prison four times — in 1995, 1996, 1998 and again in 2000 — Woods' quest for freedom was denied every time. Previous Pre-Release Decision Sheets stated the Brooklyn-born killer was prone to auditory and visual hallucinations, and suffered from an overabundance of mental disorders. Axis II, used for assessing personality disorders and intellectual disabilities, revealed Woods to have schizoid, schizotypal, and anti-social traits. Paranoid, aloof, and preoccupied with witchcraft, voodoo, telepathy and clairvoyance, he was on medication to curb his violent behaviour not only against others, but even himself. Over the decades Woods, like his co-killer Saul Betesh, attempted suicide a number of unconventional ways, including putting a plastic bag over his head to suffocate himself, snorting bleach, and asking another inmate to slash his throat.

In September of 1995, members of the Parole Board reported Woods' outlook was "Questionable as he denies culpability and continues to live in a fantasy related occult mindset." Seeking release and deportation to the United States, Woods told the parole board he would find employment as a dishwasher, and eventually a sign painter. The parole board disagreed, stating his lack of education and vocational skills would hold him back to such a degree that he would soon be living on the streets, and once again resort to criminal activity to survive. Especially concerning to them was his negative opinion of the Canadian legal system, Toronto police in particular. If he returned to the United States, he would have no obligation whatsoever to Canadian justice, and pose a serious risk to the community. At one point in 1983, Woods' vowed in writing that he would "get revenge from the other side of death" on police "for what you Nazi finks did."

Additionally, "He [Woods] presented at the hearing as mentally unstable with extremely limited insight into his past behaviour pattern and current mental condition. He minimized his own needs and rationalized his ability to obtain necessary health resources and treatment, and his ability to support himself."

Noted for his eagerness to use violence, evidence showed Woods — who said he had no involvement in the sexual assault on Emanuel — revealed he was involved sexually with adolescent boys, and required further exploration of sex offender treatment. Continuing to maintain his claims that he only attempted to revive Jaques and help dispose of the body (which he later denied), he believed police "manufactured" evidence against him, clearly indicating his inability to accept responsibility for his criminal behaviour, which was exacerbated through long-term alcohol and drug use.

Other reasons for his repeated denials for parole included his past sexual involvement with young males and need for treatment, a lack of current psychiatric/psychological assessments documenting his mental stability and ability to function, no understanding of his criminal behaviour and denial of responsibility for his role in Emanuel's death, and no basis that he had undergone sufficient attitudinal or behavioural changes necessary so he could not be deemed a risk to reoffend. His 1981 conviction for attempting to kill Betesh by slashing Betesh's throat also did not help his pleas for release.

A psychological report, dated June 3, 1998, concluded Woods' criminal behaviour originated from four control factors: "a. acceptance of antisocial attitudes and interpersonal violence, b. deficiency in social skills including assertiveness and anger management, c. psychoactive substance abuse and dependency issue, d. serious history mental health problems."

Denied once again for parole — this time day parole into a community-based residential facility — on November 22, 2000, members of the board reviewing his case determined that although Woods had attended Alcoholics Anonymous, he had not participated in any significant programs regarding his substance abuse issues. Likewise, he had acknowledged his need to attend sex offender programming, yet refused to participate, with The General Recidivism Score and violence prediction scale indicating he was at a moderate risk for general recidivism, but at a high risk for violent recidivism. Reluctance to cooperate with his parole officer, lack of openness, and no specific plans if he was released also worked against Woods' favour.

*****

In 2011, Saul Betesh was back in the news threatening *still* another hunger strike, a warning largely ignored by the media, who were reporting on his pledges to harm himself less often as the year went on. As with his earlier vows to starve himself, there were a number of conditions favourable to him, including his willingness to take only the required amount of insulin needed to stave off kidney damage, a potential consequence of his diabetes. What made headlines, however, came in September of that year when news broke about the sadistic, psychologically disturbed killer posting an online ad to expand his social circle, and meet friends from his prison cell.

"I am 60 years young," began the profile of prisoner #704938A on Inmate-Connection.com, an American-based website for prisoners in the United States and worldwide seeking pen pals and, hopefully, long-lasting relationships. Incarcerated at the time in the Warkworth Institution, a medium security Federal Correctional Facility for male offenders in Ontario, Betesh's description of himself was, typically, full of half-truths and obvious omissions. "I have short hair, blue eyes and stands [*sic*] 6 feet tall. I'm slightly overweight but active. I have three passions in life 1. Gardening 2. Computers (programming not the Internet). 3. Cooking. I am a practicing Druid and I also attend Wiccan Services. This is the most important part of my life as it concerns my interaction with the Gods and the planet earth. I will write anyone back who includes a photo."

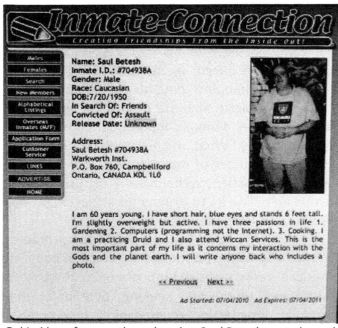

Behind bars for over three decades, Saul Betesh posted an ad on an American website in 2011 to meet pen pals. Describing his interests in Wicca, Druidism, gardening and computers, he states he was convinced of assault, instead of first degree murder.

The picture of Betesh accompanying the online ad certainly did not match his description. Wearing a dirty grey knock-off Nike 'Just Do It' T-shirt and saggy sweat pants, Betesh appears nearly bald, a considerably overweight diabetic. Unlike many other incarcerated men and women on the website, most freely admitting to an array of non-violent and violent crimes ranging from robbery to firearms possession, burglary, sexual abuse, carjacking, sex trafficking, and even murder, Saul David Betesh — responsible for committing one of the most revolting crimes in Canadian history — stated he was convicted merely of *assault*. Incarcerated for over 30 years at the time, Betesh remained incapable of telling the truth, even when he literally had nothing to lose.

Also that month, it was reported that Betesh, accused of having child pornography on his computer and having sexually assaulting another prisoner, was granted a transfer from the medium-security Warkworth facility in Campbellford to Dorchester Penitentiary, a residential-style medium and minimum security institution in New Brunswick, where the Correctional Service of Canada is the main employer.

Speaking on condition of anonymity, guards at Betesh's soon-to-be-former Ontario home were overjoyed he was leaving for the east coast. Fed-up with his never-ending threats of hunger strikes, which sometimes saw him go into diabetic shock and need to be taken to an outside hospital at taxpayer expense, Betesh constantly complained about his rights being violated, such as being denied candles to practice his Wiccan religion. "Two days before he left we thought he'd tried to commit suicide, but he'd just played with his insulin again," said one guard, noting the once-lithe murderer was now weighing about 300 pounds.

Considering his recent incidents with kiddie porn and sexual assault, which earned him confiscation of his computer and six months 'in the hole' for assault, Warkworth staff were surprised at the transfer, but relieved, as it meant they would never have to deal with him or his requests again. "Dorchester is inheriting a huge headache. For us, it was a sigh of relief," stated another guard. "He's a pompous, arrogant a****** who really thinks he's hard done by and mistreated. He believes he's owed everything in the world plus more."[57] Considering his advancing age, many Canadians believed this was the last they would hear of Saul Betesh. They were wrong.

In mid-February, 2017 — almost 40 years since Emanuel's sex slaying — Saul David Betesh was in the news once more. This time, the convicted child killer's profile was on Canadian Inmates Connect Inc., described by the Canadian Press as "a matchmaking website that helps lonesome prisoners find companionship beyond the jailhouse walls." Accompanied by a photo, as he had done with his 2011 online ad, the now-bearded Betesh appeared even more rotund (which he attributes to "eating all the great prison food for the last 41 years"), and is pictured wearing a rumpled light grey work shirt, and blue jeans. The website, featuring an overwhelming number of male inmate profiles compared to females, stated in its description that it was dedicated to Federal Inmates searching for pen pals.

Prison can be a lonely and isolated place. Time tends to go by quite slow. Contact with the outside world can become lost. Some Inmates may not have anyone at all, making communication with the outside world almost non-existant [*sic*]. Through this website, we hope to form a pathway of communication through letter writing between Federal Inmates and the outside world. By Inmates maintaining communication with society through penpalship, it may decrease the chance of institutionalization. It may also be a pro-social method of reintegration and reduce the rate of recidivism. These Inmates are obviously in jail for a reason, each with their own story to tell. Please take the time to get to know one.[58]

Betesh's profile revealed he was now incarcerated at the Pacific Institution/Regional Treatment Centre, a multi-level security complex in Fraser Valley about 80 kilometres east of Vancouver. For male offenders only, the Institution houses a psychiatric care unit, health centre, and rehabilitation unit.

Never out of the press for long, Betesh was once again posting personal ads online, this time on Canadian Inmates Connect Inc., in February of 2017.

Unlike his previous pen pal profile, where he stated he was convicted of assault, Betesh states the reason he is behind bars is first degree murder. Aged 66, although he writes he is "67 years young," Betesh says "My crime was bad, but with treatment and a bit more time I feel I can once again become a productive member of society. I will answer all letters, male or female, that are respectful, the others I will trash. I will not write anybody under the age of 20. I hope to hear from you soon." Once again, he states he is a practicing Druid, and has broadened his interests over the years to include an updated version of Dungeons & Dragons, along with chess, stained glass, working in the prison greenhouse, watching science fiction shows on TV, and sewing quilts and comforters for charity.

Although Betesh concedes for the first time the severity of his first degree murder conviction, he once again falls short of any admission of guilt or compassion for his role in the death of 12-year-old Emanuel. For Paul Tomlinson, representing Saul Betesh decades earlier proved to be one of the greatest challenges of his legal career since he was called to the bar in 1970.

What I was faced with — the law at the time, with the defense of insanity — was firstly, the Crown must prove its case beyond a reasonable doubt. That is obvious with all criminal cases. Then if that is found, and I argued that step one, they hadn't proved their case beyond a reasonable doubt as to first-degree murder, that it *could* be either second-degree or manslaughter. And then if they *had* proved it beyond a reasonable doubt, then he was insane. And the concept of that was, once the Crown had proved its case beyond a reasonable doubt, then you go into the defense of insanity at the time, and it's on the balance of probabilities, meaning the scales of justice. So it's up to the accused to show that, because the law said that everyone who commits a crime is deemed to be sane to begin with. So you're deemed to be sane, unless the defense, on a balance of probabilities, shows that he was innocent. So we've got the scales now, after the Crown has proven its case beyond a reasonable doubt, and then you heap the evidence for insanity on one side of the scales, and the evidence that he's sane on the other side of the scale, so it's 51 per cent basically. So if you prove 51 per cent that he's insane, the verdict should be not guilty by reason of insanity. The Crown had psychiatrists saying he's sane — I didn't have any psychiatrists saying he's insane — what I had was lay people or previous medical reports who testified as to what they saw and they knew of Betesh to put on my scales that he was in fact, *insane*. Obviously the jury felt that the psychiatric opinions outweighed the evidence I was presenting about all this previous behavior. And then of course, I also have the problem that Kribs had pleaded guilty. I had to address that, I had to make the changes, because that was a surprise.

Do I think Betesh should've been found not guilty by reason of insanity? Yes. Although he himself may not have been crying out for help — his personality, which was 'I don't need help, I'm Saul Betesh, I'm the centre of everything,' — and to admit that he needed assistance or help mentally will not have been within Saul Betesh's purview. But in a way he was crying out without knowing he was crying out. He was doing things almost as if, 'If I do these things, I'll get help,' but he never really did. They kept shuffling him off to places for emotionally disturbed children, instead of to a psychiatric hospital; he should've been there since he was five. Whether they could have done anything to cure, I don't know. The cure rates today aren't that good when it comes to dyed in the wool psychopaths. And for that reason, hospitals really don't want them. They disturb the hospital, and take up beds for years that could probably be used by four or five people in that time. And I think that's part of the reason the panel I put together of psychiatrists voted the way they did. And I don't think the psychiatrists wanted to be known as the doctor who testified Saul Betesh was crazy. That might've injured their professional reputation, I had that sense.

Like many high-profile crimes, the murder of Emanuel Jaques has attracted a number of bizarre, unsubstantiated, and outright ludicrous conspiracy theorists over the years. One which persists involves Dungeons & Dragons. Better known simply as D&D, the fantasy role-playing game of wizards, elves and goblins was the brainchild of creators Gary Gygax and Dave

Arneson. Introduced in 1974 and based on miniature medieval wargames, it soon became enormously popular, and was a mainstay of players at Mr. Gameways' Ark, located at the corner of Yonge and Charles Streets. Saul Betesh and Robert Kribs came into the club fairly often, while Josef Woods and Werner Gruener were spotted there occasionally.

One of the more unsettling claims dates back to 2000, with an individual making numerous, eccentric online bulletin board message posts claiming Betesh was not only innocent of the crime of murder, but that "the real murderers must be brought to justice!" Claiming to have spent years researching the case and "uncovering evidence" (despite an exhaustive police investigation and subsequent trial finding Betesh guilty of first-degree murder), and that a "demonic cult committed the murder and then forced Saul Betesh to confess the crime and implicate two others." Even more bizarre is the claim the boy's violent death was a sacrifice — made on the night of a full moon, no less — to Tlaloc, a Dungeons & Dragons rain god (originally Aztec) to whom children were offered.

While providing not one piece of evidence, the online poster stated Betesh was under the influence of the occult at the time of the murder, that he still plays D&D through the mail, and, most absurd of all, that his supporters could somehow use this "information" as a basis for Betesh's parole. "Certainly the public has a right to know the important Saul Betesh/Dungeons & Dragons connection, and take the time to evaluate such Toronto game clubs carefully, to see if they have ritual occult elements, to check them out, to question whether public space should really be offered to them. If there truly is no connection, fine, there is no connection. But withholding information from the public is not a decision to be left to weird overweight hobbyists whose psychology has been so warped from competitive wargames they can't think straight. Instead they should try to revive their atrophied consciences, and come clean, even if it is to 'outsiders' or 'mundanes' or 'zeroth levels' which they disdain. The remaining D&D community will be the healthier for it." The same individual also believed Betesh had been a member of General Staff, Toronto's first games club, and had been expelled before the murder.

Responses to claims of Betesh being framed for the murder and a covert Dungeons & Dragons 'conspiracy' were, unsurprisingly, dismissed and ridiculed, with some stating the conspiracy theorist "has a tenuous grasp on reality," and others stating the claims made them "crazy as wharf rats." As for suggesting Betesh ever be released from prison, one individual wrote: "Early parole? If there was ever a case that cried out for the perpetrators to spend the rest of their lives in prison and die there, this is it. The murder of Emmanual [sic] Jaques was one of the most cold-blooded killings in the annals of Canadian crime. So please, take your childish

Dungeons and Dragons conspiracy fantasies and stick them up your ass."

Chapter Fourteen: The Disappearing Werner Gruener

Following his controversial acquittal in March of 1978 for the death of Emanuel Jaques, police and the courts were anxious that once Werner Gruener left Toronto, it would be impossible to track him down in the event of a retrial. Although he was not required to come back to Canada, the appeal by the prosecution — to see him retried for first-degree murder, as announced by Attorney-General Roy McMurtry — could not commence unless the 31-year-old Gruener received notice in person, so he could have time to work on a defence.

Taking many months to locate him, Staff Sergeant Gerald Stevenson and Sergeant Robert McLean were able to find Gruener in Athens, Greece, where McLean served him with the notice of appeal in June of 1979, nearly two years after Emanuel's murder. At the time, Gruener was staying in a cheap Athens hostel, doing odd jobs to make a meager living, much as he had done working for body rubs back in Toronto. According to police, Gruener was completely unemotional and made no comment whatsoever when he was handed the notice of appeal in person.

Much to the dismay of police, the Ontario Court of Appeal's 41-page decision upheld Gruener's acquittal in December of 1980, along with the second-degree murder sentence of 18 years without parole for Josef Woods; at the time of the trial, the jury recommended Woods serve 10 years, but Justice Maloney decided on 18. The rationale of the decision against Woods was that he had, according to the court psychiatrist, "not developed any moral standards," with Ontario Chief Justice William Howland stating, "The murder of Jaques was a callous and cold-blooded act which showed a complete lack of any appreciation of the value of human life. It was a crime which profoundly shocked the community...there was no error in principle in the period of 18 years fixed by the trial judge. It properly marked the gravity of the offence."

Once again a free man, Werner Gruener was never out of the eye of police for long. Unable to keep himself out of trouble, he was jailed in 1980 for trying to "baptize" a group of onlookers with fire at the Canadian National Exhibition. Sentenced to one day in jail and two years' probation, Gruener was ordered by the court to undergo a psychiatric examination. A year later, living in east-end Toronto, he was charged with narcotics possession and trafficking Percodan which he obtained with a fake prescription, and sold to an undercover female police officer. In 1982, Gruener was again arrested, this time for assaulting two guards at the Eaton Centre. He was found guilty of two counts of bodily assault.

Remembering the time when Toronto detectives tracked his client to Greece following his acquittal, attorney Earl Levy went into his office one morning, when Gruener unexpectedly walked in the door. "It had been quite some time since I'd seen him, and I was surprised," he says. "He came in with his Children of God material, including some pictures. I didn't even know if Werner would've known for my office was, because he was in jail [the whole time], except for when he got out." Asking Gruener why he was there, his former client said he was served with appeal papers in Greece. Levy told Gruener he didn't have to come back to Canada, and proceed to ask him what he was going to do, since he was now in Toronto. "He said, 'Well, I learned how to eat fire.'" Asking him where he was going to do this, he said the Exhibition was opening soon, and he was going to go down there and eat fire, and earn some money. I said, 'Werner, you can't do that! You standing there eating fire, some people are going to throw gasoline on you.' He didn't seem to be concerned about it."

That was the last time Levy heard anything about Gruener until approximately 2004, when the attorney was walking on the boardwalk in The Beaches area of east end Toronto with a friend early one summer evening. He noticed Gruener with his bicycle, standing and talking to a young couple. Quickly explaining to his companion who Gruener was, Levy said he wanted to speak with his former client, who he approached as soon as the young couple left. Saying hello to Gruener was followed by a "dreamy silence," with Levy asking if he knew who he was. There was a pregnant pause, and he said, "Earl," which surprised Levy. Exchanging small talk for a few minutes, it was the final time the two men ever spoke. The whereabouts of German-born Werner Gruener — the only one of the four to elude prison — remains unknown.

*****

Two thousand and seventeen marks the fortieth anniversary of the abduction, rape and murder of young Emanuel Jaques, who would be 52 years old. As time goes on, memories fade, and those connected to the case themselves pass away. And yet, Toronto's Yonge Street continues to evolve, with new buildings replacing the old, and different crowds claiming the once-infamous Strip as their own. A new generation has emerged, unaware of the most controversial murder in the city's history. For those who remember the name "Emanuel Jaques," it will always be synonymous with the crime that changed a city.

Dismantling the sex trade: workers removing signage from a Yonge Street Strip business (Courtesy George Rust-D'Eye)

Acknowledgements

Forty years have passed since the abduction, torture, rape and murder by drowning of 12-year-old Emanuel Jaques, which remains one of the most notorious crimes in Canadian history. Widely reported at the time, the brutal death of the immigrant Shoeshine Boy still resurrects memories for those involved – including homicide detectives, politicians, attorneys, and jurors – which are unpleasant at best, horrific at worst. Of all questions raised over the decades, the most often-asked remains: *how was a child lured away to his death in broad daylight on Yonge Street?* I have done my best to explain not only the circumstances leading to the decline of the best-known street in Canada, but also its resurrection following Emanuel's murder.

Along with newspapers, magazines and books, numerous documents such as police reports, trial materials, parole board statements, and other archival sources were consulted. In a number of instances never-before published materials were loaned to me by defence attorneys involved in the trial of the four men charged with Emanuel's murder, which provided valuable information not otherwise publicly available.

For this book, I remain grateful to those who generously gave their time for interviews. They include attorney Leslie Brown, filmmaker, director and producer Colin Brunton, David Crombie, Paul V. Godfrey, attorney Earl J. Levy,

Q.C., attorney Morris Manning, attorney George Rust-D'Eye, Valerie Scott (sex worker and Legal Co-ordinator, Sex Professionals of Canada), musician Mickey Skin, and attorney Paul Tomlinson.

I also wish to thank the following individuals and organizations for their assistance with research, photos, and documents: Norina D'Agostini (Historical Researcher with the Toronto Police Service Museum), members of Toronto Police Homicide and the Access and Privacy Section, staff at the Canadian Lesbian and Gay Archives (CLGA), Fernando Nunes, Associate Professor, Mount Saint Vincent University, author Peter McSherry, Gilberto Fernandes of The Portuguese Canadian History Project, Domingos Marques (*Comunidade* – Portuguese Community Newspaper), and Julia Holland, Archives Technician, Clara Thomas Archives & Special Collections (York University Libraries).

About the Author

Robert J. Hoshowsky, author of the Arthur Ellis-shortlisted, *The Last to Die: Ronald Turpin, Arthur Lucas, and the End of Capital Punishment in Canada* and the highly acclaimed *Unsolved: True Canadian Cold Cases*. A former Researcher-Reporter at Maclean's magazine, he has contributed to top-rated television programs, including, the Canadian version of *Who Wants to be a Millionaire*. His investigative work has been published in over 100 magazines and newspapers worldwide. Presently, he is an on-air consultant for an upcoming True Crime TV series.

With a lifelong interest in criminology and forensic science, Hoshowsky's recent work has appeared in *Serial Killer Quarterly*, where he has profiled infamous murderers, including, Jeffrey Dahmer, John Christie, Leonard Lake and Charles Ng, Sheila LaBarre, and Andrei Chikatilo.

Bibliography

Books

Baum, Daniel Jay. Discount Justice. Burns & MacEachern Limited, Canada, 1979.
Boyd, Neil. The Last Dance: Murder in Canada. A Seal Book / published by arrangement with Prentice-Hall Canada Inc., Canada, 1992.
Brock, Deborah R. Making Work, Making Trouble: Prostitution as a Social Problem. University of Toronto Press, Toronto, 1998.
De Sa, Anthony. Barnacle Love. Doubleday Canada, a division of Random House of Canada Limited, Printed and bound in the USA, 2008.
De Sa, Anthony. Kicking the Sky. Doubleday Canada. Printed and bound in the USA, 2013.
Expanding the Gaze: Gender and the Politics of Surveillance. Edited by Emily van der Meulen and Robert Heynen. University of Toronto Press, Toronto, 2016.
Kinsman, Gary "The Jaques Murder: an anatomy of a moral panic," in The Regulation of Desire (Montreal: Black Rose Books, 1986).
Queerly Canadian: An Introductory Reader in Sexuality Studies. Edited by Maureen FitzGerald and Scott Rayter. Canadian Scholars' Press Inc. / Women's Press, Toronto, 2012.
Silversides, Ann. AIDS Activist: Michael Lynch and the Politics of Community. Between the Lines, Toronto, 2003.
Worth, Liz. Treat Me Like Dirt: An Oral History of Punk in Toronto and Beyond 1977-1981. Bongo Beat Books, April, 2010, Montreal, Quebec, Canada.
Wright, Richard B. A Life With Words: A Writer's Memoir. Simon & Schuster Canada, Toronto, 2015
Wright, Richard B. Final Things. The Macmillan Company of Canada, Ltd. 1980.

Warner, Tom. Never Going Back: A History of Queer Activism in Canada, University of Toronto Press, 2002.

Thesis

Yvonne Chi-Ying Ng, "Ideology, Media and Moral Panics: an analysis of the Jaques Murder" (Centre for Criminology, University of Toronto, M.A . thesis, 1981)

Magazines

Maclean's, "Mean Streets," September 5, 1977, p. 18.
Toronto Life, September 1979, "Sympathy for the Devil" (on Saul Betesh) by Stephen Williams.
Toronto Life, June 1980; Pg. 39, "Cops: COPS: the myth and the reality," by Stephen Williams.

Endnotes

[1] The Portuguese in Canada, David Higgs, Department of History, University of Toronto, Ottawa, 1982.

[2] There is some discrepancy over the purpose Emanuel had in mind for the money he earned shining shoes. Some accounts suggest he was going to buy food for a dog he was getting from a neighbor, while others state he was going to contribute money towards a family trip to Portugal the following year.

[3] The vote on Bill C-84 was a "free vote," meaning Members of Parliament could vote as they chose, not necessarily along their official party lines. With 131 to 124 in favour of abolishing capital punishment, it remains one of the narrowest margins in the history of Canada's Parliament). In a speech he made a week before the vote, Trudeau said "…it is inevitable that the defeat of this bill would eventually place the hangman's noose around some person's neck. To make that quite clear: if this bill is defeated, some people will certainly hang."

[4] This would be far from the only reference to Gordon Stuckless in the years to come. A neighbour of the Jaques family, Stuckless was a teaching assistant at a nearby school, and a part-time employee at Maple Leaf Gardens. Along with other men, Stuckless was one of the sexual predators responsible for molesting dozens of young boys over the years at the Gardens, including Martin Kruze. One of the first to testify against Stuckless, Kruze ended his life by jumping off a Toronto bridge three days after Stuckless was sentenced. An equipment manager at the famed Toronto arena between 1969 and 1988, Stuckless plead guilty in 1997 to committing sexual assaults on 24 boys. In June of 2016, after pleading guilty to 100 charges for sex crimes against 18 boys, he was sentenced to just six and a half years in prison. The sentence enraged his male victims, with one yelling in court, "I've had (expletive) nightmares longer than six years." In November of 2016, Stuckless, who had been serving his prison sentence at Kingston's Joyceville Institution, was once again arrested and faced 19 charges of sexually assaulting three boys while working at Maple Leaf Gardens between 1978 and 1984. In early October, 2017, Stuckless went on trial for the alleged incidents between 1978 and 1984, where court heard from witnesses who stated the 67-year-old

threatened to kill a boy and his family members if the child told anyone he had been sexually assaulted.

[5] The Toronto Star, Friday August 5, 1977 P. A3.

[6] *Comunidade* newspaper, 1975-1979. Part 1: Records and commentary. The Portuguese Development Committee/Movimento Comunitario Português, a community organization, was created by a group of social workers based out of the Toronto's West End YMCA, including João Medeiros and Domingos Marques, http://archives.library.yorku.ca/exhibits/show/pchp/comunidade_records.

[7] The Toronto Star, August 9, 1977, P. B1

[8] The Toronto Sun, May 9, 1976, P. 4.

[9] The Toronto Sun, May 12, 1976, P. 10.

[10] Maclean's, September 5, 1977. PP. 18-20.

[11] The Globe and Mail, August 10, 1977, page 8, "Gays on guilt: blame media."

[12] Silversides, Ann. *AIDS Activist: Michael Lynch and the Politics of Community*. Between the Lines, Toronto, 2003, PP. 12-13.

[13] The Toronto Star, August 6, 1977, P. B2.

[14] Brock, Deborah R. *Making Work, Making Trouble: Prostitution as a Social Problem*. University of Toronto Press, Toronto, 1998, P. 4.

[15] Comunidade editorial, August 1977, PP. 11-12.

[16] The Globe and Mail, August 20, 1977, PP. 1-2, "Only cure for dangerous sexiness is castration, Metro psychiatrist says."

[17] The Body Politic, Issue 39, December 1977/January 1978, P. 29.

[18] Hawkes went on trial in Kentville, Nova Scotia in November of 2016 for indecent assault and gross indecency for an alleged incident against a 16-year-old going back to the mid-1970s. Hawkes, then a teacher in the Annapolis Valley, denied the incident took place. He was found not guilty on January 31, 2017.

[19] The Globe and Mail, January 4, 1978, P. 8.

[20] *The Body Politic*, February 1978, P. 2.

[21] *Queerly Canadian: An Introductory Reader in Sexuality Studies*. Edited by Maureen FitzGerald and Scott Rayter. Canadian Scholars' Press Inc. / Women's Press, Toronto, 2012, PP. 140-141.

[22] On June 22, 2016, Toronto Police Chief Mark Saunders — at the annual Pride reception at Toronto Police Headquarters — made a historic apology for the raids on four gay bathhouses in February, 1981, which saw officers break down doors with crowbars and sledgehammers. Saunders stated: "The 35th anniversary of the 1981 raids is a time when the Toronto Police Service expresses its regrets for those very actions. It is also an occasion to acknowledge the lessons learned about the risks of treating any part of Toronto's many communities as not fully a part of society."

[23] Kinsman, Gary. *The Regulation of Desire: Sexuality in Canada.* Black Rose Books, Montreal, 1987), pp. 205-206.

[24] Treat Me Like Dirt: An Oral History of Punk in Toronto and Beyond 1977-1981, P. 195.

[25] Case Analysis, P. 17: Levy wrote this especially for a legal newsletter. It was the fourth in a series of 15 cases chosen because of the particular challenges posed to counsel.

[26] The Toronto Star, March 16, 1974, P. B5.

[27] The Globe and Mail, March 9, 1974, P. 35.

[28] Levy, P. 26.

[29] Levy case analysis, PP. 22-23.

[30] The Body Politic, Number 41, March 1978, P. 4.

[31] March 13, 1978, P. 34.

[32] Saturday, March 11, 1978, page 5.

[33] Paul Tomlinson, Jury Address, P. 1. Note that punctuation is exactly as Tomlinson wrote, while there were some changes in the oral address he presented to the jurors. Tomlinson would, on the conclusion of his address, be followed by defence attorney George Marron speaking on behalf of Josef Woods, and Earl Levy for his client, Werner Gruener; the reason Tomlinson went first was due to his client being listed at the top of the indictment.

[34] *Never Going Back: A History of Queer Activism in Canada*, p. 137, by Tom Warner, University of Toronto Press, 2002, PP. 137-138.

[35] *The Body Politic*, Number 42, April 1978, P. 4.

[36] The pen name of Lou Trifon, the late Crad Kilodney was a well-known fixture in Toronto for years, selling self-published books to passers-by on the street, with colourful titles like *Mental Cases*, *Lightning Struck My Dick*, and *Blood Sucking Monkeys from North Tonawanda*.

[37] Creating early films including *A Trip Around Lake Ontario*, Brunton went on to produce films including *Roadkill*, *Highway 61*, and *Hedwig and the Angry Inch*, along with television series *Little Mosque on the Prairie* and *Schitt's Creek*. He was the first Executive Director of The Feature Film Project from 1991 to 1995, an initiative of director Norman Jewison's Canadian Film Centre. Creating the short film *The Last Pogo* in 1978 featuring punk bands The Scenics, The Mods, Teenage Head and many others, Brunton documented Toronto's punk scene from 1976 to 1978 with *The Last Pogo Jumps Again* along with Kire Paputts, released in 2013.

[38] The Globe and Mail, July 5, 1975, P. 1.

[39] The Globe and Mail, June 7, 1977, P. 5.

[40] The Globe and Mail, Thursday July 28, 1977, P. 2.

[41] Report of the Royal Commission on Metropolitan Toronto, Volume 2, Detailed Findings and Recommendations, Honourable John P. Robarts, P.C., C.C., Q.C. Commissioner, 1977, P. 288.

[42] The Globe and Mail, August 6, 1977, P. 7.

[43] The Globe and Mail, September 1, 1977, P. 6.

[44] The Globe and Mail, September 23, 1977, P. 6.

[45] Brock, Deborah R. *Making Work, Making Trouble: Prostitution as a Social Problem*. University of Toronto Press, Toronto, 1998, P. 35.

[46] A founding member of the Sex Professionals of Canada (SPOC), Valerie Scott serves as the Legal Co-Ordinator of the organization, which is dedicated to the rights of sex workers. On March 20, 2007, Scott, Terri-Jean Bedford, and Amy Lebovitch launched a Canadian Charter of Rights and Freedoms challenge to three of the anti sex-work laws, including the communicating law. "After seven years in court, and twenty five thousand pages of evidence, on December 20, 2013, the Supreme Court of Canada unanimously ruled in our favour and agreed that the laws were causing us catastrophic harm," says Scott. "Laws are not supposed to cause harm. That defeats the purpose of law. But the Conservative government of Prime Minister Stephen Harper didn't care and used us as political fodder. The Harper government wrote new and even harsher anti sex worker laws. The new laws' stated aim is to legislate sex work, a.k.a.

sex workers, out of existence. [The new laws are causing much harm. Once again we are amassing evidence of rapes, robberies, beatings, and murders. Once again these new laws are a gift to predators.] The date they were implemented was December 6, 2014, Canada's National Day of Remembrance and Action on Violence Against Women."

[47] As one of the speakers at *The Summer of '77: How Emanuel Jaques' Murder Changed Toronto* held on June 22, 1977 at the Gallery of the Portuguese Pioneers, Valerie Scott spoke along with historians Gilberto Fernandes, Daniel Ross, and York University's Tom Hooper about how the death of the young boy impacted Toronto's Portuguese community, but also its LGBTQ and sex workers.

[48] The Globe and Mail, February 7, 1981, P. 1.

[49] The Toronto Star, April 29, 1979, P. A18.

[50] The Toronto Star, April 10, 1978, page A7.

[51] From 1867 to the last executions in 1962, hanging was the only form of execution used in Canada.

[52] The Toronto Star, March 28, 1980, P. A9.

[53] The *Canadian Jewish News*, June 4, 1981, P. 17.

[54] The Toronto Star, October 17, 2002, P. A3.

[55] Letter from Peter Ferreira, National Vice-President, Portuguese-Canadian National Congress to the National Parole Board, Ottawa, October 4, 2002.

[56] National Parole Board Pre-release Decision Sheet, October 18, 2002.

[57] The Toronto Sun online, September 15, 2011.

[58] http://www.canadianinmatesconnect.com/about.html

CPSIA information can be obtained
at www.ICGtesting.com
Printed in the USA
LVOW03s2137271117
557739LV00011B/1031/P